D1387832

SHELDON GREENBERG AND ELISABETH LAMBERT ORTIZ

A major television series by Blackrod Limited

MICHAEL JOSEPH/RAINBIRD
in association with Channel Four Television Company Limited

To Jane who put up with it all for two years and still
remains a friend – I hope.
Sheldon Greenberg

To Ortiz-Tinolo who helped me eat my way through the book.
Elisabeth Lambert Ortiz

First published in Great Britain in 1983 by
Michael Joseph Limited
44 Bedford Square, London WC1B 3DU
and
The Rainbird Publishing Group Limited
40 Park Street, London W1Y 4DE
who designed and produced the book

ISBN 0 7181 2317 4

Text set by SX Composing Ltd, Rayleigh, England
Colour origination by Gilchrist Brothers Limited,
Leeds, England
Printed and bound by Printer Industria Gráfica SA,
Barcelona, Spain

CONTENTS

AUTHORS' ACKNOWLEDGMENTS

The Spice of Life began life as a thirteen-part television series. The idea was to travel the world in search of spice, adventures, information and recipes. In the final year and a half of production, one of the unit's film directors travelled no less than 120,000 kilometres!

Everywhere, the film crews were accompanied by teams of stills photographers, the results of whose efforts grace this book. Thanks, then, not only to the well-travelled photographers, but to those many people throughout the world who planted, picked, pounded, sang, danced, cooked and ate for the cameras.

Spices, and food in general, are unusual enough topics for a popular documentary television series and accompanying book. The success of the whole endeavour is due in large measure to the talent and encouragement of Jill Roach, executive producer of the TV series and Head of Productions at Blackrod Limited.

The original task was to produce whole programmes and chapters on such apparently limited topics as 'nutmeg' or 'allspice'. Each episode not only had to be informative, but entertaining and appealing to a general audience. At first, this brief seemed daunting, but after about eighteen months of effort, the Production Unit surprised itself with the breadth and quality of the work.

No less than four talented Producer-Directors brought home pictures and information from locations as far flung as the interior of China, the Canadian Prairies and the Spice Islands themselves. The crew leaders were Nigel Maslin, Lyn Gambles, Terry Bryan and Carlos Pasini. Although working mainly on the TV series Film Editors Bob Harvey and Colin Barratt provided much appreciated inspiration. Nick Cooper contributed valuable research concerning both the ancient use of spices and their current enjoyment in Western

Europe. Jane Reeve did the same for South East Asia.

Henry Heath not only composed the tables at the end of the book, but made his undoubted expertise available for each of the chapters. Meera Taneja and Kenneth Lo, recognized authorities on Indian and Chinese cookery, both made valuable suggestions, as did Frank Robinson from the Tropical Products Institute. Guy Hallifax organized the global travellers and their information, while Kazuko Van Mechelen and Alison Fogwill serviced the production office in London.

The whole enterprise would not have happened without the efforts of Michael Blakstad, Director of Programmes, Television South plc, Clive Moffatt, Chief Executive of Blackrod Limited, Michael Rodd, a director of Blackrod Limited, the support of Television South p.l.c. and that of Masakazu Shibaoka and Yoshio Konoike of Tokyo, Japan.

The Spice of Life gratefully acknowledges the assistance of the following: Reckitt and Colman, Norwich; Bodleian Library, Oxford; National Maritime Museum, Greenwich; British Museum, London; British Library, London; Istituto Geografico de Agostini Novara, Milan; Pierpont Morgan Library; The Armand Hammer Foundation, Los Angeles; Cliche Musées Nationaux, Paris; The India Office Library, London; The Victoria and Albert Museum, London; Guildhall Library, City of London; Royal Botanic Gardens; Scala, Milan; MAS, Barcelona; National Library of Jamaica.

Many people contributed recipes for this book and some are mentioned in the text. We thank them, along with Marcella Hazan, Susan Young, Jill White, Madame Demers, Jeanie Cape, Frau Plumberger, L'Hostellerie du Vieux Peroges in France, the Kocho Restaurant in Japan and The Bakery in Penryn, Cornwall.

1
NUTMEG

It was midsummer in the year 1522. A single ship limped into the harbour of the Portuguese-controlled Cape Verde Islands. Her foremast was damaged and the members of her Spanish crew were emaciated and starving. For many months, they had played cat and mouse with their Portuguese pursuers, but now the imminence of death forced them into one last desperate gamble. They would conceal their identity from the Portuguese and explain that their ship was the damaged remnant of a squadron returning from Spanish colonies in the new world. In fact, they were returning from lands the Portuguese considered very much their own and their hold was laden with abundant treasure.

At first, the Portuguese took pity on the suffering Spaniards and rendered them help, but while a landing party was ashore the truth came out and the Spaniards on board were forced to run. Luckily, there happened to be no Portuguese warships in Cape Verde harbour and the Spaniards put to sea in safety.

One of the crew members, Antonio Pigafetta, kept a meticulous diary of the whole voyage. One thing puzzled him about the Cape Verde incident; the Portuguese said it was Thursday, yet his carefully kept records showed indisputably that it was only Wednesday.

Just over three weeks later, the ship finally reached its home port of Seville in Spain. Three years earlier, the same ship, along with four others and a total of two hundred and thirty men had set out from Seville on what was to become an epic voyage. Now, only eighteen emaciated sailors survived to tell the tale and go down in history as the first people ever to sail around the world. Their captain had been Ferdinand Magellan.

Pigafetta learned that by sailing westward around the globe, they had gained twenty-four hours, thus accounting for the discrepancy in days that he had noticed. He also learned how the Portuguese on Cape Verde discovered the real identity of the Spanish ship. Apparently, one of the landing party tried to make a purchase, using a handful of cloves as money. The Portuguese certainly knew that no cloves were to be found in Spain's American colonies.

The hold of the surviving ship, the *Victoria*, was so loaded with precious oriental spices that the king of Spain awarded its captain, Sebastian del Cano, a coat of arms emblazoned with cloves and nutmegs.

The crew of the *Victoria* unwittingly defined the world. Up until 1522 each new territorial find had expanded the known world. Now exploration and its accompanying technological achievement would only shrink it. A basic view of our planet arose which would stay virtually unaltered until almost four hundred and fifty years later when astronauts would change it once again. All this, flowed from the search for cloves and nutmegs.

It was on the island of Tidore in the Indonesian archipelago that Pigafetta first discovered nutmeg in its natural habitat.

In that island are also some nutmeg trees, the tree of which is like our walnut with the same leaves. And when the nut is gathered, it is as large as a small quince apple, having similar rind and the same colour. Its first rind is as thick as the green rind of our walnut, and under that is a thin loose rind, under which is the mace, very red and wrapped about the rind of the nut, and inside this is the nutmeg.

The fruit houses the two spices, nutmeg and mace, and is described as a 'pendulous fleshy drupe resembling an apricot in form and colour'. (A drupe is any fruit with a stone at the centre.) It looks like a small peach which, when ripe, splits open along its vertical cleft revealing its bright red inside. An apt description is found in the 1912 book *Spices* by H N Ridley:

> When quite ripe, the fleshy husk opens by splitting from top, along the groove, into two halves, nearly to the base. The husk or pericarp is of a somewhat firm texture and $\frac{1}{2}$-inch thick, rather acid in taste, with an aromatic flavour of nutmeg. Within the husk is the seed, the nutmeg of commerce enclosed in a deep brown shining seedcoat, the testa, and over this lies a crimson network, the mace, which is an arillus or outgrowth from the base of the seed.

To put it more simply, the fruit contains basically four parts. The first is the outer fleshy

Nutmeg is one of nature's greatest packaging jobs. The fruit contains four parts: the outer, fleshy, yellow layer; the bright red, lace-like coating which when dried becomes the valuable red spice, mace, and underneath, the actual nutmeg inside its shiny brown seedcoat.

layer which, while most often discarded, is sometimes preserved in sugar to produce either sweets or jelly. Next, is the bright red, lace-like coating which is the valuable spice, mace. This covers a very hard shell which has to be broken to reveal a large kernel, the nutmeg. It has been said that this is one of nature's great packaging jobs.

The nutmeg, *Myristica fragrens Houtt*, is a member of a primitive group of tropical evergreens known as Myristicaceae. They grow throughout the tropical far east, but *Myristica fragrens*, nutmeg, is the only one useful as a spice. The trees are spreading evergreens which can grow up to twenty metres, but usually stand four to ten metres high. They are 'dioecious', meaning that each tree is either a male or a female. Since each male tree is capable of fertilizing ten female trees, and only the female trees yield an abundance of fruit, this causes a problem for growers; a problem compounded because of the difficulty in distinguishing the sex of a tree until at least five years after planting. Male trees have to be culled so that ten or so females will sit downwind from each male. On account of this ratio, one writer called the nutmeg the 'pasha of tropical flora'.

It takes from fifteen to twenty years for a tree to become fully mature, but it will continue to produce fruit for thirty or forty years after that. Generally, the fruit is gathered when it falls to the ground, but this can lead to worm infestation, so often a long pole with a little basket attached is used to pick the fruit off the trees. In Indonesia, this is called a *gai gai*.

The pericarp or outer husk is stripped away with a large knife and the mace is carefully removed. It is pressed between boards and then dried in the sun. On its trip to market its colour will turn from crimson red to a dull orange. Mace from the island of Grenada is frequently 'cured' by storing it in the dark for up to three months, producing an attractive light tan colour and making it very brittle. Mace is usually sold powdered, especially in America; however, the bright orange, brittle 'blades' are available, and are splendid to have and to use.

After one week of being dried in the sun, the nut inside its shell rattles and only then is the hard outer covering broken by hammer and the nutmeg removed.

Nutmegs, along with cloves, originated on a group of tiny islands in the Indonesian archipelago called the Moluccas, but also known as 'the Spice Islands'. If the spice was known to the ancient inhabitants of the Mediterranean, they made very little use of it; however, traders from China, Java and southeast Asia have journeyed to the Moluccas for millenia and were familiar with nutmeg.

Ultimately, the spice started moving westward, but not as quickly as cloves. Nutmegs were long known and used in India, and by the year AD 500 had reached Constantinople and the Mediterranean. The Crusaders brought them northwards

into Europe, so that by the thirteenth century an English author, Walter de Bibbesworth could describe part of a banquet thus: 'The third course was rabbits in gravy, and meat cooked in Cyprus wine, with mace, cubebs and cloves, washed down with quantities of red and white wine.'

Slightly later Geoffrey Chaucer wrote in *The Canterbury Tales*:

> The herbs were springing in the vale:
> Green ginger plants and liquorice pale
> And cloves their sweetness offer,
> With nutmegs too, to put in ale
> No matter whether fresh or stale,
> Or else to keep in coffer.

What a pilgrimage nutmegs had to make to the tables of Europe from their tiny, isolated Pacific islands. The people of the Spice Islands never cultivated cloves and nutmegs, they just picked them and on occasion bartered them for a bit of rice or other basics. The islands were indeed remote, a backwater of civilization with nothing

Facing page: Harvesting nutmeg on the Banda Islands in the Moluccas using a *gai gai*, a long pole with a basket attached to one end. At one time all the world's nutmeg was grown on these tiny islands.

Above: After harvesting, the fleshy outer husk is removed and the bright red coating is carefully taken off. To turn it into mace, this coating is then dried in the sun on large mats for several hours.

Left: Indonesian mace before drying. Indonesian mace is usually exported in its scarlet state whereas Grenadian mace is 'cured' prior to export and becomes a paler, dull orange colour.

to offer the emerging empires far to the west but cloves and nutmeg. Yet this was enough to break their ancient tranquillity and make them the focal point of dispute between nations.

By the year 1493 the Spanish already had landed in America and the Portuguese were on the verge of their push to India. In order to keep the peace between two great Christian states, the Pope drew an imaginary line from north to south in the middle of the Atlantic Ocean with Portugal receiving the right to exploit all 'heathen' territory to the east of the line and Spain to the west. The location of the magic line was moved slightly the following year with the Pope's blessing, in an accord between Spain and Portugal called the Treaty of Tordesillas. This treaty became the legal and moral justification for European conquest in all the other continents of the world.

How different the history of the past five hundred years could have been had the Pope counselled Spain and Portugal that they could go throughout the world and trade, but in all instances they must respect the lives, sovereignty and religions of the peoples they encountered. The Pope, however, was Alexander VI, Rodrigo Borgia.

The Portuguese, sailing eastward from India, were the first to reach the Moluccas in 1512 and quickly captured the lucrative clove and nutmeg trade. In 1519, a disgruntled Portuguese navigator convinced the King of Spain that the Spice Islands could be found by sailing westward into the Atlantic and then somehow on into the Pacific. Such a voyage could put the islands into the Spanish sphere of influence or, at the very least, would give rise to a powerful Spanish claim. The Portuguese navigator was Ferdinand Magellan, who was chosen to lead the fateful expedition.

Magellan and his five ships set off from Seville, crossed the Atlantic Ocean and proceeded slowly

The people of the Moluccas still remember in ritual dances the coming of the Portuguese and the Dutch in the sixteenth and seventeenth centuries in search of lucrative spices that was to change the whole way of life of the islanders. The ancestors of the present-day Bandanese were brought to the islands by the Dutch to work on the nutmeg plantations after they had massacred and dispersed the original inhabitants.

down the east coast of South America searching for a passage to the Pacific Ocean. Fifteen months and the loss of two ships later Pigafetta wrote, 'On Wednesday the 28th of November, one thousand five hundred and twenty, we issued forth from the straight and entered the Pacific Sea.' The three ships were, of course, at the westerly end of what is now known as the Straits of Magellan, near the most southerly tip of South America. They then headed north and for twenty-three days clung to the coast of what is modern Chile. Magellan's next move was into the unknown for he turned left towards the west, away from the mainland, and headed directly out into the Pacific. Magellan had no charts, no maps, no evidence that anyone had ever gone before him and he had already been out of communication with the civilized world for well over a year. Even the feats of modern astronauts cannot compare. His crude instruments provided a reasonable estimate of his latitude. Longitude remained sheer guesswork.

We entered the Pacific Sea, where we remained three months and twenty days without taking on board provisions or any other refreshment, and we ate only old biscuit turned to powder, all full of worms and stinking of the urine which the rats had made on it, having eaten the good. And we drank water impure and yellow . . . and of the rats which were sold for half an écu apiece, some of us could not get enough. Besides the aforesaid troubles, this malady was the worst, namely that the gums of most part of our men swelled above and below so that they could not eat. And in this way they died, inasmuch as 29 of us died . . . there remained very few healthy men.

Before bumping into the island of Guam three months and twenty days later, the three tiny ships had travelled no less than 20,000 kilometres throughout the Pacific Ocean.

We have already recorded that the expedition did find the Spice Islands and that only one ship and eighteen sailors made the return journey back to Spain. Magellan himself was one of the majority who perished. It seems strange to us today that the quest which drove Magellan's men round the world was not principally for gold nor silver but for cloves and nutmegs.

Of course, it would be foolish to underrate spices like nutmeg. Only in modern times have people made the distinction between the pantry and the medicine chest. The great plagues which regularly visited and devastated Europe in the first half of the present millenium certainly helped shape the medieval mind and nutmeg was believed to be a powerful antidote.

In 1826 a book, *The Materia Indica*, claimed that 'nutmeg is considered by the natives of India as one of their most valuable medicines . . .' In fact, both mace and nutmeg have been integral to Indian medicine since ancient times, both being used for a variety of ailments.

Throughout the ages, three areas of complaint seem to have responded best to nutmeg treatments; illnesses concerning the liver and digestion, freckles and other discolorations of the skin and madness! Today nutmeg is still prescribed as a sedative both in cases of epileptic convulsions and asthma.

Nutmeg became important to Arabic medicine sometime later than in India, but certainly over a thousand years ago. Again as in India, the Arabs used nutmeg to help digestion and defects of the skin and liver. Nutmeg, and especially mace, was also widely touted as an aphrodisiac.

Western medicine simply followed on from the Arabs. In the late Middle Ages, nutmegs were so valuable that carved wooden imitations were being sold in the streets. The arrival of nutmegs directly from the Far East caused their popularity to soar and according to the herbals of the sixteenth and seventeenth centuries there was virtually no ailment which nutmeg could not cure.

De Nuce Moschata, a short book extolling the glories of the spice, written in 1681 by J. H. Dietz, caused the already considerable reputation of nutmeg to soar. This was increased in 1704 by a massive tome praising nutmeg written by C. F. Paullini. This was called *Moschocaryographia seu Nucis Moschatae.*

People carried nutmegs everywhere and around their necks wore little graters made from either silver, ivory, wood or bone. These contained usually a compartment for the nuts along with a grating surface and often were made in imaginative shapes. Graters styled in the form of a mace were particularly popular. By the middle of the nineteenth century, the era of nutmeg, the wonder drug, had ended, but another of its properties was beginning to be appreciated.

In 1576, a physician, Lobelius, wrote: *Memini generosam Anglam gravidam esu 10 aut 12 nucum myristicarum ebriam delirasse.* (I remembered a pregnant English lady who, having eaten 10 or 12 nutmegs, became deliriously inebriated.)

Mulled Wine

In the past mulled wine was usually served in pewter mugs and heated with a red hot poker.

SERVES SIX

½ orange, sliced	½ teaspoon/2.5 ml ground ginger
¼ lemon, sliced	1½ oz/40 g (3 tablespoons) dark brown sugar
¼ stick of cinnamon	18 fl oz/500 ml (2¼ cups) dry red wine
10 cloves	4 fl oz/100 ml (7 tablespoons) brandy
½ teaspoon/2.5 ml grated nutmeg	11 fl oz/300 ml (1¼ cups) water

In a saucepan combine the oranges and lemon slices, spices and sugar. Add the wine, brandy and water and heat but do not allow to boil. Taste and add more sugar or water if necessary. Strain into mugs.

Nobody really knows the origin of the idea that nutmeg could bring on a period or cause miscarriage, but for centuries this notion persisted in the popular imagination. Most of the standard herbals claimed the opposite, that nutmeg was helpful in preventing miscarriages. There is no medical evidence that nutmegs influence miscarriages one way or the other, but still, even in the 1980s books are written which warn pregnant women of the dangers of nutmeg. In the late nineteenth and early twentieth centuries the belief that a sufficient dose of nutmeg would bring on a miscarriage was so strong that medical surgeries were constantly handling cases of pregnant women suffering from nutmeg poisoning. Symptoms varied, but usually patients were delirious or suffering from hallucinations.

In the seventeenth century, the botanist Rumphius visited the Spice Islands and in an enormously detailed study of their flora, retold tales of the mind-altering properties of nutmeg. One fanciful story is about a group of soldiers who, apparently, became drunk from nothing more than sitting under a nutmeg tree. It was a good excuse and could not have worked more than once, but it did reinforce the association between nutmeg and hallucinations.

Jan Evangelista Purkinje was a brilliant Czech physiologist, who, in the 1820s taught at the University of Breslau in Germany. He was the first to describe the 'purkinje effect', that dim light appears bluer to the eye than it really is, but he is most famous for developing the basic concept of 'protoplasm'. Less well known were his self-experiments with nutmeg. Here he describes the effect of eating three whole nuts:

At half-past six, when it was almost dark, I woke up in order to go to the Royal Theatre from Brueder Street where I lived. The distance was long, but this time I thought it had no end. My movements appeared entirely adequate, but were lost momentarily in dream pictures, from which I had to extricate myself with considerable force in order to keep on walking. My feet did their duty and, since I had to stick to a straight road, there was no danger of going astray. I went forward in this dream, for, if I attempted to orient myself, I could not even recognise the cross streets. Time seemed long, but I got to the opposite side of the place where I was going. During this time dreams and physical activity battled one another. The return journey was good, and I slept well that night and next day.

Nutmeg's psychoactive element, isolated around the turn of the century, is called myristicin. It constitutes about 4 per cent of nutmeg's volatile essential oil and seems to work differently in humans and animals. Experiments show that the effect of myristicin is felt in two stages. There is first a primary action which can include hallucination and distortions of space and time, followed by a secondary coma which, with sufficient dosage, can cause death.

Certain animals, cats for example, require an absolutely massive dose before there is any effect whatsoever. If sufficient is administered to cause the primary action, such as hallucinations, secondary coma is virtually inevitable leading to the animal's death. Probably, this is why so many books warn of the dangers of large quantities of the spice, but human reaction seems somewhat different. A relatively small dose can produce the primary action without the secondary coma. In fact, there is but one recorded case of human death from nutmeg poisoning, that of an eight-year-old boy who swallowed two nutmegs.

Tests have also shown that pure myristicin has less effect than freshly ground nutmeg itself, suggesting that some other trace chemical may also play a part. A possible candidate is safrol which is also found in saffron and has chemical similarities to the drug MDA. The essential oils which contain the psychoactive substances are highly volatile and are probably long gone from the powdered spice. In much smaller quantities myristicin occurs in parsnip, parsley, scotch lovage and dill.

All this leads to a consideration of the 'recreational' use of nutmeg. In the 1960s one Italian jail held a number of middle-class minor drug offenders from various countries. Prisoners were able to cook their own meals and buy groceries from a local seller who took orders once a week. He was astounded by the numbers of whole nutmegs ordered. Prisoners ground them and then added boiling water to the powder to make a very strong tea. In small quantities, nutmeg makes a rather pleasant tea. In order to experience the slightest feeling of being drugged, prisoners had either to brew the tea to the point of vileness or drink a virtual ocean's worth, either way an unappetizing prospect. Yet they persisted.

Being a 'legal narcotic' nutmeg has been popular in prisons for years. Also during the 1960s, one George Weiss undertook a study of nutmeg use in the state prison at Trenton, New Jersey in the United States. He found that its use amongst some prisoners was extensive, and wrote: 'Doses of two to three tablespoons of powdered nutmeg tended to narcotize the subjects against the unpleasant experience of incarceration without blurring the boundaries between the self and the outer world.' Perhaps because Weiss had drawn undue attention to it, nutmeg was banned from the prison.

Recreational use in the Far East is rather difficult to determine because so many other substances are widely available; however, in parts of India nutmeg is eaten with the traditional betel nut, *pa'an*, in order to give it just a bit more kick, and in rural Indonesia it is sometimes found in snuff.

It was in the banana-smoking days of the late 1960s that the recreational use of nutmeg reached its peak. Thousands of experimenting university students on at least two continents were terribly disappointed upon discovering that all they suffered was the terrible taste of the brew and an upset stomach. With all psychoactive drugs, and especially one as weak as myristicin, there is a large element of the subjective. It is not surprising that women, distressed by unwanted pregnancies, had unpleasant experiences or 'bad trips'. It is equally unsurprising that prisoners, yearning for mental relief from their confinement, would find it delightful. A much fuller consideration of the subject can be found in an old but still valid article by Andrew T. Weil, 'Nutmeg as a Narcotic', published in 1963 in *Economic Botany*.

Shortly after the Magellan/Del Cano circumnavigation of the earth, the King of Spain bartered away to Portugal Spain's claim to the Moluccas, the Spice Islands. Later, it would be proved that despite the heroics of Magellan's crews, Spain never really had anything to barter, as the islands had always been on Portugal's side of the Pope's magic line.

The Banda group of islands is a set of tiny volcanic islands forming the southerly limit of the Moluccas. For centuries, they were visited regularly by Javanese traders. The traders came because, except for the odd tree here and there throughout the Moluccas, Banda housed all the world's nutmeg. The Portuguese preferred not to interrupt age-old trading patterns and were content to deal with the Javanese but the Dutch changed everything.

The Dutch came in the first years of the seventeenth century not as glory-seeking emissaries from a medieval king but as representatives of a corporation eager to show profits to a board of directors and shareholders. While their fortunes were waxing, those of the Portuguese were definitely on the wane. The first objective of the Dutch in snatching the nutmeg trade from the Portuguese was to cut out the Javanese middlemen and deal directly with the natives of Banda. This they accomplished with an impressive show of military force and a treaty with Banda's council of headmen, the Orang Kayas. The Dutch quickly became frustrated because despite their best efforts, the Bandanese simply refused to trade honourably. They were given to selling the same shipment several times over, pocketing money and not delivering, and worst of all, sticking low-quality nutmeg and mace at the bottom of piles. Moaned one Dutch captain, 'A man needs seven eyes.'

All this the Dutch bravely tolerated, but patience finally broke when the Bandanese took Dutch money and then resold the nutmeg and mace to the other new boys, the English. The Dutch hurried to refortify an old Portuguese fort on the islands, but while so doing were drawn into a trap

Lemon Curd Nutmeg Tart

SERVES SIX

For the pastry

4 oz/100 g (1 cup) plain (all-purpose) flour

pinch of salt

1 oz/25 g (⅛ cup) caster (superfine) sugar

2 oz/50 g (4 tablespoons) butter, cut into pieces

1 egg, lightly beaten

cold water if necessary

For the filling

12 oz/350 g (1½ cups) cottage cheese

juice and grated rind of 2 lemons

2 oz/50 g (¼ cup) caster (superfine) sugar

2 oz/50 g (½ cup) currants

1 oz/25 g (⅓ cup) flaked (slivered) almonds

1 teaspoon/5 ml freshly grated nutmeg

6 fl oz/175 ml (¾ cup) double (heavy) cream

4 thin lemon slices

To make the pastry, sift the flour, salt and sugar into a large bowl. Rub in the butter with the fingertips until the mixture resembles coarse meal. Stir in the beaten egg. Add water if necessary to make a pliable dough. Form the dough into a ball and put into a plastic bag or wrap in wax paper. Chill in the refrigerator for at least 1 hour.

Roll the dough out on to a lightly floured surface, first pressing it with the heel of the hand to flatten it. Beat it lightly with the rolling pin to make it pliable. Roll the dough into a circle and drape it over a buttered 7-inch/18-cm flan case, pressing the pastry lightly into the bottom of the case. Leave about ½-inch/1.5-cm pastry over the edge of the flan case, then trim away any excess. Fold over the border pastry to make an even rim round the inside of the flan case. Prick the bottom of the pastry at ½-inch/1.5-cm intervals with a fork. Line the pastry with buttered aluminium foil and fill it with dried beans. Bake in a preheated moderate oven, 400°F, 200°C, Gas Mark 6, for 20 minutes. Remove the foil and beans and return the pastry to the oven for a further 10 minutes or until the shell is lightly browned. Unmould the flan case and gently slip it on to a cake rack to cool.

Meanwhile, to make the filling, put the cottage cheese in a bowl and stir in the lemon juice and rind. Add the sugar and currants. Arrange the almonds on a baking sheet and bake in a preheated moderate oven, 350°F, 180°C, Gas Mark 4, until lightly browned. This should take about 5 minutes. Allow the nuts to cool and add to the bowl with the freshly grated nutmeg. Whip the cream until it stands in firm peaks and fold gently but thoroughly into the cottage cheese mixture. Turn the mixture into the prepared flan case, chill for several hours and decorate with the lemon slices cut and twisted into butterfly shapes.

by the Bandanese. Perhaps emboldened by promises of help from the English, the natives ambushed and slaughtered a Dutch admiral and thirty of his men, under the pretext of meeting for talks. Quickly, the Dutch declared war, and on 10 August 1609, the Bandanese island of Neyra was declared the first territorial acquisition of a Dutch empire which would last right into modern times.

One person who witnessed the treachery at Banda was a young Dutch administrator, Jan Pieterzoon Coen, who later turned out to be the most intelligent and able Dutch officer in the Far East. As the company's bookkeeper-general, an exalted post, he drafted the actual plan for the Dutch empire which was based on a tight monopoly over the trade in both cloves and nutmegs. As the years passed, however, the Bandanese again became restive, a situation the English were delighted to exploit.

In 1621 Coen sailed for Banda with a force of one thousand men, including eighty Japanese mercenaries. After a series of bitter battles Coen again forced the Bandanese to submit to Dutch will, but he heard rumours of further revolutionary activity in the hills. He seized the whole of the Orang Kayas, forty-five elders, and sent an expedition inland. When this was ambushed,

The extensive Dutch empire in the Far East grew on profits from spices. The Dutch had a monopoly of the wealthy nutmeg trade for 150 years until the mid-eighteenth century and the scale of this trade is evident in this painting showing the Dutch East India Company's base at Hooghly in 1665.

Coen ordered six of his Japanese mercenaries to kill the whole of the Orang Kayas. In addition, the Dutch rounded up hundreds of islanders, packed them aboard ships and literally dumped them on the island of Java. The remainder of the population fled inland where most died of starvation. Coen effectively depopulated the whole of Banda. The nutmeg groves were offered to 'decent' Dutch settlers along with slaves to do the work and nutmeg trees on all other islands were destroyed. The Dutch had achieved their monopoly. Dutch history has always treated Coen as a controversial, if not villainous, character, yet, the company, and nation willingly accepted the profits.

The Dutch nutmeg monopoly lasted for one hundred and fifty years, which was also the Netherland's golden age of affluence, art and culture. It was finally broken by the French whose story is told in the chapter on cloves. Nutmegs were later cultivated by the British in Penang and, by way of Kew Gardens in England, eventually reached the West Indian island of St Vincent. In 1843 they came to the island of Grenada which now calls itself 'The Nutmeg Isle'. In 1955, the Grenadian crop was destroyed by hurricane, but with help from new Moluccan plants it has now recovered. Today, Grenada supplies 30 per cent of the world's nutmeg while Indonesia provides most of the rest.

Nutmeg contains a high fat content, much of which can be removed by solvent extraction. A nutmeg oleoresin is produced as well as a butter-like orangey substance unsurprisingly called nutmeg butter. The oleoresins are used to flavour processed foods while the butter is used widely in the cosmetic and pharmaceutical industries.

Nutmeg flavour is almost entirely created by the volatile oil which is present from 7 to 16 per cent in nutmeg and 4 to 15 per cent in mace. Indonesia is the major producer of these oils which manufacturers of processed food and drinks employ. Only unmarketable nuts are used for oil production. The grade of nut which produces the

Rum punch, the famous Caribbean drink. The Caribbean island of Grenada is known as 'The Nutmeg Isle'.

Rum Punch

Whether made individually or in great quantity for a party, rum punch is a great Caribbean contribution to entertaining. The spices marry with rum to produce a splendid drink for hot days.

SERVES ABOUT 24	
8 fl oz/225 ml (1 cup) lime juice, strained	12 fl oz/350 ml (1½ cups) sugar (simple) syrup
2 pints/1.1 litres (5 cups) white rum	1¾ pints/1 litre (4 cups) water
4 fl oz/100 ml (½ cup) clear honey	¼ teaspoon/1.5 ml ground cloves
	1 teaspoon/5 ml freshly grated nutmeg

Combine all the ingredients, except the nutmeg, in a large bowl and mix well. Pour the mixture into bottles or carafes and refrigerate. When ready to serve, pour the mixture into a large punch bowl over ice cubes or cracked ice. Sprinkle with the freshly grated nutmeg and serve in punch glasses.

SERVES ONE	
2 fl oz/50 ml (¼ cup) white rum	2–3 dashes Angostura bitters
1 tablespoon/15 ml lime juice, strained	3–4 ice cubes
1 tablespoon/15 ml sugar (simple) syrup	freshly grated nutmeg

Combine all the ingredients, except the nutmeg and ice cubes, in a cocktail shaker and shake vigorously. Strain over ice cubes into a small tumbler and sprinkle with grated nutmeg.

highest yield of oil is known as BWP—Broken, Wormy, Punk. These nuts are infested with weevil larvae which eat the fixed oils and other starchy compounds permitting a much greater yield of the valuable volatile oils. As has been said, these oils have wide application in food industries, especially soft drinks and most especially in colas. Ponder that next time you pause for refreshment.

To the average person, nutmeg and mace are kitchen spices. Nutmegs are used primarily in baked goods and with sugar. Mace is a meat savoury spice; however, often nutmeg and mace can be interchanged without disastrous consequence and both can be used to flavour meats. For example, Henry Heath, the flavour technologist, describes mace as accounting for 20 per cent

Steak, Kidney and Oyster Pie

There are many versions of this traditional British dish. Some versions use sliced mushrooms and others, such as this recipe, use oysters. This version, therefore, was particularly popular around Colchester and Whitstable, the famous oyster centres of England. Either shortcrust, hot-water crust or puff pastry can be used. The recipe here is made with shortcrust pastry. The steak may be

raw, partially cooked or braised before being topped with pastry. If a less tender meat such as stewing steak is used, it is better to cook it in advance. Let the meat mixture cool before covering it with the pastry lid so that the pastry does not become soggy. Use a 2½-pint/1.5-litre enamelware or ceramic English pie dish with a rim edge or a casserole with a rim edge.

SERVES SIX

For the pastry

12 oz/350 g (3 cups) plain (all-purpose) flour

½ teaspoon/2.5 ml salt

3 oz/75 g (6 tablespoons) butter

3 oz/75 g (6 tablespoons) lard

about 4 tablespoons/60 ml iced water

For the filling

12 oysters

3 tablespoons/40 g plain (all-purpose) flour

salt and freshly ground black pepper

⅛ teaspoon or pinch freshly grated nutmeg

1½ lb/700 g lean steak cut into 1-inch/2.5-cm cubes

8 oz/225 g kidney, cut into 1-inch/2.5-cm cubes

½ oz/15 ml (1 tablespoon) gelatine

2 tablespoons/30 ml hot water

6 oz/175 ml (¾ cup) beef stock

1 egg, lightly beaten

To make the pastry, sift the flour and salt into a mixing bowl. Cut the butter and lard into small pieces and then rub quickly into the flour, using the fingertips until the mixture resembles coarse meal. Add enough iced water to make a pliable dough. Gather the dough into a ball and put into a plastic bag or wrap in wax paper. Refrigerate for 1–2 hours.

Meanwhile, open the oysters and drain them, reserving the liquid. Put them into a small bowl. In a large bowl, combine the flour, salt, black pepper and freshly grated nutmeg. Toss the meat, kidneys and oysters in the seasoned flour and put into the rimmed pie dish. Dissolve the gelatine in the hot water and stir into the beef stock. Add the oyster liquid and put into the pie dish. The liquid should just cover the meat. If there is too much, spoon off a little and use it as a gravy with the pie.

To use the dough, press it out partially with the heel of the hand on to a lightly floured surface. Flatten it lightly with a rolling pin and roll it out to the size and shape required. Cut a strip of pastry to fit round the rim of the pie dish and press it firmly into place. Brush the strip lightly with beaten egg and cover with the large piece of pastry. Press the edges firmly into place, cutting off any excess. Crimp the edges with a fork or with the fingers. Brush the pastry with the remaining egg and make a steam hole in the centre. Bake in a preheated moderate oven, 375°F, 190°C, Gas Mark 5, for 25 minutes. Reduce the heat to 325°F, 170°C, Gas Mark 3, and cook for 1½ hours longer or until the pastry is cooked and golden brown. If the pastry browns too quickly, cover it lightly with aluminium foil. Remove the foil for the last 10 minutes of cooking.

Béchamel Sauce

Sauces are the basis and glory of French cuisine. Béchamel is one of the basic sauces of the French kitchen, *a mother sauce giving rise to other sauces. It is also the base for soufflés, and is infinitely useful in the kitchen.*

MAKES $\frac{3}{4}$ PINT/450 ML (2 CUPS)	$\frac{3}{4}$ *pint/450 ml (2 cups) milk*
$1\frac{1}{4}$ *oz/30 g (2 tablespoons) unsalted butter*	*salt and white pepper*
$1\frac{1}{2}$ *oz/40 g (3 tablespoons) plain (all-purpose) flour*	$\frac{1}{8}$ *teaspoon/pinch of freshly grated nutmeg*

Melt the butter in a medium-sized heavy saucepan over a low heat. When the foam begins to subside, stir in the flour and cook, stirring with a wooden spoon for 2 minutes without letting the mixture colour. Remove from the heat and gradually stir in the milk. When all the milk has been added and the mixture is smooth return the saucepan to the heat and bring to the boil, stirring constantly. Simmer, stirring for 5 minutes. Season with salt, pepper and nutmeg.

For a very thick sauce, for example, for making a soufflé base, reduce the liquid to half the amount. For a thinner pouring sauce, increase the liquid used by 4 fl oz/100 ml ($\frac{1}{2}$ cup).

---

of the flavour of fresh beef sausages, and 10 per cent respectively for pork sausages, frankfurters, meat loaf and pork pie. Nutmeg is responsible for 20 per cent of the flavour of both fresh beef sausages and meat loaf and 10 per cent for pork sausages and bologna.

In the seventeenth and eighteenth centuries, nutmeg was essential to virtually every sweet dish. Here is an American recipe from Mrs E. Smith's *Compleat Housewife* published in Williamsburg in 1742.

TO MAKE AN ALMOND PUDDING

Take a Pound of the best Jordan Almonds blanched in cold Water, and beat very fine with a little Rosewater; then take a Quart of Cream, boiled with the whole Spice, and taken out again, and when 'tis cold, mix it with the Almonds, and put to it three Spoonfuls of grated Bread, one Spoonful of Flour, nine eggs, but three Whites, half a Pound of Sugar, a Nutmeg grated; mix and beat these well together, put some Puff-Paste at the bottom of the Dish; put your Stuff in, and here and there stick a Piece of Marrow in it. It must bake an Hour and when 'tis drawn, scrape Sugar on it, and serve it up.

Today, there are any number of sauces, soufflés, baked goods and potted meats all requiring as essential either nutmeg or mace; but it is surprising how many people, even those somewhat sophisticated in the kitchen, have never seen, held or tasted mace in blade form. If you have not—do! It is magic. It is the most elegant way of truly understanding the essence of *Myristica*.

As for nutmeg, 40–45 per cent of the world's supply is used in ground form for industrial purposes, 25–35 per cent is used in ground form as a domestic culinary spice, about 25 per cent goes into the oils and only 1–2 per cent is used in whole form in domestic kitchens. This is not only incomprehensible, but tragic. It is so simple to grind a nutmeg. Every kitchen has some grinding surface and it is just as easy to reach for the nut as for the box of powder. Whole nutmeg is vastly superior because the volatile oils which are the basis of the flavour quickly vanish after grinding and the nutmeg is its own best container. The difference is remarkable.

Finally, Waverley Root in his book *Food* quoted the French gourmet Curnonsky on nutmeg:

'. . . anyone who has tasted this spice no longer desires others, just as anyone who has made love with a Chinese woman no longer desires to make love with other women.' Figure that out for yourself.

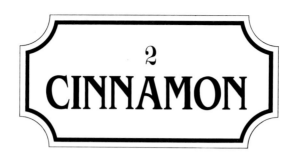

2
CINNAMON

I have perfumed my bed with myrrh, aloes, and cinnamon.

Come, let us take our fill of love until the morning; let us solace ourselves with loves.

(PROVERBS Chapter 7: 17, 18)

At one time or another, every spice or herb has been touted as an aphrodisiac. Cinnamon, with its warm, sensuous aroma, has been so regarded more than most. The Queen of Sheba brought it to King Solomon who sang its praises:

Spinkenard and saffron; calamus and cinnamon, with all trees of frankincense; myrrh and aloes, with all the chief spices: . . .

Awake, O north wind; and come thou south; blow upon my garden, that the spices thereof may flow out, let my beloved come into his garden, and eat his pleasant fruits.

(SONG OF SOLOMON Chapter 4: 14, 16)

But Solomon knew that the use of cinnamon, and its sister spice cassia, was commanded for less frivolous purposes, by no less an authority than the Lord himself. These spices were essential in the ointment for the holiest of holies, the ark of testimony.

Moreover the Lord spake unto Moses, saying,

Take thou also unto thee principal spices, of pure myrrh five hundred shekels, and of sweet cinnamon half so much, even two hundred and fifty shekels, and of sweet calamus two hundred and fifty shekels.

And of cassia five hundred shekels . . .

And thou shalt make it an oil of holy ointment, an ointment compound after the art of the apothecary; it shall be an holy anointing oil.

And thou shalt anoint the tabernacle of the congregation therewith, and the ark of the testimony.

(EXODUS Chapter 30: 22 to 26)

Solomon was living in about 1000 BC and Exodus of course was written much earlier; yet, even in most ancient times a distinction was made between cinnamon and cassia and they were both precious. Two questions arise; where did cinnamon come from? And, how did it get to Egypt and the Holy Land?

Neither cinnamon nor cassia grow, or have ever grown in the land of the Bible. The ancient Egyptians used them for both cosmetics and embalming. In about 1500 BC, five hundred years before Solomon, the Egyptian Queen, Hatshepsut, sent out an expedition of five ships. It passed through an open waterway on the site of the present Suez Canal into the Red Sea and sailed down the African Coast to 'The Land of Punt', present-day Somalia. There the expedition was able to find precious metals, ivory, baboons, panthers, various spices and cinnamon. There was another recorded ancient voyage to Punt, a full thousand years before Hatshepsut, by the Pharaoh, Sankhare, who also sought cinnamon and other aromatics. It is no wonder that the areas of Ethiopia and Somalia which lie close to the Arabian peninsula were known to the ancients as 'the cinnamon-growing lands'.

For millenia, myths and stories of the origin of cinnamon and cassia circulated throughout the Mediterranean. Herodotus, the great historian, wrote in about 450 BC:

When the Arabians go out to collect cassia, they cover their bodies and faces, all but their eyes,

Cinnamon quills on the left and cassia on the right. Cinnamon being sweeter and milder is thought to be the more elegant spice. They both come from the bark of tropical evergreens of the genus *Cinnamomum*.

with ox-hides and other skins. The plant grows in a shallow lake which, together with the ground round about it, is infested by winged creatures like bats, which screech alarmingly and are very pugnacious. They have to be kept from attacking the men's eyes while they are cutting the cassia.

The process of collecting cinnamon is still more remarkable. Where it comes from and what country produces it, they do not know: the best some of them can do is to make a fair guess that it grows somewhere in the region where Dionysus was brought up. What they say is that dry sticks, which we have learnt from the Phoenicians to call cinnamon, are brought by large birds, which carry them to their nests, made of mud, on mountain precipices, which no man can climb, and that the method the Arabians have invented for getting hold of them

is to cut up the bodies of dead oxen, or donkeys, or other animals into large joints, which they carry to the spot in question and leave on the ground near the nests. They then retire to a safe distance and the birds fly down and carry off the joints of meat to their nests, which, not being strong enough to bear the weight, break and fall to the ground. Then the men come along and pick up the cinnamon, which is subsequently exported to other countries.

Sad to say, this is not how cinnamon and cassia are harvested. These and similar tales were spread deliberately in order to protect trading monopolies. Herodotus's story does, however, contain three interesting clues to the real source. Firstly, cinnamon comes from 'the region where Dionysus was brought up'. This means India, or at least lands to the east. Secondly, we (the Greeks) 'learnt from the Phoenicians' to call the spice cinnamon. And finally, it is the Arabs who collect the cinnamon and export it to other countries.

The truth about cinnamon and cassia is as amazing as the fables. Both cinnamon and cassia are the dried bark of tropical evergreens of the genus *Cinnamomum*. This belongs to the family Lauraceae, which makes cinnamon and cassia distant cousins of bay leaves and avocados. That is about as far as the authorities can agree. One problem is that the genus *Cinnamomum* contains between fifty and two hundred and fifty different species, depending upon which expert you want to believe. Another problem is that over the centuries the distinction as to which *Cinnamomum* is cinnamon and which is cassia has changed. Some people do not even bother to distinguish between the two; for example, the French word *cannelle* covers both, and the French certainly know something about food. It is, however, generally agreed that cinnamon being sweet and mild is the more elegant of the two, while cassia is strong and bitter. It is also probable that the cinnamon and cassia used by the ancient Hebrews and Egyptians would both be classified today as cassia.

Cassia (*Cinnamomum cassia*) is one of the great spices of China. It was mentioned in ancient herbals written even before Pharaoh Sankhare's expedition to Punt. Along with anise pepper (*Xanthoxylum*), star anise, cloves and fennel seed, it forms the five-spice powder essential to Chinese cooking. The word 'cassia' may derive from the Chinese *Kwei-shi* meaning cinnamon branch; however, since cassia has never grown wild in China this is probably wrong. The spice *does* grow wild in Assam, that part of India lying north of Bangladesh, and it is virtually certain that it entered China from this region. The people of northern Assam are known as 'Khasi' and, to this day, their mountains are called the Khasi Hills.

From very ancient times, Chinese goods were transported westward along the very arduous and

dangerous trail which came to be known as the silk route. Starting in central China, the route wound south of the Gobi desert and north of the Himalayas and then on to Kashgar, Tashkent, Samarkand, Baghdad and the Mediterranean. Certainly, some cassia must have passed this way. It is most likely that the spice gave its name to both the great trading post of Kashgar and the northern Indian state of Kashmir. But that

Cassia is sometimes called Chinese cinnamon and has been used widely in Chinese cooking for many centuries. It is one of the essential spices in the Chinese five-spice mixture. The fishermen of this region of Gwilin use cormorants to catch fish which are then cooked with cassia on their houseboats.

does not explain why the ancients travelled to Africa to obtain both cinnamon and cassia. There had to be another route. The Indonesians were the ancient world's greatest mariners. They sailed the oceans to Easter Island, New Zealand and Hawaii, whose name is a corruption of 'Java'. They traded with the Chinese and India was, for them, but a hop across the Bay of Bengal. Undoubtedly some Chinese cassia reached India with the help of the Indonesians. From there it was carried on to the Red Sea and the Mediterranean by the Arabs.

Cinnamomum burmanii, sometimes called Batavia or Java cassia, grew wild on the Indonesian islands of Sumatra, Java and Borneo. Noticing the similarity between their *Cinnamomum burmanii* and Chinese cassia, the islanders probably started harvesting and trading the local bark. This could have been the cinnamon of old. The quest does not end here, for there was another route to the west, the most fantastic of all.

'Arabia produces neither cinnamon nor cassia', wrote the Roman historian Pliny in about AD 70, '"Happy" Arabia! False and ungrateful does she prove herself in the adaptation of this surname, which she would imply to have been received from the gods above; whereas, in reality, she is indebted for it far more to the gods of hell. It is the luxury which is displayed by man, even in the paraphernalia of death, that has rendered Arabia thus "happy"; and which prompts him to burn with the dead what was originally understood to have been reproduced for the service of the Gods.' Pliny, was commenting critically on the Emperor Nero's burning of a whole year's supply of cinnamon at his wife Poppaea's funeral. Pliny was an official of the Roman Empire and was very concerned about a growing balance of payments problem. He was determined to describe accurately the source of the eastern luxuries which were eating away at the reserves of Roman gold.

He easily dismisses Herodotus: 'All these tales . . . have been invented evidently for the purpose of enhancing the prices of these commodities.' He was often wrong, but his description of the Indonesian cinnamon carriers was probably accurate. '(They) carry it over vast tracts of sea, upon

Arroz con Leche · Rice Pudding

Rice was introduced into Mexico after the Conquest and can be said to have been an instant favourite. This is a purely colonial dish owing nothing to the pre-Columbian past. This pudding is served cold.

SERVES SIX

2 oz/50 g (⅓ cup) seedless raisins	1¾ pints/1 litre (4 cups) milk
2 fl oz/50 ml (¼ cup) sherry	8 oz/225 g (1 cup) sugar
4 oz/100 g (½ cup) long-grain rice	½ teaspoon/1.5 ml ground cinnamon
1 x 2-inch/5-cm piece of lemon peel	2 eggs, well beaten
pinch of salt	toasted flaked (slivered) almonds
8 fl oz/225 ml (1 cup) water	cinnamon

In a small bowl combine the raisins with the sherry and set aside. Wash the rice in cold water until the water runs clear. Put the washed rice into a bowl with hot water to cover and let it soak for 15 minutes. Rinse in cold water and drain.

Put the rice into a saucepan with the lemon peel, salt and water. Bring to the boil, reduce the heat to very low, cover and cook until all the water has been absorbed. Remove and discard the lemon peel. Add the milk, sugar and cinnamon, stir and cook, uncovered, over a very low heat until all the milk has been absorbed. When the rice is cooked, stir in the eggs and raisins and cook for about 5 minutes longer. Turn into a serving dish and sprinkle with the almonds. If liked, sprinkle with more ground cinnamon. Chill in the refrigerator.

Café Brûlot

Coffee and cinnamon seem to go together naturally from the Café Brûlot of New Orleans to the Café de Olla of Mexico. Brûlot, literally translated, means burnt brandy and when the hot alcoholic coffee is served in a darkened room the effect of the flickering flames is wonderfully dramatic.

SERVES SIX	
1 x 3-inch/7.5-cm stick of cinnamon	6 sugar cubes
10 whole cloves	8 fl oz/225 ml (1 cup) brandy
peel of 1 orange or grapefruit	2 fl oz/50 ml (¼ cup) Curaçao (optional)
	1 pint/500 ml (2 cups) strong, hot, freshly made coffee

Put the cinnamon, cloves, orange peel and sugar into a silver *brûlot* bowl, or chafing dish and mash them together with the back of a ladle. Pour in the brandy and the Curaçao, if using, and stir until the sugar has dissolved. Ignite the brandy, standing well back, then pour in the hot coffee, gradually mixing with the brandy until the flame flickers out. Ladle the coffee into *demi-tasse* or *brûlot* cups.

Café de Olla   *Mexican Coffee*

SERVES FOUR

1¼ pints/700 ml (3 cups) water	4 oz/100 g (½ cup) brown sugar, preferably Mexican
4 tablespoons/60 ml strong dark roasted coffee	1 x 2-inch/5-cm stick of cinnamon

Heat the water in an earthenware pot. Add the coffee, sugar and cinnamon and bring to a boil.

Bring to the boil twice. Strain and serve in small earthenware or other cups.

---

rafts, which are neither steered by rudder, nor drawn or impelled by oars or sails. Nor yet are they aided by any of the resources of art, man alone, and his daring boldness, standing in place of all these.' He goes on to describe how they put out to sea at the beginner of winter when the south-east wind is at its height and how they travel from gulf to gulf. Ultimately, a north-east wind takes them up the coast of Africa into the Gulf of Aden to Ethiopia, 'the cinnamon-growing land'. The whole journey takes almost five years and many perish.

One historian, J. I. Miller in his *Spice Trade of the Roman Empire* uses Pliny and other sources to show that the south-east wind first carried the Indonesians to the island of Madagascar off the African coast. It is a fact that in the first millenium AD the Indonesians colonized Madagascar. The Malagasy language spoken there is unquestionably derived from Malaysian. Although colonization began in the first millenium, some authorities find evidence of trading voyages much earlier, perhaps back to the time of the Pharaoh Sank-hare. If this is true, then at a time when the most advanced of Western civilizations could only fumble along the tiny Mediterranean coast, Indonesian cinnamon traders were navigating 6500 kilometres of open ocean, and back!

The cinnamon was then taken to an ancient and mysterious metropolis called Rhapta. The best guess is that Rhapta was located on the East African coast opposite the island of Zanzibar. The name 'Rhapta' comes from the Arabic root *rbt* to bind, as in binding the planks of a raft. In describing the Indonesian boats, Pliny used the Latin words *ratis, ratibus*, meaning raft. Most etymo-logical dictionaries show the origin of the English word 'raft' to be Old Norse, but the similarity to the Arabic seems too close for coincidence.

According to Professor Miller, from Rhapta, Arab or perhaps Phoenician traders sailed with the cinnamon north to the Red Sea and ultimately to the Mediterranean. *Kayu manis* is Malay for 'sweet wood' and is the origin of the word cinnamon. The Hebrews and Phoenicians took the name and called it *guinnamon*. As Herodotus pointed out, the Phoenicians passed it on to the Greeks as 'Kinnamon' and finally to the Romans as 'Cinnamomum' and 'cinnamon'.

Much of the cinnamon followed yet another route from Rhapta. This was an arduous land journey, northward past Mount Kilimanjaro and into present-day Kenya, then westward at Lake Turkana (Rudolf) to Juba which sits on the Nile 1000 kilometres south of Khartoum; then through the marshes to Malakal and up the length of the Nile to Alexandria. Remember that cassia could have started its journey in the interior of southern China. The cinnamon route was one of the most fantastic voyages not only of ancient times, but of all time.

Before he described the journey Pliny wrote: 'At the very lowest computation, India, the Seres, and the Arabian Peninsula withdraw from our empire one hundred millions of sesterces every year—so dearly do we pay for our luxury, and our women.'

Finally, of the brave Indonesians, what did they get for their troubles? Pliny tells us:

In return for their wares, they bring back articles of glass and copper, cloths, buckles, bracelets and necklaces; hence it is, that this traffic depends chiefly upon capricious female fidelity to fashion.

By Pliny's time, the Romans themselves started sailing and trading across the Indian Ocean. They had learned that the wind which carried the Indonesians to Africa was the winter, or north-east, monsoon. The summer, southwest, monsoon brought them back. The Romans traded extensively with India and ultimately Ceylon, now Sri Lanka. On the latter they found what is now regarded as true Cinnamon, *Cinnamomum verum* or *Cinnamomum zeylancium*. Its yellowish-brown quills are regarded as the finest in the world. Today, Sri Lanka grows most of the world's true cinnamon but methods of harvest have changed little from the time of the Romans.

The best cinnamon grows along the coastal strip near Colombo, just inland from the white sandy beaches which are gaining in popularity with tourists from all over the world. In its wild state,

trees grow high on stout trunks. Under cultivation, the shoots are continually cropped almost to ground level. The result is a low bush, dense with thin leafy branches. From these come the finest quills. Harvesters work in families, each member responsible for a specific task. Cutting begins soon after first light. The idea is to take two or three branches from each tree, allowing new shoots to grow in their place. Cutting is best done during the rainy season because the humidity helps the bark to peel easily. A special axe called a 'katty' is used.

After a few hours, the cut branches are taken to the *wadi* or peeling shed. The *wadi* is a large room, open on one side. The workers sit in rows on the floor. To the left are the 'establishers', skilled workers who remove the cinnamon bark itself.

The best cinnamon in the world grows along the coastal strip of land near Colombo in Sri Lanka. The finest cinnamon bark comes from these young, tender shoots in the centre of the bush. Cutting is best done during the rainy season because the humidity helps the bark to peel off more easily.

To the right, are the women and children who carry out the preparatory tasks.

First the thin outer bark is scraped away, then the branch is rubbed with a brass rod. The valuable inner bark is bruised so that it will lift away more easily. Two long slits are made in the bark, which is then lifted off the stick. Drying in the sun causes the separated bark to curl inward, forming the familiar quills. The quills are cut to a standard length and are left for further drying in the roof of the *wadi*. Nothing is wasted. Small chips are used to fill the longer quills. Even the leaves and small branches trimmed at the start are saved for making cinnamon leaf oil. The remaining naked sticks provide fuel. Sri Lankan land reform legislation now ensures that no one person owns more than fifty acres of cinnamon, but most plantations are considerably smaller. The Seychelles and the Malagasy Republic (Madagascar) are today the other major producers of true cinnamon.

Facing page above: The cut branches are taken to the nearby *wadi*, or peeling shed, where the workers sit in rows on the floor. On one side are the 'establishers', the skilled workers who remove the cinnamon bark itself, and on the other side are the women and children who carry out the preparatory tasks.

Facing page below: The thin outer bark is stripped off by the women and children before the men prepare the cinnamon quills from the valuable inner bark.

Above: The inner bark is bruised and two long slits made in it so that it will lift off in layers more easily. Finished cinnamon quills are put up in the ceiling of the *wadi* for further drying.

Left: Nothing is wasted and small chips of cinnamon are used to fill the longer quills.

In Europe cinnamon reached its peak of popularity in the late Middle Ages. Along with ginger, it was a staple ingredient of many medieval recipes. Normally, households had only one cooking utensil, a large cauldron hung in the hearth. There was no cutlery and few plates. Food was served on slabs of stale bread called 'trenchers', which themselves were often eaten at the close of the meal. Opposing flavours, sweet and sour, were thrown together. Boiling away in the hearth could be a single casserole containing both meat and fruit. Later, returning Crusaders brought home sugar which was also thrown into the cauldron along with meat and fruit. A survivor from the period is mince pie in which fruit, meat and sugar are mixed together. Cinnamon was

found to be the ideal spice to bridge the gap between sweet and sour flavours.

So great was the craving for cinnamon, that immediately after reaching India, the Portuguese invaded Sri Lanka. In 1536, they occupied the island and extracted a tribute of 110,000 kilogrammes of cinnamon annually from the Sinhalese King. The Dutch captured Sri Lanka from the Portuguese in 1636 and established the system of cinnamon cultivation that still exists. The Dutch, however, were soon faced with a decreasing demand for cinnamon and they were forced into extreme measures to maintain its price in the market place. One can imagine the aroma over Amsterdam as whole warehouses of the spice were burnt.

Left The finished cinnamon quills are taken to the local cinnamon merchant where they are graded and exported all over the world.
Above: The cinnamon merchant packs up the quills for export. The Sri Lankan cinnamon trade was well established by the eighteenth century.

Ultimately, in the eighteenth century the cuisine of Europe changed. The various flavours were appropriated to distinct courses which were cooked in separate pans and eaten with cutlery on plates. A new taste, neither sweet nor sour, rose to dominate the culinary scene: savoury. Pepper, not cinnamon, became the prime spice of choice. Cinnamon was shifted mainly to the pudding or dessert course where it still acts as the bridge between sweet and sour. Apple strudel, for example, with its sweet sugar and sour apples, would be unthinkable without cinnamon.

Today, the confusion between cassia and cinnamon continues. On account of its stronger taste, cassia, and its extracted oils, is preferred by the processed food industry. Quilled cassia is, however, sold in several countries as cinnamon. Many commercial powders contain both cassia and cinnamon and even the best experts are baffled as to which is which.

The largest importer of Sri Lankan cinnamon is Mexico. There, it is drunk with coffee and chocolate and brewed as a tea.

A touch of the festive and exotic still accompanies cinnamon. It makes many dishes a bit 'special'. As for being an aphrodisiac, cinnamon does exude a sensuous warmth. Its essential oils and those of cassia are widely used in perfumes, soaps and cosmetics.

So, the circle closes. Solomon, in his wisdom, had the right idea all along. As for cinnamon and cassia, their ancient secrets have been revealed but there are new secrets: their essential oils form part of the closely guarded formulae of the major colas.

The Austrians have always used a lot of cinnamon in their cooking and their famous pudding, *apfelstrudel*, uses cinnamon to bridge the gap between sweet sugar and sour apples. Here, the Plumbergers of Bad Ischl are enjoying the warm *apfelstrudel* freshly made by Frau Plumberger.

Apfelstrudel

Apple Strudel

To make this famous Austrian pudding sheets of strudel dough can sometimes be bought frozen but it is worth while going to the extra trouble of making the pastry which bakes into a deliciously crisp, parchment-thin covering for the cinnamon-flavoured filling of apples and nuts.

SERVES SIX TO EIGHT

For the pastry

4 oz/100 g (1 cup) plain (all-purpose) flour

⅛ teaspoon/large pinch of salt

1 egg, lightly beaten

½ fl oz/15 g (1 tablespoon) vegetable oil

1 teaspoon/5 ml lemon juice

2 fl oz/50 ml (¼ cup) lukewarm water

For the filling

1½ lb/700 g (6 cups) tart cooking apples

2 oz/50 g (¼ cup) sugar

2½ oz/65 g (½ cup) sultanas (golden raisins)

2 oz/50 g (½ cup) flaked (slivered) almonds

or 2 oz/50 g (½ cup) coarsely chopped walnuts

½ teaspoon/2.5 ml ground cinnamon

grated rind of 1 lemon

4 oz/100 g (½ cup) melted butter

4 oz/100 g (2 cups) breadcrumbs, lightly toasted

icing (confectioners') sugar

To make the pastry, sift the flour and salt together into a large bowl. In a small bowl combine the egg, oil, lemon juice and water. Make a well in the centre of the flour, add the egg mixture and mix to a fairly soft dough which will be slightly sticky. Knead the dough until it is silky and pliable. Form it into a ball, coat it lightly with oil, cover it with a cloth, and leave it to rest in a cool place for 1 hour.

Use a workspace (a table) 3 feet/1 metre square. Cover the table with a lightly floured cloth of the same size. Put the dough in the centre of the cloth. Flour the dough very lightly, then roll it out into a circle of about 12 inches/30 cm. Using floured hands, gently pull the dough from all sides until it is the same size as the cloth. Be careful not to let your nails pierce it. It is a good idea to take off any rings. Pull and stretch the dough very gently over the backs of the hands. It will be paper thin when it is ready to fill. Traditionally it is said that you can read a newspaper through it.

Peel, core and slice the apples. In a bowl combine the apples, sugar, sultanas (golden raisins), nuts, cinnamon and grated lemon rind. Mix well. Trim the edges of the dough and brush with half of the melted butter. Spread the dough with the bread-crumbs, leaving a margin all round. Cover the breadcrumbs with the apple mixture. Lift the cloth from one end, and using the cloth to help, roll up the dough. Tuck the ends under to seal in the filling. Brush with the remaining butter. Slide the strudel on to a large buttered baking sheet and form it into a horseshoe. Bake in a preheated moderate oven, 400°F, 200°C, Gas Mark 6, for 45 minutes to 1 hour, or until the strudel is golden brown. Sprinkle generously with icing (confectioners') sugar and serve warm.

3
PEPPER

Leo Steiner is certain that his Carnegie Delicatessen in Mid-Manhattan, New York, is the best in the world. With his broad grin and white apron, Leo is also experienced in front of the camera. 'Gimme a countdown', he begs. 'This Deli sells about two tons of pastrami a week!' Lunchtime in New York is pastrami and Leo knows a lot about it; but first he wants to talk about the gaggle of musicians and show-business types that flock to the Deli.

'Woody Allen eats here,' whispers Leo who grimaces, 'But he only eats oatmeal!' The Carnegi Deli shines with neon, glass, stainless steel and arborite but really is a creature of the past.

'We make everything here ourselves,' shouts Leo, drawing attention to the perpetual motion of the slicing machine, an unnecessary attention, for no nose could miss the aroma, nor eye miss the mountains of rich red meat. Heaping sandwiches inspire guilt, then puzzlement. How does one get a mouth around that? One bite and hesitation vanishes into sublime contentment. Leo hovers. His grin broadens as eyes close and spirits soar.

'Years ago, they had to preserve meat,' explains Leo with the passion of the true guardian of ancient wisdom, 'And the way you preserve meat is with salt and saltpetre in vacuums in a cool place. This all runs together with the natural juices of the meat. After meat had lain from seven to fourteen days, it became a little . . . well . . . mildewed. It formed a light taste over the mouth. Now, how to get rid of this mildew taste? . . . They cooked the meat with cloves of garlic, bay leaves . . . and especially, all sorts of different spices.'

The food of medieval Europe was bland. Potatoes and tomatoes had not yet arrived from the new world. Vegetables and fruit, limited in

Leo Steiner's Carnegie Delicatessen in New York sells about two tons of pastrami a week.

both variety and quantity, were mistakenly considered unhealthy. People liked meat, but supply was unpredictable. Techniques for keeping fodder over the winter had not yet developed, so excess animals had to be slaughtered in the autumn. To make culinary matters even more difficult, church edict prohibited meat on at least half the days of the year. Smoking and curing were essential.

Mustard, garlic, saffron and a multiplicity of local herbs were employed to create some variety and, indeed, to mask the various mildew tastes, and worse. Nothing, however, could compare with the spices of the orient . . . pepper, cloves, cinnamon, nutmeg and mace. Only in the tropics could the blazing sun burn such intensity of flavour and aroma into such tiny packages. Spices were treasured; they were kept under lock and key; they were demanded as dowries and bequeathed in testaments. They were traded in gold, a substance in which they were, literally, worth their weight. But one spice was sought and

Top: Pepper comes from the plant *Piper nigrum* and is mainly produced by Indonesia, Malaysia and Brazil. Black pepper is produced from whole, unripe, fully developed berries. White pepper berries are picked slightly later, just as they are turning red.
Above: Picking pepper in Sarawak, Malaysia. The pepper is picked here when it is slightly more red than in Sri Lanka where the pepper is picked at its green stage.
Right: Picking peppers in Sri Lanka; here the berries are picked in a green or unripe state.

cherished above the rest; it was what made pastrami pastrami; the master spice . . . pepper.

Pepper is indigenous to the southerly part of India's east coast, an area known as Malabar. The name 'pepper' comes from the Sanskrit *pippali*, meaning berry. It originally referred to a related plant known as *Piper longum* or long pepper. Although it was valued by the Romans, today long pepper is not important commercially. The pepper of commerce is *Piper nigrum*. It still grows in India, but Indonesia, Malaysia and Brazil are now the major producers.

Black pepper comes from berries picked in a green or unripe state and allowed to dry in the sun until black. White pepper berries are picked slightly later, just as they are turning red. They are soaked in water to remove the reddish pericarp or outer skin before drying. White pepper has the milder flavour of the two.

In the first century AD the Romans came to the Malabar coast of India for pepper. They used pepper much as today, both in cooking and as a condiment. They kept their supply in *horrea piperataria* or giant warehouses built in the 'spice quarter'. In AD 408 the Romans paid the Gothic King Alaric 1200 kilograms of pepper not to sack their city. It did not work. The Goth took the pepper and sacked the city anyway.

Later, the Islamic Arabs seized control of the trade routes to the east and but a trickle of pepper reached the West. The Crusades marked an awakening of European interest in the East and its luxuries, including pepper. The enterprising merchants of the emerging city of Venice established strong and profitable trading links with the Arabs.

In 1204 the Venetians were supposed to lead the Fourth Crusade against Alexandria, then controlled by the Arabs. Instead, they turned their great warships north and attacked and looted

In Asian countries pepper is put out to dry in the sun on bamboo mats. The drying takes between seven and ten days during which time the green peppercorns gradually turn to the more familiar black colour.

Li commence li liures du grant Caam qui parole de la grant Ermenie de perse...
et destrtans et dynue. Et des granz mervielle qui p le monde sont...

A view of Venice in 1338 when the city was beginning its long period of wealth and magnificence as a result of its thriving trade with the East. Pepper was one of the valuable commodities that Europe could obtain only through Venetian merchants, the middlemen. It is ironic that the very success of Venice led to a European conquest of the world.

the centre of the Byzantine Empire, Christendom's greatest city, Constantinople. In the subsequent carving-up of the Byzantine Empire, Venice took the best bits for itself. Naturally, the Venetians continued to control the profitable pepper trade with Alexandria.

By the beginning of the fifteenth century, Venice was at her most magnificent. Ships clogged her harbours and canals; the hum of business reverberated through the Rialto; Venetians, Greeks, Arabs, Jews, Turks, some buying, some selling, all bargained passionately for the silks, perfumes and spices of the East. Venice's arsenal was the most formidable shipyard and fortress in the Mediterranean. As Lord Byron said, ' . . . Venice, sat in state, throned on her hundred isles'.

The Venetians passed a law that all trade goods from the East had to be brought to Venice prior to distribution throughout the rest of Europe. This meant that eastern pepper on its way west would pass western gold journeying east. No doubt, as middlemen, the Venetians made a profit on both. Since pepper was more easily produced than gold, Europe began to suffer the beginnings of a balance of payments problem. Europeans resented Venice, not only for draining their gold, but for passing it on to the hated sons of Islam. But Europeans still craved their pepper.

La Pearà
Pepper Sauce for Boiled Meats

This Venetian sauce is medieval in origin. It is made from breadcrumbs, a rich beef broth, marrow and lots of *freshly ground black pepper. Indeed, the pepper trade made medieval Venice rich.*

SERVES SIX
8 oz/225 g (1 cup) beef marrow
$\frac{2}{3}$ oz/20 g ($1\frac{1}{2}$ tablespoons) butter

2 oz/50 g ($\frac{1}{4}$ cup) freshly made breadcrumbs
16 fl oz/450 ml (2 cups) rich beef broth
salt and freshly ground black pepper

Put the marrow and butter into a small, heavy saucepan. Ideally, flameproof earthenware should be used, but cast-iron enamel does almost as well. Cook over a moderate heat, mashing the marrow with a wooden spoon until the marrow melts and the mixture begins to foam. Stir the breadcrumbs into the fat for 1–2 minutes.

Add 3 fl oz/75 ml (about $\frac{1}{3}$ cup) beef broth and cook over a low heat, uncovered, stirring until the broth evaporates and the breadcrumbs thicken. Season with salt and a generous amount of freshly ground black pepper. Continue to add the rest of the broth, little by little, letting it evaporate before adding more, and stirring from time to time. The finished sauce should be thick and creamy. Serve over sliced boiled meat or in a sauceboat on the side.

The last pepper merchant of Venice is Dr Fabio Zoppolata whose family has been buying and selling spices for generations. The Zoppolata warehouse is only a short distance from the central market in the Rialto district where Dr Zoppolata talked about the long relationship between Venice and pepper which had lasted many hundreds of years.

We are in the centre of Venice, in the centre of the market of Venice. Since the old days, this area has been important for trade. It was most important for the spice trade especially pepper. The state even appointed special pepper officials to act as brokers between buyers and sellers. These brokers kept information secret. Exchanges of information between sellers and clients were whispered in the ear.

So influential was the square that here, the fathers of Venice proclaimed their decrees; on that stone over there, supported by a statue called the dwarf of the Rialto. For us, the dwarf has always been a popular character.

So jealous were the Venetians of their secrets, that they did more than just whisper them. They kept all foreigners away from the market to prevent them from learning the true quotations for spices, especially pepper.

The Germans, for example, were kept locked on the other side of the Rialto bridge in their own warehouse or *fondaco*. They never knew the wholesale prices.

The Germans were very important. In the fifteenth century, they bought more than half of all Venetian spices, but traders came from everywhere in Europe, all prepared to exchange gold for pepper. The Venetians treated them very well, why not? They were customers, but they also kept them in the dark about current prices. The Venetians traded with everyone, Turks, Arabs, everyone . . . religion or ideology were unimportant. Just gold and spices.

'Pastrami', proclaims Leo Steiner, rapidly circling his own belly, 'comes from the navel, yes, the navel.' 'We use only the finest corn-fed beef', he says, plunking a dripping slab of beef on the table. 'We take it and pickle it up. Now this piece of meat is about fourteen days old, as you can tell, the ageing has started . . . '

Using his own body with anatomical precision, Leo demonstrates that corned beef, or salt beef, comes from the side of the steer, the brisket. It is too thick properly to absorb both spices and smoking, but the navel is just right.

Reaching for a large bowl, he explains that in the pickling process, spices, especially pepper, are used whole. At first the meat is soaked in a marinade in large plastic containers. This is to prevent the incursion of outside tastes . . . just meat and spices. After twenty-four hours, the meat and marinade are transferred to wooden barrels for a long steep. Crushed spices are added next. Pointing to a shallow bowl, Leo continues, '. . . as you can see there's all sorts of spices . . . you see here mustard seed, allspice, a little thyme and, of course, black pepper . . . Everything! As we grind it, it changes value . . . in grinding it up, we've dried out.' Leo lifts the meat and sets it into the spices, first one side and then the other. Dry spice coats the wet meat. Then Leo lovingly massages and caresses the meat with the spice mixture.

'In rubbing it in, we add the moisture of the meat back into the spices'. As the massage progresses, Leo becomes more ecstatic. 'We rub the spices right into it . . . into the cavity here with the fat in it . . . see as we rub everything in to it how it turns the colouring of the meat . . .' Indeed, the meat does respond. It turns from bright red to dark purple.

'This is a process that takes hours because our tonnage of meat takes a lot of it. You see, most of the places today are commercial, they have machines that prepare this stuff in twenty-four hours. They don't rub the spices in, they get it on both sides and press it on. We don't do that.'

Breathing slightly faster, Leo gasps, 'after we rub the spices in, we leave the meat to stand on this table here and the flavour goes right through it. Then we smoke it.'

It was May, 1498; the place was Calicut on India's Malabar coast. The Portuguese admiral Vasco Da Gama was leading his thirteen officers through the narrow streets. Just ahead of them marched two hundred Indian troops with swords bared. Trumpets blared; drums beat; crowds pressed from all sides. Faces filled every window. Calicut was a major trading centre, but for over a thousand years since the days of the Romans, it had not seen the sight of a European ship. Da

No European ship had sailed in Indian waters since the days of the Romans, and even they did not sail directly from Europe. Imagine the surprise of the Indian and Muslim traders in Calicut when they saw Vasco da Gama who had sailed around Africa from Portugal.

Gama and his crew were the first Europeans to sail directly to India from their home port.

'We have come looking for Christians and spices', proclaimed Da Gama, and when asked why the Venetians or Spanish had not come, replied, 'the King of Portugal would not permit them!'

Da Gama and his men were ushered into the chamber of the local king, the Zamorin. The ruler reclined on a high green couch and munched slightly phsycoactive betel nuts. The guard around him all covered their mouths, a gesture of humility. Fruit was brought to refresh the visitors. Da Gama said he wanted to trade for pepper and other spices, but the relationship quickly soured when it became apparent that he had nothing of value to interest the sophisticated Zamorin. Da Gama's beads and baubles were considered an insult.

Da Gama and his men rummaged the waterfront attempting to purchase some of the spices which lay everywhere. But the Portuguese were blocked at every turn by Muslim traders who resented Christians interfering with their monopoly. The Portuguese even tried bartering their personal belongings, shirts, belts, shoes, for handfuls of spice . . . Finally, in humiliation they left, facing a gruesome, scurvy-ridden voyage home, determined to return.

The planning for Vasco Da Gama's journey had started in Portugal some eighty years earlier. A young prince, Henry, second son of King John I, had already distinguished himself in battle against the Muslims. Henry had read the journeys of the thirteenth-century explorer Marco Polo and was impressed with the description of spices in India and beyond. He also hated Venice, not only for draining Portugal's gold, but for dealing with Christendom's mortal enemy, Islam. If only, he thought, 'a way could be found to obtain pepper at its source, a double blow would be

dealt to both Venice and Islam. It could also be good business'.

To lesser men, the thought would have been mere fancy. Portugal lay at the end of the earth. Wherever India was, the forces of both Venice and Islam had to lie in between. Portugal's doorstep was the Atlantic Ocean. Since the time of the Vikings, some four hundred years earlier, no ship had sailed even out of the sight of land, let alone the thousands of leagues it would take to get to India. In any event, Africa was in the way. Nobody knew where, or if, it ended. Ships venturing even short distances down the African coast had a habit of not returning. This gave rise to tales of hideous monsters, giant whirlpools and the host of assorted horrors available to the medieval mind. Henry, however, was determined to find the solution.

Aside from spices, two other things lured the Portuguese to action. There were tales of gold

Marco Polo's journeys to the East in the fourteenth century caught the imagination of Europe. This inaccurate illustration of the pepper harvest by a Western artist is one of a series in the fifteenth-century French manuscript *Le Livre des merveilles de Marco Polo.*

Ananas au Poivre Jean et Pierre   *Pineapple with Crème de Cacao*

Jean and Pierre, the famous Troisgros brothers, are the namesakes of this dish. The famous chef, Anton Mosimann, says that he had the privilege to work with them in France for a few weeks, and experienced at first hand the efficiency with which their hotel and restaurant kitchens run. Les frères Troisgros are among the most imaginative chefs in the world, which, combined with their self-discipline and hospitality, makes them unforgettable and earns them a place in the evolution of French cooking.

SERVES FOUR
1 small pineapple weighing about 11 oz/300 g
freshly ground black pepper
1½ oz/40 g (3 tablespoons) butter
2 tablespoons/30 ml Crème de Cacao
4 scoops vanilla ice cream

For the sauce

1 oz/25 g (2 tablespoons) butter
4 oz/100 g (½ cup) sugar
4 tablespoons/50 ml orange juice
1½ tablespoons/20 ml lemon juice
4 tablespoons/50 ml Crème de Cacao
zest of orange, blanched

To make the sauce, heat the butter in a small saucepan over low heat and let it brown. Set it aside. In another small, heavy saucepan melt the sugar over moderate heat until it forms a light brown caramel. Stir the orange and lemon juice into the caramel. Add the Crème de Cacao and cook for a minute or two. Add the melted butter and stir in the blanched orange zest.

Peel the pineapple and cut it into 4 crosswise slices, approximately ½ inch/1.5 cm thick. Cut out the central core. Sprinkle the pineapple with freshly ground black pepper. Heat the butter in a frying pan. Add the slices of pineapple, pour in the Crème de Cacao and ignite it. Add the sauce and heat it through gently. Arrange the pineapple slices on four plates. Put a scoop of vanilla ice cream in the centre of each slice and pour the sauce on top. Serve immediately.

---

down the coast, but more important was the belief that a great Christian King, Prester John, ruled a mighty empire in the east. He could be an ally in the struggle against Islam. Henry's idea was simple. The Portuguese would sail around Africa, attack the Arabs from the rear and take over the pepper trade. At first this seemed like madness.

Henry, however had read *The Histories* written in about 450 BC by the Greek historian Herodotus. One small passage caught his imagination:

As for Lybia (Africa), we know that it is washed on all sides by the sea except where it joins Asia, as was first demonstrated, so far as our knowledge goes, by the Egyptian King Neco who, after calling off the construction of the canal between the Nile and the Arabian Gulf, sent out a fleet manned by a Phoenician crew with orders to sail westabout and return to Egypt and the Mediterranean by way of the straits of Gibraltar. The Phoenicians sailed from the Arabian Gulf into the southern ocean, and every autumn put in at some convenient spot on the Lybian coast, sowed a patch of ground, and waited for next year's harvest. Then, having got in their grain, they put out to sea again, and after two full years rounded the pillars of Hercules (Gibraltar) in the course of the third, and returned to Egypt. There men made a statement which I do not myself believe, though others may, to the effect that as they sailed on a westerly course round the southern end of Lybia, they had the sun on their right—to northward of them. This is how Lybia was first discovered to be surrounded by sea.

As is shown in the chapter about cinnamon, Herodotus was something less than a reliable reporter; however, it was the last few lines which fascinated Henry. '. . . As they sailed on a westerly course round the southern end of Lybia, they had the sun on their right . . .' Henry is known to history as 'The Navigator'. He knew the world was round, and the description of the phenomenon by the Phoenicians would be accurate provided the tip of Africa lay on the opposite side of the Equator. The fact that caused Herodotus to doubt, convinced Henry. Africa was surrounded by sea; its tip lay across the Equator; it could be circumnavigated; and there was a sea route to India.

In 1418 Henry built a school of navigation at Sagres on Portugal's most southerly tip. Anyone with a knowledge of navigation was welcome. Italians, Scandinavians, Jews, Arabs, shipbuilders, instrument designers and chartmakers assembled. All set to work for the same goal . . . the circumnavigation of Africa and the spices of the east.

At the time, there were two basic types of ship in use in Europe. Northern 'cogs' used in Germany and Scandinavia were sturdy, square-sailed and capable of ocean travel. Unfortunately, they were not very manoeuvrable and could only sail when the wind was right. Mediterranean 'lateeners' had triangular sails and could tack against the wind, but, could not cope with the open ocean. The Portuguese combined the best features of both into new ship designs.

The caravel was developed first. It is a swift 'lateener' with a stern rudder. For sailing with the wind it could be rerigged with square sail in which form it was called 'Caravela Redonda'. This was the workhorse of the age. It could brave open oceans, tack against the wind and was sufficiently shallow drafted to explore unknown coves and inlets. Later came the 'Nāo' which was much larger and rigged with both square and triangular sails. Vasco Da Gama's flagship, the Sāo Gabriel, was a Nāo, but his small fleet also contained a caravel.

Almost immediately, Henry started sending probes down the African coast. In 1434 they passed the dreaded cape Bojador, a spit of desert lying twelve hundred kilometres south-west of Gibraltar. Bojador was the limit of previous

European exploration. As they ventured down the African coast, the Portuguese naturally seized anything of value, including the Africans themselves. Henry used the slaves to finance further voyages, but in so doing started a trade in human suffering which would continue for the next four hundred years.

Henry's men also established a series of colonies down the coast, the first European colonies in Africa. In 1487, twenty-seven years after Henry's death, Bartholomew Diaz rounded the Cape of Good Hope and proved, conclusively, that Henry was right. There really was a sea route to India. Further exploration was carried out in secret. For Venice, what had started out as an impossible dream, was now a genuine and troublesome threat.

Suddenly in 1492, there occurred an unexpected event which shook the world. The Spanish, like the Portuguese, sought eastern spices. Christopher Columbus convinced the young Queen of Spain that India could be found by sailing westward into the Atlantic. The Portuguese had known for a long time that it was possible, at least in theory, to find India by sailing west. They calculated, quite correctly, that sailing around Africa would be the shorter route. It was also safer because of the numerous landfalls.

Christopher Columbus opened a whole new world to European exploitation, yet he never found the spices he was seeking and went to his grave broken and disappointed. What he did find is matter for other chapters but his first voyage put pressure on the Portuguese for their own thrust to India five years later when Da Gama first sailed there.

It was a Saturday morning, 8 July 1497 and the whole of Lisbon, it seemed, crowded the docks to watch four ships weigh anchor. Flags fluttered, priests chanted and women wailed as the imposing figure of Vasco Da Gama on horse-back cut through the throng on his way to the wharf. It was a very different scene from the humiliating retreat from Calicut just over a year later. The rulers and merchants of India would soon learn that Vasco Da Gama was not a man to trifle with. He was determined to have the spices

Entrecôte Sautée Dorchester *Steak with Pepper and Cream Sauce*

The famed chef, Anton Mosimann, of the Dorchester Hotel in London created this dish which exemplifies his culinary philosophy. Make it simple, but make it perfect. Professional chefs and devoted cooks make their own brown veal stock for use in cooking. The rich, subtle flavour adds greatly to any sauce. This veal stock recipe makes $1\frac{3}{4}$ pints/1 litre (4 cups). For the mirepoix use diced carrots, onions, turnips and herbs.

SERVES FOUR
4 x 6 oz/175 g entrecôte (boneless sirloin) steaks
2 tablespoons/30 ml crushed black peppercorns
2 tablespoons/30 ml crushed white peppercorns
salt
4 tablespoons/50 ml peanut oil
3 tablespoons/40 ml Cognac
7 fl oz/200 ml ($\frac{1}{4}$ cup) brown veal stock
7 fl oz/200 ml ($\frac{1}{4}$ cup) double (heavy) cream
$1\frac{1}{2}$ oz/40 g (3 tablespoons) butter, cut in bits

freshly ground black pepper
$\frac{1}{2}$ teaspoon each pink and green peppercorns
For the veal stock
$2\frac{1}{4}$ lb/1 kg veal bones and trimmings, cut into small pieces
4 teaspoons/20 ml vegetable oil
2 oz/50 g ($\frac{1}{2}$ cup) mirepoix
1 lb/450 g diced tomatoes
$2\frac{1}{2}$ pints/1.4 litres (6 cups) beef stock
$1\frac{3}{4}$ pint/1 litre (4 cups) water
salt and freshly ground black pepper

To make the veal stock, put the veal bones and trimmings into a baking pan with the oil and brown in a moderate oven. Pour off any accumulated fat and discard. Add the *mirepoix* and tomatoes and bake for 4–5 minutes longer. Add half the stock and bring to the boil. Add the remaining stock and reduce to a glaze. Remove the baking pan from the oven and transfer the contents to a saucepan. Add the water and simmer for 2 hours, skimming occasionally to remove the fat. Strain through a muslin cloth, or fine sieve and season to taste.

Season the steaks on both sides with the black and white peppercorns and salt. Heat the oil in a heavy frying pan (skillet) and sauté the steaks for 3–4 minutes on each side for medium rare. Transfer the steaks to a dish and keep them warm. Discard the fat in the pan. Add the 7 fl oz/200 ml ($\frac{1}{4}$ cup) veal stock and reduce it to half its volume over a moderately high heat. Add the cream and reduce again until the sauce is lightly thickened. Beat in the butter, bit by bit. Taste for seasoning and add salt and pepper to taste. Stir in the pink and green peppercorns, cover the steaks with the sauce and serve immediately.

Jus Lié (*Quick Brown Sauce*)
An acceptable shortcut for home cooks when you need veal stock is to simmer $\frac{3}{4}$ pint/425 ml (2 cups) beef stock in a saucepan for about 15 minutes, then stir in 2 teaspoons/10 ml arrowroot dissolved in 4 tablespoons/60 ml cold water and simmer until the mixture has thickened.

of Malabar and to avenge his humiliation.

In 1503 Da Gama assembled a new squadron of ten fighting ships. He returned to India, not with gold, but with guns. On the way they encountered a Muslim vessel loaded with women and children. By Da Gama's order it was set afire and sunk. The fleet bombarded Calicut into submission. Da Gama's first act was to forcibly expel the Muslim traders. He then hung thirty fishermen, cut up their bodies and flung them into the sea. The pepper was taken not with gold coin, but lead shot. The white beaches of Malabar were stained red.

In 1524 when Vasco Da Gama died, it was he, not the Zamorin, who ruled the Malabar coast. The Portuguese had pushed east and taken the Spice Islands. Their empire now stretched from Brazil to Macao at the gates of China, the most extensive empire the world had yet known. As for India, four hundred and fifty years would pass before it could rid itself of its European masters.

In just one generation, the search for spices, and

Sauce au Poivre   *Pepper Sauce*

This recipe comes from chef Laurier Therrieu of the Restaurant La Tanière, Ste-Foy, Quebec. The demi-glace sauce he uses is made from wild boar stock, not a practical thing for most of us so I have given an easier recipe here to use instead. Serve the finished sauce with cold meat.

MAKES 25 FL OZ/700 ML (3 CUPS)

1 tablespoon/15 ml shallots, peeled and finely chopped

½ oz/15 g (1 tablespoon) salted butter

4 fl oz/100 ml (½ cup) dry red wine

16 fl oz/450 ml (2 cups) demi-glace sauce

1 fl oz/25 ml (⅛ cup) Cognac or other brandy

freshly ground black pepper to taste

1 oz/25 g (½ cup) fresh mushrooms, thinly sliced

4 fl oz/100 ml (½ cup) double (heavy) cream

For the demi-glace sauce

1 tablespoon/15 ml butter

1 medium carrot, peeled and finely chopped

1 medium onion, peeled and finely chopped

1 oz/25 g (½ cup) fresh mushrooms, sliced

4 sprigs parsley

2 pints/1.1 litre (5 cups) rich brown stock

4 fl oz/100 ml (½ cup) dry Madeira or Sherry

To make the *demi-glace* sauce, melt the butter in a saucepan and add the carrot and onion. Cook until they are soft. Add the mushrooms, parsley and stock and simmer until reduced to 16 fl oz/450 ml (2 cups). Stir in the dry Madeira or Sherry and simmer for a few minutes longer. Strain before using.

Sauté the shallots in the butter in a medium-sized saucepan until they are golden. Add the wine, *demi-glace* sauce, Cognac, pepper to taste and the mushrooms. Simmer, uncovered, over a very low heat for about 15 minutes. Stir in the cream and heat through.

---

in particular the pepper of the Malabar coast, not only changed the world, but gave birth to our modern age. From now on, politics would be worldwide; events in one place could effect every other place. Age-old patterns of movement and trade were smashed and replaced by a new super-structure generally dependent upon Europe. But most of all, the era of European colonialism had begun and would dominate global affairs for the next half millenium.

'It's ready!' shouts Leo. 'In here is a batch of Pastrami that's been smoking. It's ready now.' Leo pulls open the door. The aroma! Once en-joyed, it's never forgotten. In our Western world of refrigeration and regular food supplies, none of this is really necessary. People could easily sur-vive without smoking, pickling or flavouring with spices. New Yorkers, however, consume thousands of tons of pastrami each year—simply because they like it. Spices make lunch a little more interesting and therefore life a little more worth living.

'You have to know food in order to like it', says Leo, 'now, I've eaten the finest food in the world . . . like French hout or hoot cuisine, however you pronounce it. Eh? It doesn't mean anything to me. I don't know it. But delicatessen food and pastrami, I eat it every day. I know it. I love it. Good food. More than that I can't tell you, folks. Just enjoy!'

4
CLOVES

When I compare the figure which the Dutch make in Europe with what they assume in Asia, I am struck with surprise. In Asia I find them great Lords of the Indian Seas; in Europe the timid inhabitants of a paltry state.

OLIVER GOLDSMITH, *Citizen of the World*, 1760.

Most of the cloves used throughout the world are grown on the coast of the African state of Tanzania, at Zanzibar and the nearby island of Pemba. In some years, however, Indonesia grows even more cloves than Tanzania but, surprisingly, it also imports most of the Tanzanian crop. On a *per capita* basis, Indonesians consume almost twenty-five times as many cloves as the Americans and fifty times as many as the French. Indonesia is far from being a small country and it has the fifth largest population of any nation on earth. So we are talking about a considerable quantity of cloves.

It is not that the officially Muslim Indonesians have developed a passion for glazed ham; it is because they smoke cloves in cigarettes onomatopoeically called *Kretek*, because they crackle and

Indonesia is one of the largest producers of cloves in the world but is also the largest importer as the Indonesians have a passion for clove cigarettes called *kretek*. The cloves are mixed with tobacco and the cigarettes give off the familiar aroma of cloves.

pop as they burn. The cloves are mixed with tobacco and the cigarettes give off the familiar aroma of cloves.

If you are curious, it is simple enough to try yourself. Next time you are studding the festive ham, grind the leftover cloves, mix them with about twice the amount of tobacco and smoke. If you think you have stumbled across a legal high, save yourself the disappointment. Smoking cloves may be pleasant but it is no easy ticket to Nirvana.

For most of history, and for that matter pre-history, cloves grew only on a few tiny islands in the Moluccas, later called the Spice Islands, and which are now part of modern Indonesia. The spice is the dried, unopened flower buds of a tropical evergreen tree belonging to the myrtle family. Depending upon which system of botanical classification you follow, the tree is known scientifically as either *Syzgium aromaticum* or *Eugenia caryophyllus*. *Eugenia* is a very large genus

and *Syzygium* is simply an attempt by some botanists to narrow it down. *Caryophyllus* was the ancient Greek name for cloves. It comes from *Karcuon* meaning 'nut' and *phullon* meaning 'leaf', and is remembered today in the name used to describe certain fragrant flowers, 'gillyflower'. The word 'clove' itself, is from the old French *clau* which in turn is from the Latin *clavus* or nail. The idea, 'nail', carries through in many languages. In Chinese, clove is *ting-hiang* or nailspice; the

Persian is *Nekhak* or little nails; and Germans say *Nelkin* or *Nägelchen*, again, little nails.

In the wild, clove trees grow high, forming substantial forests, but cultivated trees generally are kept to reasonable heights for easier picking, averaging 12–15 metres. The cloves grow in clusters at the ends of branches, making picking a difficult operation. In Zanzibar, women and children harvest the lower branches while men climb ladders or branches to reach the upper parts

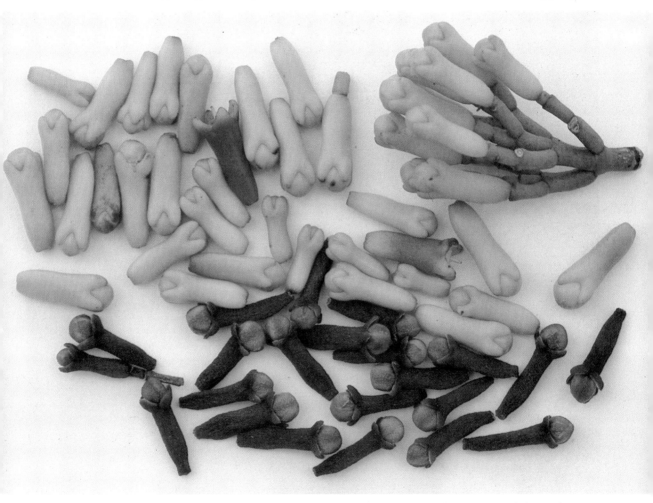

Left: The clove in various stages on the plant; the unopened flower buds which are ideal for picking; the bud in flower which gives off the aroma of cloves and the remnant of the flower known as 'mother of cloves'. This is of inferior quality to the unopened bud as the essential oils have already been released, but is sometimes mixed with the dried, unopened flower buds, the cloves, to form inferior-quality spice.

Above: The raw clove and the dark, dried clove. Clove clusters are picked ideally when the buds have reached full size and have a pinkish flush.

Left: Picking cloves by hand in Ambon, Indonesia. The pickers pick only the ripe clusters. Women and children pick the lower branches while the men have the more difficult job of harvesting the upper branches.

Below: After picking the clusters, the process of stemming, removing the buds from the flower stalk, takes place. The stalk is pushed from one hand to another with a twisting motion and the buds snap off.

of the tree. The pickers pull clove clusters towards themselves, holding long, hooked poles in one hand and with the other hand snap the buds free and deposit them into baskets. To make things more difficult, the trees are often covered with torturous red ants. Branches broken either on purpose or by accident can be the entry point for the disease called 'die-back', which if left untreated will kill the particular tree.

For high-quality cloves, the buds must be picked at precisely the right moment, that is just as they reach their full size and start to turn pink, but before they flower. The folded petals with the stamens inside are the heads of the cloves. If the buds are not picked, they will flower and eventually turn into oblong, drooping fruit containing one or sometimes two seeds. This fruit is known as 'mother of cloves' and is sometimes mixed with the dried buds to form inferior-quality spice.

By late afternoon pickers return to a central processing-area for stemming, which is the removal of the buds from flower stalks. The inflorescence is held in the right hand and pressed against the left with a twisting motion. The buds snap off and are then set out to dry on leaf mats spread upon concrete platforms. Three days in the tropical sun and they become the familiar dark brown cloves of commerce. In drying they lose two-thirds of their weight and become brittle and even painful to grasp in a cluster.

There are two crops a year, but often only one is harvested as picking and branch-breaking throw trees into a state of shock reducing future yields. Clove crops fluctuate wildly, mostly in four-year cycles, each of which is likely to contain at least one bumper crop and one disaster. To make matters even more uncertain, since the 1890s the groves of Zanzibar and now elsewhere have been subject to a disease bearing the ominous title, 'sudden death'. Fortunately, young trees are immune so, although trees can live upwards of one hundred years, continual programmes of replanting are necessary.

The Moluccas straddle the Equator and most of the world's cloves grow near the sea within ten

Sorting the dried cloves at the clove merchant's to remove any impurities. Not only does the yield of cloves vary enormously from year to year but so also does the international price paid for cloves.

degrees of the magic line. Penang on the west coast of Malaysia, Sri Lanka, French Guiana, and, of course, Zanzibar and Pemba all fall within this limit. The Malagasy Republic and the Comoro Islands lie off the east coast of Africa just to the south, while the Caribbean island of Grenada is slightly to the north. Cloves are tropical and should be grown within sight of the sea.

These aromatic buds came later to the civilizations of the ancient Mediterranean than did cinnamon or pepper; however, cloves were well known in the East from very early times.

Chinese records reveal that in the third century BC, during the Han dynasty, officers of the court were required to carry cloves in their mouths when addressing the emperor. It is not surprising that the Chinese, who were so conscious of bad breath, were among the first to discover some of clove's true medicinal benefits. They were aware that the spice is a mild anaesthetic which can relieve the suffering of toothaches.

To this day in China, cloves are available principally through pharmacies, not grocers. For part of the nineteenth century, China was ruled by an unpopular dowager empress, called Xi Ci. This empress normally lived with her family in the Forbidden City of Peking, but during the hot season she moved with her entourage to the Summer Palace some miles away.

It was the Imperial family's habit to wander into a room full of sumptuous dishes and nibble at just a few of them. This was excessively wasteful, especially as the peasant masses of China were starving, but the cuisine at the Imperial Court was excellent and constantly varying. Perhaps it was because they were having such a wonderful time that the family became fascinated by the idea of longevity. The décor, the furniture, the art, even the food of the palace bore the motifs and symbols of long life.

A favourite dish was *Xiang Su Ji* or crispy chicken with cloves. A young bird was parboiled and then flavoured with cloves, Sichuan pepper, dried ginger, fresh ginger, onions, chopped nutmeg, Chinese five-spice mixture and bay leaves. The chicken was then covered with stock from a previous boiling, further seasoned with salt, sesame oil, soy sauce, monosodium glutamate and wine, and steamed for two hours. Just before eating it was fried in oil to make it crisp.

Today, the Summer Palace is occupied by a restaurant, Ting le Laun, meaning 'place for listening to the birds'. The restaurant still serves '999' dishes created for Xi Ci's birthday, including *Xiang Su Ji*, which is as crispy and spicy as ever. '999' is a magic number in China and has been for many centuries.

No doubt some ships from ancient China visited the Moluccas, but the Indonesians who were, and still are, magnificent navigators probably delivered the cloves to China themselves. Even today the sailors of nearby South Sulawesi or Makassar ply the seas between the Indian and Pacific Oceans. They are more likely to be carrying refrigerators or aluminium furniture than spice, but in their spare time they create clever replicas of ancient sailing ships out of cloves which are readily available and cheap.

Well over two thousand years ago, cloves became rooted firmly in Indian culinary tradition.

They are one of the 'warming' spices still commonly used in the spice mixture called garam masala and it would be difficult to find a *pilau* rice made without their unique aroma and pungency. The people of ancient India, like the Chinese, used them to dispel bad breath, especially the odour of garlic.

In *pa'an pati*, cloves have a very significant part to play. A mixture is prepared consisting of chopped areca nut, lime and perhaps cardamom and nutmeg. This mixture is placed in a leaf of the betel vine which is folded into a parcel fastened by a clove. The *pa'an* is not only mildly stimulating, but it causes the eater's saliva to turn bright crimson. The anaesthetic property of the clove is essential for the whole effect which is designed to aid digestion. The *pa'an* has been known since ancient times and to satisfy demand, the finest quality cloves are still shipped to India.

Whether or not the Roman writer Pliny knew of cloves is still being debated. Around the year AD 70 he wrote: 'There is in India another grain which bears a considerable resemblance to pepper, but is longer and more brittle; it is known by the name "caryophyllon". It is said that this grain is produced in a secret grove in India; with us it is imported for its aromatic properties.'

It seems from this passage that if Pliny was talking about cloves then whoever brought them to the West was intent upon hiding their original source, as happened with cinnamon.

Just a hundred years after Pliny, cloves made a definite appearance in the customs records of Alexandria and within a further hundred years or so they became popular throughout the Mediterranean. In the fourth century AD the Emperor Constantine presented a gift to the Bishop of Rome which contained 70 kilograms of cloves. As lovers of pork, the Romans appreciated cloves as a new culinary spice, but also used them for perfume and medicine.

As with pepper and cinnamon, the fall of the Roman Empire reduced the supply of cloves to Western Europe to barely a trickle. When the Crusades reawakened a taste for spices in Europeans, they found in cloves something new.

Left: The pa'an seller is found on nearly every street corner of India. Cloves play a vital part in pa'an and to satisfy demand the best quality cloves are still shipped to India, where the Indians on a per capita basis eat more cloves than anybody else in the world.
Below: A selection of spices used to make pa'an. Cloves are frequently used to hold the pa'an package together.

Essential oils are those organic compounds in aromatic plants which are mostly responsible for the plant's distinctive smell. They are often called 'volatile oils' because when the plants cellular tissue is broken they are released into the air causing an aroma. In the Middle Ages, the Islamic Arabs perfected techniques for separating out essential oils by distillation. Clove oil has many of the magic properties of the spice itself and is much more highly concentrated.

It is difficult to imagine what Europe suffered during and immediately after the Crusades. Terrible plagues were commonplace. Wave after wave of horrible epidemics left no family untouched. It was widely believed that pestilence was carried by the air, and, since spices could alter the character of the air, they were considered a sort of cure-all. At least they were worth a try, but they were expensive because they could also relieve the monotony of salted meat and cover the taste of turning flesh.

One great advantage of cloves was that sometimes they actually fulfilled the claims made for them. The spice, and especially its essential oil, could really relieve toothache and had strong germicidal and antiseptic qualities. Cloves were,

and in some quarters still are, highly regarded as a carminitive, or a reliever of excess and uncomfortable gas.

By the thirteenth century, the aristocracy, especially, was given to carrying balls of blended aromatic substances as prophylactic charms against the plague. These 'apples of amber' came to be called 'pomanders' and if at all possible contained cloves. They were used as protection against pestilence and foul smells. It is not certain whether people really believed that the odour of cloves itself stopped the plague or that it marshalled the blood to a supreme effort of resistence. In any event, what else was there to do? If anything, the belief in cloves as a protector and healer grew over the following centuries.

Early in the history of printing, a book was published in Holland in the mid-sixteenth century which caught the public's imagination. It was called the *Intinerio* by Dr Bernardus Paladanus, an influential physician. In it he proclaimed that cloves were the wonder drug: 'Cloves give a clear breath, force the wind, stop diarrhoea and cure upset stomachs.'

Also in the sixteenth century a theory called the Doctrine of Signatures came to full flower. The

Pomander

Pomanders were widely used in the past for sweetening the air and are still available in various forms, sometimes as ceramic containers filled with spices. An old-fashioned way of making a pomander goes back to the Middle Ages when the need for sweetening the air was often a *necessity. Nowadays, pomanders are usually hung in clothes cupboards (closets) or put into bureau drawers. An orange, lemon or lime, but more usually an orange is stuck with cloves, dusted with orris root and cinnamon, and then left to dry. Its fragrance lasts for a long time.*

FOR EACH POMANDER	
1 fine-skinned orange	*1 teaspoon/5 ml orris root*
cloves	*1 teaspoon/5 ml ground cinnamon*

To make pomander balls choose fine-skinned oranges and wash them. Dry them thoroughly. Using a skewer if necessary to start the holes, insert cloves all over the orange in a close, random pattern. Use plenty of cloves. Put the orris root and ground cinnamon into a bag, add a clove-stuck orange and shake to coat it well; or roll the orange in a mixture of the two spices.

Place the orange in a basket lined with aluminium foil, or on a foil-lined tray but do not let the oranges touch each other. Leave the fruit in a cool, dark place to dry out and harden. This takes three to four weeks. Turn the oranges from time to time. Wrap the oranges in a cradle of coloured cord with a loop so that the pomander can be hung up; or wrap in net and tie with a ribbon.

idea was to treat like with like—a sufferer of yellow jaundice would be treated with, say, yellow turmeric. The concept had existed for a long time, but in the middle of the seventeenth century there was a concerted intellectual attempt to find new relationships of order in the universe. At some time or another, every spice and herb has been touted and sold as an aphrodisiac or at least as a restorer of vital energy. The clove is the only spice shaped like a human penis, and an erect one at that! Combined with the Doctrine of Signatures (treat like with like), it is easily understandable why cloves themselves became the object of such lust.

Increasingly, cloves were being used as a seasoning for food. In the fourteenth century, *Le Ménagier de Paris*, an early guide to domestic science, never hesitated to call for their use and soon, along with cinnamon, the spice was deemed an essential bridge between sweet and sour tastes and an important flavouring for hot alcoholic beverages. It is, however, more likely that the belief in the clove's medicinal and restorative powers was responsible for the spice's major role in shaping human history. As much as pepper, cloves were the object of the quests of Christopher Columbus and Vasco da Gama.

The Portuguese under da Gama reached India in 1497. By 1511 they were in the Moluccas trading for cloves and by 1514 had started building a series of factories and forts to protect their trading interests. Cloves, as much as nutmegs, caused Magellan and the crew of the *Victoria* to embark upon the first voyage around the world. Magellan was dead in November 1521 when the *Victoria*, under Sebastian del Cano, reached the Moluccan island of Tidore. There the chronicler, Pigafetta, described the clove tree:

Its branches extend very wide about the middle of the trunk, but at the summit terminate in a pyramid. Its leaf resembled that of Laurel and the bark is of an olive colour. The cloves grow at the end of small branches, in clusters of from ten to twenty; and the tree, according to the season, sends forth more on one side than the other. The cloves at first are white; as they ripen they become reddish, and blacken as they dry. There are annually two crops gathered, the one at Christmas, the other about St John the Baptist's day.

The *Victoria* loaded enough cloves and nutmeg not only to pay for the whole voyage, but also to yield a handsome profit for the Spanish who backed the voyage. The Moluccas became a convenient stopping place for circumnavigators, and why not? On the European market, cloves fetched triple the price of pepper and were just as easy to carry.

In 1579 Francis Drake and his ship, the *Golden Hind* landed at Tidore's sister island, Ternate, and loaded up with cloves. Not far from the Moluccas on the journey home, the ship hit a rock and in order to save the ship, Drake was forced to throw overboard three tons of the spice. This loss was more than made up when Drake later attacked and took a Spanish vessel, itself just leaving the islands. Drake brought his treasure home and was knighted by Elizabeth I for his efforts.

The combination of Drake's exploits and the growing reputation of cloves spurred the Dutch into action. The Dutch people had recently won their independence from Spain and were anxious to assert their newfound national identity. Near the end of the sixteenth century, ships sailed to the East Indies from several Dutch ports. At first they met with success, but then things became more difficult. The Portuguese, who for almost a century had had their own way, were initially unprepared for competition but they soon learned to show resistance. In response, the Dutch who had also been competing with one another, banded together and in 1602 formed the United East India Company. The business of trading on the other side of the world required new systems of finance and organization and like the English who had formed their own East India Company in 1599, the Dutch turned to the joint stock company and so ushered in a new era. Capital was raised by spreading the risk amongst a number of shareholders who could forfeit no more than their original investments. The United East India Company was run by a group of seventeen directors known as the Herren Seventeen. They had little interest in empire for its own sake, the saving of souls or personal glory, but they did care very much about profits, which meant, as always, buying low and selling high. Unfortunately, the assets and interests of the company had to be protected and this meant substantial military expenditure so, at the beginning of the seventeenth century, the Dutch came to the eastern seas in force.

The Portuguese were not easy to displace everywhere, but in the Moluccas the Dutch managed to assert their influence very quickly. In fact, the Portuguese were never very strongly lodged there. Although they had built a series of forts, they preferred to purchase their cloves from natives at the trading port of Malacca near modern Singapore. More important, the crusading zeal of the Portuguese offended the predominantly Muslim islanders and they made a dangerous enemy of the Sultan of Ternate. At first, the Dutch were welcomed as liberators from the hated Portuguese and the United East India Company became the world's leading trader in cloves.

Things then started turning sour for the Dutch. With the benefit of hindsight it is difficult to condone colonial imperialism; however, the seventeenth-century Dutch felt themselves to be the aggrieved parties and their actions justifiable.

For tens of centuries the Moluccas had relations with the civilizations of China, India, Arabia and Java. Traders came and went and left their mark on an increasingly heterogeneous population. Business was conducted on an opportunistic basis where contracts, handshakes and word of mouth meant nothing. A 'no scruples' system is fine provided everyone understands and is willing to play the game, but it affronted everything the Dutch meant by the phrase 'fair dealing'. In doing business with the natives they felt themselves being robbed at every turn. Cloves were soaked in water to add to their weight and adulterated with stems, mother of cloves and non–cloves. Lots were sold

Batavia, now called Jakarta, the capital of Indonesia, in
the seventeenth century. It was from here that the Dutch
controlled their monopoly of the clove trade for 150 years.

Tourtière   *Minced (Ground) Pork Pie*

This pie is a popular French Canadian dish which, in the past in the days of the French colonies in Canada, *was always served at Christmas. Use a 9-inch/23-cm pie tin.*

MAKES ONE PIE

1½ lb/700 g minced (ground) lean pork

1 medium onion, peeled and finely chopped

2 cloves garlic, peeled and crushed

1 teaspoon/5 ml salt

½ teaspoon/2.5 ml ground cloves

1 lb/450 g shortcrust pastry

egg wash (1 small egg yolk plus 1 teaspoon/5 ml water)

Combine the pork, onion, garlic, salt and ground cloves in a heavy saucepan with enough water, about 8 fl oz/225 ml (1 cup), to come about three-quarters way up the meat. Bring to a simmer and cook, uncovered, for 45 minutes, stirring from time to time. Check the seasoning and add more salt if necessary. Let the mixture cool.

Roll out the pastry into two circles, one larger than the other to fit the pie tin. Line the pie tin with the smaller circle. Fill with the pork mixture, and cover with the larger circle of pastry, crimping the edges to seal. Brush with the egg wash. Bake in a preheated hot oven, 450°F, 230°C, Gas Mark 8, for 10 minutes, then reduce the heat to moderate, 375°F, 190°C, Gas Mark 5, and bake for 30 minutes, or until the crust is golden brown. Serve hot.

several times over and deliveries, if they happened at all, hardly ever met contract specifications. It was the same with other spices such as nutmeg. To add to all this, the Dutch had taken on as enemies two of the most powerful empires the world had yet seen, Spain and Portugal. Forts had to be built and maintained and merchant ships making the long voyage around Africa and across the Indian Ocean needed military protection.

Most bothersome of all were those sometimes-allies sometimes-enemies, the English. In order to get the Moluccans to harvest the cloves, the Dutch often had to pay in advance with hard goods such as cloth or utensils. The English developed a habit of then swooping in and buying the harvested cloves from the already-paid natives. A Dutch writer spoke of the 'English pursuing the Dutch through the Indies like gadflies'. The English response was 'you do the fighting; we reap the benefits'.

In the company books at Amsterdam, cloves were becoming a liability. For one thing, there was now a glut of them. A ten-year supply had accumulated at the Dutch eastern capital of Batavia, now called Jakarta, and the people of Amsterdam were being treated to the aroma of officially burned spice. The situation was so bad that the company was forced to pay off its share-holders not in money, but in cloves. Imagine the fury. Realising that without a new approach the whole enterprise could be lost, the Dutch were forced to take drastic action to reduce the amount of cloves coming on the market. The 'extirpation', as it was called, meant simply that all the clove trees in the Moluccas (ie the world) would be destroyed except for those on the one island of Amboyna which could then be strictly controlled.

The Dutch justified the policy by declaring that the loss of trees was compensation for previous unfulfilled contracts. In any event the Dutch also paid off the nominal owner of the islands, the Sultan of Ternate, who considered the payments a windfall. In order to make this plan work, other strict laws had to be passed and enforced. Growing cloves, transporting cloves or even mere possession of a seedling were all serious offences, punishable by death.

The Dutch had managed to create a nutmeg monopoly on the island of Banda, but cloves grew on a number of islands stretching for hundreds of miles throughout the Moluccas. The extirpators, however, took their work seriously and in 1625 alone, 65,000 clove trees were cut down. To help grasp the effect of these actions on the Moluccan people, here are two excerpts from Sir James George Frazer's famous work, *The Golden Bough*:

> In some parts of Amboyna, when the state of the clove plantation indicates that the crop is likely to be scanty, the men go naked into the plantations by night, and there seek to fertilise the trees precisely as they would impregnate women, while at the same time they call out 'More Cloves'. This is supposed to make the trees bear fruit more abundantly.
>
> When the clove trees are in blossom, they are treated like pregnant women. No noise may be made near them; no light or fire may be carried past them at night; no one may approach them with his hat on, all must uncover in their presence. These precautions are observed lest the tree should be alarmed and bear no fruit, or should drop its fruit too soon like the untimely delivery of a woman who has been frightened in her pregnancy.

It is difficult to trace the source of this informa-tion and it is unlikely that any such rituals con-tinue to the present day. There is, however, an element of truth in the spirit of the quotations. Today, Moluccan villages are either Christian or Muslim but on occasion traces of old animistic beliefs appear and cloves seem to have a special status. In some villages the religious head must be present at both the planting of young seedlings and on the first day of harvest. Trees can only be planted when there is no moon and they must be shaken during an eclipse. At the time of the extirpation, many Moluccans planted clove trees at the births of their children and firmly believed that the fate of the trees was bound with that of their offspring. Extirpation was a traumatic experience in more ways than one.

On most of these islands the people had been in the habit of trading cloves for rice. When the cloves went, so did their means to buy rice and the population was forced to turn to the less satisfactory sago palm which is still essential to the local diet.

One historian, George Masselman has written recently in *The Cradle of Colonialism*: 'Deprived of the two main sources of their former prosperity, the cultivation of spices and free shipping, the renowned principalities of the Middle Ages, Ternate, Tidore, Matjan and Batjan, were reduced to little more than subsistence level. Such was the penalty for having a valuable produce that was coveted by a determined group of European entrepreneurs.'

In some respects extirpation harmed the Dutch themselves. For example, they eliminated a market for their own manufactured goods and so jealous was the company of its own trading rights that it prevented the rise of a Dutch entrepreneurial class. Today, throughout the spice trading areas of South East Asia, the middlemen who buy from local producers and sell for export are almost invariably of Chinese descent.

So, the Dutch had their monopoly and it survived for over a hundred years, but we now know that corporations, like people, have lifecycles and by the mid-eighteenth century, the United Company was exhibiting the strains of age. Idealism had given way to corruption and problems of cash flow, but by sheer momentum the company still remained a force.

Literature is full of characters whose names reflect their tasks or stations in life. In history they are more rare, but one surely was Pierre Poivre, called in English Peter Pepper or Peter Piper. Poivre was the administrator of the French island of Isle de France, now called Mauritius. He is quoted by Madeline Ly-Tio-Fane in her essay *Mauritius and the Spice Trade* (1958): 'I then realised that the possession of spices which is the basis of Dutch power in the Indies was grounded on the ignorance and cowardice of the other trading nations of Europe. One had only to know this and be daring enough to share with them this never-failing source of wealth which they possess in one corner of the globe.'

It was in 1745 that Poivre had the idea of breaking the Dutch embargo and forcing the Netherlands to share the spice trade with France to the benefit of Poivre's own bailiwick, Isle de France. What he did not count upon was that his own countrymen would be even less receptive to the idea than the Dutch. On several occasions, by stealthy trips of his own or others, Poivre managed to obtain clove and nutmeg seedlings and even plant a garden. Each time his efforts were thwarted by one court intrigue or another. Poivre had his enemies who preferred that he did not get credit for a profitable scheme and rival French colonies were jealous of a possible bonanza on the Isle de France.

However, Poivre persisted, but it was not until 1776, long after he had left the Isle de France, that his plan bore fruit, or rather buds, as the first batch of French cloves was harvested. Instead of

Pierre Poivre, the eighteenth-century administrator of the French island, Isle de France, now called Mauritius. Poivre made many attempts to break the Dutch clove monopoly and to establish clove trees on the island. Finally, long after he had left the island, the first batch of French cloves was harvested in 1776, and the Dutch monopoly was broken.

following Poivre's plan and making an accom-modation with the Dutch for a new monopoly, the French spread the cloves throughout their various colonies, including those in the new world. Ultimately plants reached Kew and the Royal Botanic Gardens in England and were quickly planted in tropical British colonies.

Ly-Tio-Fane comments: 'The outstanding suc-cess of Zanzibar (still a British colony in 1958) as the foremost producer of cloves at the present time has at last vindicated Poivre's views on the culture of the spices on the islands of the Indian Ocean. It is one of the ironies of history that the profits accruing from the trade go to the nation which Poivre and his collaborators sought to keep out.'

In 1799 the United East India Company went bankrupt, at least in part because it could no longer enforce its spice monopolies. It was not, however, the end for the Dutch. The Dutch government assumed the assets of the company and controlled a mighty East Indian empire for another hundred and fifty years. By the time modern Indonesia was established, *kretek*-smok-ing had caused the country to develop from being the largest exporter to the largest importer of cloves.

The story goes that the spice was brought to Zanzibar in 1818 by Harameli bin Saleh, who had been banished from the principality for the crime of murder, and who had spent some time on the French Indian Ocean islands. The cloves he brought with him earned bin Saleh his pardon. The Sultan of Zanzibar ordered all landowners to plant cloves or risk confiscation of their property. Records show that by 1835 an American ship, the USS *Peacock* was able to obtain a whole cargo of the spice at the colony.

Salem custom house; the first American millionaires were made during the height of the lucrative clove trade between Salem in Massachusetts and Zanzibar during the period 1830–1870.

In 1837 the brig *Leander*, anchored in Zanzibar harbour, gave a thirteen-gun salute on the arrival of the first American consul, Richard Palmer Waters, a native of the Massachusetts port of Salem. Trade between Salem and Zanzibar flourished, despite the fact that Waters was a crusading abolitionist and slavery was legally practised in Zanzibar until 1897. In order to pay for the cloves and other raw materials from Zanzibar, manufacturing industries were established at Salem, which themselves survived the clove trade until recent times.

Throughout most of the twentieth century, the cloves of Zanzibar and Pemba were grown on private small holdings but in the political upheavals of the 1960s the Tanzanian government nationalized large portions of the industry. There is some fear amongst spice professionals that adverse economic conditions in Tanzania are forcing growers to turn from cash to subsistence crops and let the clove plantations run down.

The Malagasy Republic is the world's second largest clove exporter and could probably fill any gap should Zanzibar cease to be a source of cloves, but Malagasy cloves are neither as large nor as desirable.

Cloves work because their essential oils contain about 90 per cent eugenol. The buds are the best source of clove oil containing about 16 to 17 per cent. The stems and leaves also contain the oil but in not nearly as great a quantity.

After *kretek* the most popular use of the spice is as a food flavouring. Cloves are widely available either whole or ground and find their way into any number of foods. For centuries no stew was considered complete without either an onion or a

Right: Joe Froggers molasses.

Joe Froggers

These spicy molasses cookies have an interesting history. In American colonial times they were originally baked by a half-black, half-Gayhead Indian called Black Joe who lived by a pond on Gingerbread Hill in Marblehead, Massachusetts. The cookies were named after Black Joe and the frogs that sat on the lily pads in this pond. He kept the recipe a secret, but after his death his wife, Aunt Crese, gave it to a fisherman's wife. With the secret out, Joe Froggers accompanied by a pitcher of milk, became a favourite Sunday supper. They were sold at a local bakery where the children bought them for a penny each. Many recipes have since appeared in print. This one is from a Marblehead woman whose family has had it for over a hundred years. The cookies can still be bought at the Rusty Rudder, a shop in Marblehead where it all began.

MAKES A DOZEN BISCUITS	
3 fl oz/75 ml (about ⅜ cup) hot water	14 oz/400 g (3½ cups) plain (all-purpose) flour
2 fl oz/50 ml (¼ cup) dark rum	1½ teaspoons/7.5 ml salt
1 teaspoon/5 ml baking powder	1½ teaspoons/7.5 ml ground ginger
8 fl oz/225 ml (1 cup) treacle (molasses)	½ teaspoon/2.5 ml ground cloves
4 oz/100 g (½ cup) butter or vegetable shortening	½ teaspoon/2.5 ml ground nutmeg
8 oz/225 g (1 cup) sugar	¼ teaspoon/1.5 ml ground allspice

Combine the hot water and the rum together and set aside. Mix the baking powder with the treacle (molasses). Cream the butter with the sugar. Mix all these ingredients together and set aside.

Sift the flour, salt, ginger, cloves, nutmeg and allspice into a bowl. In another bowl mix the dry and liquid ingredients alternately until all are used up, mixing well. Chill in the refrigerator for 1 hour.

Roll out on a lightly floured board to ¼ inch/ ½ cm thick. Cut into 4-inch/10-cm rounds with a cookie cutter or a glass. Arrange on a baking sheet and bake in a preheated moderate oven, 375°F, 190°C, Gas Mark 5, until lightly browned. This takes about 10–12 minutes.

Apple Cream Pie

SERVES SIX

½ lb/225 g shortcrust pastry

1½ lb/700 g tart cooking apples

4 oz/100 g (½ cup) sugar

4 fl oz/100 ml (½ cup) water

½ teaspoon/2.5 ml ground cloves

1 large egg

4 fl oz/100 ml (½ cup) double (heavy) cream

Line a 9-inch/23-cm pie tin with the shortcrust pastry. Peel, core and slice the apples. Combine the apples, sugar, water and ground cloves in a saucepan and simmer for 10 minutes, or until the apples are tender. Cool. Then drain the apples, reserving the syrup.

Arrange the apple slices in the pastry-lined pie tin. Beat the egg with the cream. Beat in the apple syrup and pour the mixture over the apples. Bake in a preheated, moderate oven, 350°F, 180°C, Gas Mark 4 for 30–40 minutes, or until the custard topping is firm and the pastry is golden brown.

---

scallion stuck with two or three cloves. Some people regard them as essential for apple pies but others feel it is an acquired taste. Along with cinnamon they are popular in festive, hot, spicy drinks and, of course, glazed hams.

The food-processing industry generally uses the spice in the form of oleoresins or essential oils. Clove bud oil is regarded as the best and is generally distilled in the user countries. This oil is found in fine soaps, men's brands of cosmetics and perfumes and expensive or up-market sauces. Clove bud oil is almost certain to be used in all dental applications, for instance mixed with zinc oxide to make temporary fillings for cavities. Clove stem oil comes from Zanzibar and leaf oil from the Malagasy Republic and, for most applications, both are considered inferior to the bud oil. Blended with bud oil, they do, however, find their way into a large variety of sauces, pickles, preserves and meat products.

Cinnamon leaf and pimento oils are also mostly eugenol and a great deal of blending takes place amongst them all. In the past, one of the major uses of eugenol was in the production of the flavouring vanillin used to make ice cream; however, today it is generally made from by-products of the pulp and paper industry.

It should be noted that while the use of cloves in processed foods has increased during the past half century, its domestic culinary use has declined. Time and again cookery writers call for

their use but warn against actually being able to taste them.

As for the people of the Moluccas, they plant them, pick them, make model boats of them, identify the spirits of their children with them and, of course, smoke them; but, do they eat them? After considerable search, you may find a sort of stewed banana dessert sprinkled with the odd clove but that is just about all.

5
SAFFRON

Johst Findeker's sobs cut the cold pre-dawn air. Torches cast tall shadows upon the walls of the small market square in Nürnberg, Germany. A circle of merchants and curiosity seekers watched, with silent stalls standing empty behind them. At its centre, a circle of faggots and kindling surrounded an upright stake. Tied to the stake was the sobbing Findeker. The year was 1444. Findeker had been adjudged an adulterer, but it was not for sharing his bed out of wedlock that he was about to die. A soldier stepped forward carrying a large burlap sack. He ripped it open with a small knife and spread its orangey-red contents over the kindling. He then reached for a torch and touched its flaming head several times to the woodpile. Findeker's sobs turned to screams.

The *safranschau*, Nürnberg's committee of saffron inspectors, or perhaps one should say, inquisitors, sealed his fate. Findeker had committed one of the oldest crimes. He had adulterated pure saffron with other less valuable but similarly coloured substances, and had been caught. One would expect that Findeker's harsh end would act as a deterrent to other like-minded merchants, but alas, just two years later, one Elss Pfagnerin was buried alive for an identical offence.

Pure, immutable, rare and precious, gold has always been the royal metal and saffron, the gold of spices. It is somewhat surprising that this, the most exotic spice of all, comes from lovely violet-coloured, autumn-blooming crocuses, not at all unlike the typical garden crocuses seen in early spring. They are said to have been cultivated originally in Cilicia, the southern part of modern Turkey, at an ancient town called Corycus. It is

not certain whether the town gave its name to the flower or *vice versa*.

Theophrastus, the pupil of Aristotle and the founder of botanical science, described it thus:

> The saffron crocus is herbaceous in character . . . but has a narrow leaf. Indeed, the leaves are, as it were, hair-like; it blooms very late, grows either late or early, according as one looks at the

The flower of the saffron crocus is violet and saffron is the orangey-red, string-like stigmas which droop out between the petals.

season; for it blooms after the rising of Pleiad (autumn) and only for a few days. It pushes up the flower at once with the leaf, or even seems to do so earlier. The root is large and fleshy and the whole plant vigorous; it loves even to be trodden on and grows fairer when the root is crushed into the ground by foot; wherefore it is the fairest along the roads and in well-worn places. It is propagated from the root.

The flower of the crocus is violet, but saffron is the orangey-red, string-like stigmas which droop out between the petals. It contains three basic chemical substances: a tiny amount of volatile oil, which provides its aroma, picrocrocin, which makes it bitter and crocin, which gives the spice its characteristic colour. Crocin is water soluble and intensely yellow. Only one part added to one hundred and fifty thousand parts will turn water bright yellow.

The flavour is delicate but slightly bitter and is perhaps an acquired taste. It has a faint odour of iodine or seaweed, so it is not surprising that over the millenia the spice has been so associated with the sea. In 'The Ballad of Bouillabaisse' Thackeray wrote:

Green herbs, red peppers, mussels, saffern, soles, onions, garlic, roach and dace;
all these you eat at Terrés Tavern in that one dish of bouillabaisse.

Those ancient mariners, the Phoenicians seemed so addicted to saffron that they took it wherever they went. The crocuses grew in abundance in what was then the Phoenician homeland and is now modern Syria and Lebanon. When they arrived at the Mediterranean coast of what is now France, they found such a multitude of every variety of rock fish, that a new dish had to be invented. Today, on the waterfront of Marseilles, boats dock at the quay right beside the outdoor fish market. Fishermen rush with trays of new catch through the market to a nearby local landmark, the Restaurant Michel. Inside, diners crowd long communal tables across a large, bright, noisy room. The only concession to fancy décor is the glittering display of fresh fish on crushed ice just by the entrance. One glance and it is obvious why the French call seafood *fruits de mer*. Perfected here is the subtle art of preparing

The ingredients for Restaurant Michel's *bouillabaisse*.

Bouillabaisse

This is a robust, highly seasoned dish relying for its success on a mixture of different types of fish, all of them non-oily, half of them firm-fleshed, and half of them delicate. Shellfish may be added but are not essential. Also necessary are a good olive oil, and above all, saffron. Some of the fish traditionally used in Marseilles, home of the bouillabaisse, are not available outside Provence, but there are acceptable substitutes.

Provençal Fish Stew

The delicate, non-oily fish such as lemon sole, red mullet, John Dory, or brill should each weigh less than 1 lb/450 g. Use them whole if they are small or halved if they are larger. For the firm-fleshed, non-oily fish, use fish such as monkfish, sea bass, sea bream, halibut, cod or conger eel, thickly sliced except the eel which should be cut into 1½-inch/4-cm slices. Ask your fishmonger to clean and prepare the fish.

SERVES SIX TO EIGHT

For the fish stock

1 lb/450 g fish heads, trimmings and carcasses

1 medium onion, peeled and coarsely chopped

6 parsley stalks

branch of fresh fennel, or ½ teaspoon/2.5 ml fennel seeds

green part of leeks used in the bouillabaisse

1 x 2-inch/5-cm strip of dried orange peel

sprig of thyme

bay leaf

salt and freshly ground black pepper

2–3 cloves garlic, peeled and minced

5 pints/2.8 litres water

For the bouillabaisse

1 lb/450 g leeks

6 fl oz/175 ml (¾ cup) olive oil

---

1 large or 2 medium onions, peeled and finely chopped

4 cloves garlic, peeled and chopped

1 lb/450 g tomatoes, peeled, seeded and chopped

1 teaspoon/5 ml saffron threads

1 x 1-inch/2.5-cm piece of dried orange peel

1 teaspoon/5 ml dried mixed herbs

1 bay leaf

salt and freshly ground black pepper

4 fl oz/100 ml (½ cup) Pastis

3 lb/1.4 kg delicate, non-oily fish

2 lb/900 g firm-fleshed, non-oily fish

12 large prawns (shrimp) or langoustines

18–24 x ½-inch/1.5-cm slices French bread

olive oil

garlic cloves for the bread

To make the fish stock, combine all the stock ingredients in a large saucepan, bring to the boil, cover and simmer over moderate heat for 30 minutes. Strain through a fine sieve into a bowl, pressing down hard on the solids with the back of a large spoon to extract all the flavour possible.

Thoroughly wash the leeks and finely chop the white part. The green tops have been used in the fish stock. Pour the oil into a large, heavy saucepan. Add the onions and leeks and cook over moderate heat, stirring from time to time with a wooden spoon for about 5 minutes until the onions are soft. Add the garlic and cook for a minute longer. Add the tomatoes, saffron crumbled in the fingers, dried orange peel, herbs and bay leaf and cook for about 5 minutes longer until the mixture is well blended. Pour in the prepared fish stock, stir to mix and season to taste with salt and pepper. Stir in the Pastis. Bring to the boil over a high heat. Add the

firm-fleshed fish and cook, uncovered, at a rapid boil for 5 minutes. Add the delicate fish and cook for 5 minutes longer, or until all the fish is tender. In the last 3 minutes add the prawns. Meanwhile, sprinkle the bread with olive oil, rub it with garlic and arrange it on a baking tin. Bake it in a preheated slow oven, 250°F, 130°C, Gas Mark ½, until it is dried out but not toasted.

Carefully lift out the fish on to a heated serving dish. Moisten it with a ladleful or so of the broth. Pour the broth into a warmed tureen and send to the table with the garlic bread and the fish. Put a couple of slices or more of garlic bread into the bottom of large soup plates and pour the broth over them. If liked, spread the bread with *rouille* (Garlic Hot Sauce) before putting it into the soup plates, or stir a spoonful into the broth. Serve the fish separately, accompanied by the *rouille,* or add it to the soup plate with the broth as preferred.

Rouille

Garlic Hot Sauce

Rouille *is traditionally served with* bouillabaisse *or with Provençal fish soups and is made with garlic and hot red peppers. The hot pepper used is very hot so it is wise to remember the rule that it is a good* idea to wash the hands with warm soapy water after handling hot peppers and never, never, to let 'peppery' fingers get near the eyes. It will not do any lasting harm but it will be temporarily very unpleasant.

SERVES SIX TO EIGHT	or *1 teaspoon/5 ml cayenne pepper*
3 oz/75 g (1½ cups) freshly made breadcrumbs	*salt and freshly ground black pepper*
3 large cloves garlic, peeled and crushed	*2 tablespoons/30 ml olive oil*
3 fresh hot red peppers, seeded and chopped	*4 fl oz/100 ml (½ cup) broth from* bouillabaisse

Soak the breadcrumbs briefly in a little cold water. Squeeze them out and fluff the bread. Reduce the garlic to a paste in a mortar or in a blender with the hot peppers, salt and black pepper. Combine the breadcrumbs with the garlic and hot pepper mixture and beat in the oil. Thin the sauce to the consistency of a medium-white sauce with the broth from the *bouillabaisse.*

bouillabaisse, handed down from the Phoenicians. Three things are essential . . . the freshest possible selection of coastal fish, the best olive oil and the finest saffron.

As Theophrastus pointed out, saffron seemed to grow everywhere, especially along highways. Presumably this contributed to the Greek and Roman custom of strewing it on the paths of emperors and kings, providing a sort of ancient yellow carpet. Fussy and extravagant Roman nobility thought that saffron possessed cleansing qualities and spread it willy-nilly around theatres and other public places to fumigate them.

Saffron soon made its way east. Legend tells us that when Alexander the Great's troops descended into the valley of the Indian province of Kashmir, they broke ranks and ran wildly, crazed apparently by the abundant fields of autumn-blooming crocuses. The name 'kashmir' itself may have come from *Kasmiraja* meaning saffron. (It is interesting to note that the spice cassia also lays claim to providing the name for Kashmir.)

Today, saffron is used in northern Indian Mogul food, but the influence, and possibly the spice itself, came first from Persia or Iran. It was there that one of the great events in food history took place, the meeting of saffron and rice. Turmeric had long been used in the east to colour food yellow. It is an essential ingredient in curries, but it is not water soluble. Turmeric will turn rice yellow, but the yellow is composed of billions of tiny turmeric particles. Saffron, dissolved in water, penetrates the rice itself. If you want saffron rice, there is no substitute for saffron.

Modern Iran is dominated by the Shia'h branch of Islam. After the prophet Muhammad's death, his followers split into two groups, each laying claim to his true succession. Shia'hs follow the line of Muhammad's son-in-law Ali and hold special reverence for his son, Husayn. They believe that in the person of Husayn was merged the true succession from the prophet with that of the pre-Islamic kings of Persia. Husayn was slain in battle on the tenth day of the Muhammadan month of Moharram. His death occupies a central place in Shia'h religious observance. The first ten days of Moharram are especially intense. In street processions, men strip to the waist and flay themselves with thongs; large platforms draped in black ribbon seem to float across the solid crowds; people dance, sing, call out the name of Husayn and generally work themselves into religious frenzy. It is also traditional that during these ten days, people give to one another a very special gift, a bowl of a sweet yellow rice pudding called *sholezard.*

Sholezard

Persian Yellow Rice Pudding

This recipe for a delicious cold rice pudding is taken from Claudia Roden's A Book of Middle Eastern Food. *This excellent dish is traditionally served on the* anniversary *of the death of a member of the Prophet Muhammad's family. Saffron gives it its elegant colour and distinctive taste.*

SERVES SIX

4–5 oz/100–125 g pudding rice

¼ teaspoon/1.5 ml powdered saffron

1 lb/450 g sugar

1 teaspoon/5 ml lemon juice

2 oz/50 g (½ cup) blanched almonds, chopped (optional)

1 teaspoon/5 ml ground cinnamon (optional)

Wash the rice well. Bring it to the boil in 2 pints/900 ml (5 cups) water in which you have dissolved the saffron. Simmer gently for about ¾ hour until the rice is soft and swollen. Add a hot syrup made by simmering together the sugar, lemon juice and ¾ pint/100 ml (½ cup) water. Cook all together for about ½ hour, until much of the liquid has been absorbed.

If you like, stir in some chopped, blanched almonds. Allow to cool a little and pour into a glass serving bowl. Chill and serve dusted with a little cinnamon if you wish.

Saffron and rice also figure in the ceremonial life of India. Each morning Hindu women come to their temple bearing gifts of spices, food and fruit for the gods. The women, wearing necklaces of fragrant yellow French marigolds, chant continuously as each individual carries her gift to the altar and receives in exchange a dab of saffron paste in the middle of the forehead. A few grains of rice are stuck on to symbolize the fertile and bountiful goodness of the universe. The mark, or *tillak*, placed by one person on the forehead of another is an all-purpose gesture of blessing, good luck and beneficence. In late October, in associa-

tion with the festival of light, Diwali, a touching ceremony happens in the home. It is called *bhaiya-dooj*, brothers and sisters. The sister places a saffron paste mark on the brother's forehead. He in return, gives her a gift. In some parts of central India, after the brothers have left the ceremony, the women of the household remain behind and sprinkle saffron in honour of all the male members of the family.

Each flower of the saffron crocus (*Crocus sativas*) has only three drooping stigmas. Today, as in more ancient times, the only way to remove them is by hand. To give an idea of the tediousness of

Zaffrani Chawal

This dish from Uttar Pradesh in the north of India is traditional on the feast day of Basant which marks the

Saffron-Flavoured Rice

beginning of spring when the fields are yellow with mustard (colza) blossom.

SERVES EIGHT	
10 oz/275 g (1¼ cups) Basmati or other long-grain rice	20 fl oz/575 ml (2¼ cups) water
2 oz/50 g (⅓ cup) sultanas (golden raisins)	2 oz/50 g (4 tablespoons) ghee
⅛ teaspoon/large pinch saffron threads	1½ oz/40 g (⅓ cup) flaked (slivered) almonds
3 tablespoons/45 ml warm water	1 oz/25 g (¼ cup) pistachio nuts, coarsely chopped
4 green cardamom pods	3 leaves silver
3 oz/75 g (⅜ cup) sugar	**ghee** (Indian clarified butter)
	1 lb/450 g (2 cups) unsalted butter

To make the ghee, cut the butter into small bits, put into a medium-sized heavy saucepan and melt it over a very low heat. When the butter has melted, 5–15 minutes according to the size of the pieces, increase the heat to moderate. Simmer the butter for 10 minutes. It will crackle and be covered with foam. At the end of that time the foam will subside and the crackling noise stop. Now stir the butter constantly with a wooden spoon and as soon as the butter fat solids turn brown, remove the ghee from the heat, let it cool and pour off the liquid, taking care not to let any of the brown bits get into the clear butter. If necessary strain through a double layer of dampened cheesecloth. Pour the ghee into a screwtop jar and keep in the refrigerator where it will stay fresh for several months. It can be kept, unrefrigerated in a cool kitchen for about 1 month.

Wash the rice until the water runs clear, drain and put into a bowl with cold water to cover and let it soak for 30 minutes. Put the sultanas into

another bowl and soak for 15 minutes. Drain and set aside. Put the saffron threads into a small bowl with the warm water and leave to soak. Remove the cardamom seeds from the pods and crush them lightly. Dissolve the sugar in the water.

Heat the ghee in a medium-sized heavy saucepan. Drain the rice and add it to the pan. Sauté, stirring with a wooden spoon, for 1 minute. Add the cardamom seeds and the dissolved sugar and if necessary a little more water. The water should come to about 1 inch/2.5 cm above the rice. Add the saffron and the soaking water. Stir the rice and bring to the boil over a high heat. Reduce the heat, cover and cook for 10 minutes, or until the rice is almost tender. Add the almonds and sultanas. Cover and cook over a very low heat for 5 minutes longer or until the rice is tender and all the liquid is absorbed. Remove from the heat and let the saucepan stand, covered, for a few minutes. Fluff the rice with a fork and garnish with the pistachios and silver leaf.

Saffron plays a part in the ceremonial life of India. The *tillak*, or saffron paste mark, placed by one person on the forehead of another is an all-purpose gesture of blessing, good luck and beneficence.

the process, it takes from between 200,000 and 400,000 individual stigmas to make just 450 g of saffron. This means that thousands of flowers are needed for even several grams.

The flowers must be picked as soon as they bloom, and they bloom only for a two-week period in the autumn. Just a few yellow strands can represent an enormous amount of back-breaking, tedious work.

Because its cultivation demands an enormous effort, saffron is dependent upon societies possessing both a noble class sufficiently sophisticated to appreciate its culinary subtleties, and a class of slaves or workers which can be forced or per-suaded to harvest it. For this reason, when the western Roman Empire fell, saffron usage ceased in Europe.

Zahafaran is Arabic for saffron, and it is the Arabs who gave Europe both the spice and its name. First they introduced rice to the lakes of the Spanish region of Valencia and in about the year AD 900 they started to cultivate saffron to go with it. The rice of the lakes met the saffron of the fields, and, as if by magic, a new treasure was born.

Raco D'Lolla is a small provincial restaurant on the shore of a Valencian lake famous for its rice. The door from its dining-room opens onto a terrace which extends to the water's edge. It is here that the *Paellero* Juan Castillo practises his art of fusing saffron, rice and seafood into Valencia's great dish, *paella*. The sumptuous aroma is almost too much to bear as Juan patiently works a wok-like pan over an open fire. *Paella* takes its name

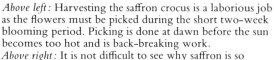

Above left: Harvesting the saffron crocus is a laborious job as the flowers must be picked during the short two-week blooming period. Picking is done at dawn before the sun becomes too hot and is back-breaking work.
Above right: It is not difficult to see why saffron is so expensive. Each saffron crocus has only three stigmas and it takes from between 200,000 and 400,000 stigmas to make 450 g (1 lb) saffron. The bowl represents the yield from an average-sized field. The farmer is holding in his hand all that remains after the stigmas are dried.

from the pan, a *paellera*. Winds off the lake fan the fire; golden liquids boil and bubble, but all is well for Juan Castillo has personally cooked over twenty thousand *paellas*!

The Spanish town of Consuegra overlooks the brown barren plains of La Mancha. A mule cart bumping along the dusty road winding up to the town suggests that little has changed since Cervantes chose this area to be the home of his immortal character, Don Quixote. This is also the home of saffron.

In La Mancha, saffron is very much a family affair. It is just possible to eke out a few pesetas, maybe, if everything goes well. The impossibility of mechanization because of bad terrain and the size of the plots, permits fields to be used which are too small for any other purpose. These are the only plots of land available to the poor, and saffron is the only possible crop.

The Cassas family is a typical example. Three and possibly four generations all exert themselves to make one tiny, dry field pay. On September

Paellero Juan Castillo's Valencian *paella* which fuses together saffron, rice and seafood.

Paella Valenciana

Paella, *usually called* Paella Valenciana, *is almost certainly the best known Spanish dish. The word* paella *actually refers to the special metal pan, a paellera, in which dishes of rice, poultry, fish and shellfish are cooked on Spain's Mediterranean coast. The pan is round with shallow, sloping sides and two flattened handles. A 12–13-inch/30–33-cm pan holds enough to serve four to six people. No two cooks, and no two culinary authorities agree on the contents of the dish. Originally it was made from snails, eels, olive oil, rice and green beans. Purists in Valencia make it with chicken, snails, tomato, green beans, peas, rice and garlic. The luxurious and complicated dish that is the popular* paella *of today contains olive oil, poultry, prawns, mussels, clams, squid, saffron, vegetables and rice. The dish is so versatile that it can be claimed the only essentials are olive oil, rice and saffron. This recipe here is a suitable version for cooking at home. A heavy frying pan (skillet) or shallow flameproof casserole can be used instead of a* paella *pan.*

SERVES FOUR TO SIX

1 x 2¼-lb/1-kg chicken, cut into 8 serving pieces
salt and freshly ground black pepper
4 fl oz/100 ml (½ cup) olive oil
8 oz/225 g lean pork, cut into ¼-inch/0.75-cm cubes
8 oz/225 g chorizo or other spicy sausage, sliced
1 medium onion, peeled and finely chopped
2 cloves garlic, peeled and chopped
2 sweet red peppers, skinned, seeded and chopped
¾ lb/350 g tomatoes, peeled, seeded and chopped
24 mussels, thoroughly scrubbed and soaked
1 lb/450 g (2 cups) long-grain rice
1¾ pints/1 litre (4 cups) chicken stock
½ teaspoon/2.5 ml ground saffron, or saffron threads
4 oz/100 g green beans cut into 1-inch/2.5-cm pieces
8 oz/225 g peas, if frozen thoroughly defrosted
8 oz/225 g uncooked prawns (medium-sized shrimp)
or 4 oz/100 g defrosted frozen prawns (shrimp)
12 snails, cooked and shelled, optional

Season the chicken pieces with salt and freshly ground black pepper. Heat the oil in a *paella* pan or heavy frying pan and sauté the chicken pieces and the pork cubes until they are lightly browned all over. When the chicken is half cooked, add the sausages. Add the onion, garlic and peppers. When the onion is soft, add the tomatoes. Simmer the mixture for about 10 minutes. Add the mussels and cook, covered, for 3–4 minutes, or until the mussels have opened. Discard any that do not open.

Add the rice and stir it into the mixture. Mix the stock with the pulverized saffron and pour it into the pan. Bring to the boil, cover and cook over a very low heat for 20 minutes or until the rice is tender and has absorbed all the liquid. When the rice has been cooking for 5 minutes, add the green beans and peas. Five minutes before the rice is finished, add the prawns (shrimp) and the snails, if using. Let the *paella* rest, covered, for 3–4 minutes before serving. Serve directly from the pan.

nights during harvest time, the whole family huddles together around a large table in a remote one-room cottage. There is no electricity; just enough candle light to define the cluster of faces, young and old. On the table is a heap of purple flowers. On the floor are pans for collecting separated stigmas. Fingers move endlessly . . . flower, separate stigmas, drop it . . . and on and on. They talk, sometimes they even sing, but there are long stretches of numbing silence. In just a few hours, before dawn, they will leave the hut and make their way back to the field to spend another day stooped under the blazing sun collecting yet another load of purple flowers.

No one survives on saffron, explains Doña Felicia, the white-haired grandmother. It simply gives them a bit of cash to purchase things at the local store, like boots or clothes. Everyone in the family works. Year round the hard soil must be kept dug over, and in August, when the burning sun bakes the surface too hard for the new shoots, the field must be reploughed with a harrow.

The saffron crocus has ceased to exist in the wild. Its seeds are barren so it must be cultivated vegetatively. Each year two or three cormlets form on the base of the main corm. These are harvested and used for the new crop. Although plants can live up to fifteen years, in practice they are permitted no longer than four years as older corms become highly susceptible to disease. This means that crops will run in four year cycles . . . year one, small flowers, small crop; year two, better but still small crop; year three, large flowers, best crop; year four, also good, but it is the last year and the field now requires a long rest.

Not only will the crop for each grower fluctuate, but world-wide prices and demand also vary. Some years when there is very little money for saffron, the farmers will try to hold the crop over until prices rise. Doña Felicia explains that the family keeps the whole crop in a little wooden drawer, and tries to preserve it so that it does not lose weight.

The boys have lit a small charcoal fire. The thread-like stigmas are spread on large sieves for slow drying over the glowing coals. Eighty per

Above: The Spanish town of Consuegra in the brown, barren plains of La Mancha. Saffron is an important crop in this region because it can be grown in tiny, dry plots which are unsuitable for growing anything else.

Left: The stigmas have to be removed by hand from the blooms, a tedious process that goes on night and day during the short harvesting season. Beautiful as they are, the violet petals have no use and are discarded.

cent of what little weight there is, is lost during the drying process, but it is here that the characteristic flavour of the spice comes alive. Since the crocus blooms for only two weeks this final day and night spurt of effort is harsh, but brief. In the year 1981 the whole of the Consuegra region produced only 675 kilograms of saffron!

The weeks finally pass; crowds gather and flow into Consuegra's central square. Flags fly, bands blare and on a large stage costumed dancers step lightly to Spanish rhythms. *Rosa del azafrán*, the annual festival is here. Now, for a brief moment, the people of La Mancha can pause from their toils and revel, just a bit, in the fruits of their labours.

Each year, as part of the festival, the Spanish government restores and dedicates one more of the region's many windmills. But the highlight is the crowning of a Queen, a *Dulcinea* who then presides over, no less, a saffron-separating contest. As the music plays and the crowd sings, the contestants, all women like Doña Felicia, sit at long tables piled with purple flowers. Well-practised fingers select a flower, separate the stigmas, drop it . . . select a flower, separate the stigmas and so on, and so on!

By the time the Renaissance dawned in Europe, saffron was one of the most important spices. It was grown everywhere and used in everything. People seemed to think that food should be mostly yellow. Meals were eaten smothered in a saffron concoction known simply as 'the yellow sauce'. In winter, people preferred it slightly redder, so a bit of sandalwood was added. The sauce was even hawked from door to door.

Even at the height of its popularity, saffron remained very expensive. A cook would have to pay more for locally grown saffron than for an equal weight of pepper which originated half way around the world. Of course, even then nobody used saffron like pepper, just a small amount was sufficient. It was and is expensive because it is labour intensive in the extreme.

Richard Hakluyt, the sixteenth-century English geographer and historian, considered saffron cultivation as a possible solution to the even then growing problem of unemployment. He heaped praise upon the patriotic traveller who first brought the crocus to England.

It is reported at Saffron Walden that a pilgrim purposing to doe good to his country stole a head of saffron, and hid the same in his palmer's staff, which he had made hollow before of purpose, and so he brought this root into this realme, with venture of his life; for if he had been taken, by the law of the country from whence it came, he had died for the fact. If the like love in this our age were in our people that now become great travellers, many knowledges, and many trades, and many herbs and plants might be brought into this realme that might doe the realme good.

In fact, some years later Hakluyt's wish came true with the establishment of the botanical gardens at Kew. Hakluyt was convinced that saffron was already of major benefit for England. Here is an excerpt from a letter he wrote in 1582 to a gentleman who was about to set off to Turkey to be a factor for one of the new trading companies

Left and below: In October of each year in Consuegra there is a saffron festival after the harvest is over. The highlight of the festival is a saffron-separating contest.

emerging at that time. Hakluyt wants him to sell English saffron to the Turks.

> Saffron, the best of the universall world groweth in this realme, and forasmuch as it is a thing that requireth much labour in divers sorts, and setteth the people on worke so plentifully, I wish you to see whether you can finde ample vent for the same, since it is gone out of great use in those parts. It is a spice that is cordiall, and may be used in meats, and that is excellent in dyeing of yellow silks.
>
> This commodity of saffron groweth fifty miles from Tripoli in Syria, on a high hill called in those parts Garian, so as there you may learne at that port of Tripoli the value of the pound, the goodness of it, and the places of the vent.
>
> But it is said that from that hill there passeth yearly of that commodity fifteene moiles laden, and that those regions notwithstanding lack sufficience of that commodity. But if a vent might be found, we would in Essex about Saffron Walden and in Cambridge shire revive the trade for the benefit of the setting of the poor on work. So would they doe in Hereford shire by Wales, where the best of all England is, in which place the soil yeelds the wilde saffron commonly, which sheweth the naturall inclination of the same soile to the bearing of the right saffron, if the soile be manured and that way employed.

Despite Hakluyt's novel solution for problems of the dole, by the end of the eighteenth century northern European saffron cultivation had all but died out. The growers of Saffron Walden were known as Crokers and, it is said, they were constantly 'croaking' or complaining. Apparently the moisture in the English soil encouraged corm disease. But the principal reason cultivation ended was the labour demands of the Industrial Revolution. With the decline in cultivation came a corresponding decline in use. In 1877 E. S. Kettner, a noted culinary author, lamented the fact:

> It is the elegiac muse that ought to write the account of saffron, for its glory is departed. The stigmas of this autumnal crocus were once all important in European cookery, and were supposed to possess the rarest virtues and attractions . . . There was a time when England was known as merry England; and Lord Bacon in his *History of Life and Death* says: 'The English are rendered sprightly by a liberal use of saffron in sweetmeats and broth.' Saffron is now but little used anywhere in human food to please the eye, to tickle the palate, or to strengthen the stomach; and in England it has been so completely ousted by curry that what once rejoiced the heart of man is now only sprinkled on water to cheer the melancholy of canaries . . . Let us be thankful that one thing will last while man lasts—the saffron-coloured morn.

Fortunately, pockets of saffron culture managed to survive. In the eighteenth century, a German grower named Schwenfelder brought it with him to Pennsylvania, where it is still cultivated. Saffron is an important seasoning in Pennsylvanian Dutch food and is essential for their golden Schwenfelder cake.

As for golden cake, in 1908 the naturalist W. H. Hudson, after a visit to west Cornwall, wrote the following:

> As I wished to know how they (the Cornish) lived, I had the ordinary fare and found it quite good enough for any healthy person: pork fattened on milk and homecured; milk (from the cow) and Cornish clotted cream, which is unrivalled; sometimes a pasty, in which a little chopped-up meat is mixed with sliced turnip and onion and baked in crust, and finally the thin Cornish broth with sliced swedes which give it a sweetish taste.
>
> Then there was a very excellent home-made bread, and saffron cake, on which the Cornish child is weaned and which he goes on eating until the last day of his life.

Even at the end of June, low grey clouds threaten the remote Cornish fishing village of Porthleven. This does not, however, stop the children of the village from gathering and march-

Saffron Buns

8 fl oz/225 ml (1 cup) warm water	1 lb/450 g (4 cups) plain (all-purpose) flour
1 teaspoon/5 ml ground saffron	1½ teaspoons/7.5 ml salt
½ oz/50 g (2 packets) active dried yeast	5 oz/150 g (⅝ cup) each lard and butter
1½ oz/40 g (3 tablespoons) sugar	¾ lb/350 g (2¼ cups) mixed sultanas and currants
	a little peel, chopped

Heat half the water until lukewarm. Stir in the saffron. Put the yeast into a bowl with 1 tablespoon/15 g of sugar. Add the water, mixing well. Leave in a warm place for about 10–15 minutes until it bubbles. In a large mixing bowl combine the flour, salt and the rest of the sugar. Cut the lard and butter into small pieces and rub into the flour with the fingertips to make a coarse meal. Add the mixed fruit and peel. Make a well in the centre and pour in the yeast mixture. Stir to mix, adding enough of the remaining water to make a soft but not sticky dough. Turn the dough out onto a lightly floured board and knead it for 15 minutes. It will be smooth, satiny and elastic. Lightly grease the bowl. Form the dough into a ball and return it to the bowl. Cover with a clean cloth and let it stand in a warm, draught-free place until it has doubled in bulk. This should take about 2 hours.

Divide the dough into six equal portions and pat into circles about 7 in/18 cm in diameter. Put the buns on greased baking sheets and stand, covered, in a warm, draught-free place for about 30 minutes until risen again. Bake in a preheated, moderately hot oven, 400°F, 200°C, Gas Mark 6 for about 35 minutes or until they are lightly browned and sound hollow when they are tapped on the bottom with the knuckles. If preferred, the dough may be divided into twelve equal portions for smaller buns.

ing in procession throughout the town. It is St Peterstide and the children of fishermen are honouring another fisherman of long ago. It is the Methodist chapels of the area who march. Banners and bands lead the way followed by ragged lines of striding young, and in prams pushed by mums, riding young. The whole parade cheerfully winds over the sea walls, through the high street, past the harbour and up the hill to a grassy common at the top of the town. There, awaiting the marchers is the tea treat. To each child is presented a round golden bun chock-full of currants and so ample that both hands seem required for its proper negotiation. Some children tear pieces and put them in their mouths, others attack more directly . . . there are no complaints. The adults gather in a nearby marquee where at long communal tables they sip tea and feast upon the more traditional saffron cake.

There are various stories and legends of how saffron came to Cornwall. Some say it was brought by the ancient Phoenicians who were interested in the product of the local tin mines. Others even claim that after its defeat, the remnant of the Spanish Armada was blown off course and floundered on the Cornish coast. Amongst the spoils, the locals found and took a fancy to saffron. More likely, saffron was grown and used extensively in Cornwall as it was everywhere else. When the tradition died, the Cornish were fortunately too stubborn to give it up.

Here is a recipe for saffron cake written in 1760 by the wonderful cookery writer, Hannah Glasse. Commenting on the recipe, another superb but modern writer, Elizabeth David, wondered in her *English Bread and Yeast Cookery* (1977) whether Mrs Glasse had family interests in the East India Company or with the West Indies spice and sugar trade.

Take a quarter of a peck of fine flour, a pound and a half of butter, three ounces of carraway seeds, and six eggs; beat well a quarter of an ounce of cloves and mace together very fine, a pennyworth of cinnamon beat, a pound of sugar, a pennyworth of rose water, a pennyworth of saffron, a pint and half of yeast, and a quart of milk, mix all together lightly with your hands thus; first boil the milk and butter, scum off the butter, and mix it with the flour and a little of the milk, stir the yeast into the rest, and strain it; mix it with your flour, put in your seed and spice, rose water, tincture of saffron, sugar, and eggs; beat all up with your hands very lightly, and bake it in a hoop or pan, minding to butter the pan well; it will take an hour and a half in a quick oven; you may leve out the seed if you chuse it, and I think it the best.

HANNAH GLASSE, *The Compleat Confectioner*, 1772, first published c. 1760.

The Sabbath is one of Judaism's great gifts. It is the only festival ordered by the ten commandments and it represents the very first labour legislation. Once a week human beings are permitted to enter the kingdom of the eternal. Jews, for millenia, scrimped and scraped throughout the week in order to make the Sabbath very special. The Sabbath begins at sundown on Friday night. In the Orthodox tradition, the men return from the synagogue, it is said, escorted by angels. Mother has already laid her best table and lights the Sabbath candles. The whole family gathers for the *kiddish*, or blessing, before the meal. Two giant loaves of the golden Sabbath bread, *Challah*, dominate the table.

When first asked, the British cookery expert, Evelyn Rose, could not recall saffron being used in the *Challah*. On further investigation, she discovered that often it was, but for a rather unexpected reason. In Russia or eastern Europe, eggs essential for *Challah* were sometimes too expensive or even unavailable. A few strands of saffron would colour the bread the necessary gold. On very special occasions, a wedding or festival Sabbath, both eggs and saffron could be used together. Saffron was also used to enrich the hue of the *goldene yoich,* the golden chicken soup, and, on occasion, the famous Sabbath appetizer, *gefilte* fish.

Challah

Although refrigerated doughs have become popular only recently the method is similar to the old Russian way of leaving bread dough outside the kitchen door overnight to rise in the winter cold. This method gives very good texture and taste. For a large loaf, double the amount given. For a quite spectacular loaf the dough is divided into five pieces which are then plaited. Evelyn Rose, *who created the recipe, says it is impossible to describe plaiting with five strands. It must be seen to be understood.*

Saffron, which lends a yellow colour and fragrance to the bread, is closely associated with the fragrant spices of the Psumim or Spice Box traditionally used on Sabbaths and holidays when this bread would be eaten.

MAKES ONE LOAF

½ teaspoon/2.5 ml saffron threads	or 1 cake fresh yeast
2 tablespoons/30 ml hot water	2 teaspoons/10 ml salt
4 fl oz/100 ml (½ cup) lukewarm (43°C, 110°F) water	1 tablespoon/15 ml vegetable oil
8 oz/225 g (2 cups) bread flour	1 egg, lightly beaten
1½ teaspoons/7.5 ml sugar	1 egg yolk beaten with 1 teaspoon/5 ml cold water
1 tablespoon/15 ml (1 package) active dried yeast	poppy seeds

Pulverize the saffron threads in a mortar, transfer to a cup or small bowl and pour the hot water over them. Leave to infuse for a few minutes. Pour the lukewarm water into the bowl of a food processor or a mixer. Add the saffron water. Add one-third of the flour, the sugar and the yeast and mix for about 15 seconds until smooth. Cover and leave for about 20 minutes or until the mixture is frothy. Add the rest of the flour, half the salt, the oil and the beaten egg. Process the mixture to form a ball, then continue to process for 45 seconds.

Turn the dough out on to a lightly floured board and knead for 30 seconds to shape it into a ball. The dough should be smooth and elastic. If necessary knead until it is so. If the dough is made by hand, it should be kneaded at this stage for 5–6 minutes or until it is smooth and elastic. Lightly oil the inside of a plastic bag large enough to hold the dough when it has doubled in bulk. Put the dough into the bag and fasten it loosely. Place on the bottom shelf of the refrigerator for 12–24 hours.

When ready to shape the loaf, remove the dough from the refrigerator, take it out of the bag and let it stand on a lightly floured surface for about 30 minutes to come to room temperature. Divide the dough into three equal pieces. Roll each piece into a 12-inch/30-cm sausage shape. Press the pieces firmly together at one end, then plait tightly. Place on to a greased baking tin, then slide, tin and all, into a large greased plastic bag and leave in a warm, draught-free place until doubled in bulk. This takes about 1 hour. Mix the remaining teaspoon/5 ml salt with the egg wash made from the egg yolk and the cold water. Remove the dough from the plastic bag and, using a pastry brush, brush the bread with the egg mixture. Sprinkle the surface with poppy seeds.

Bake the loaf in a preheated hot oven, 425°F, 220°C, Gas Mark 7 for 15 minutes. Lower the heat to 375°F, 190°C, Gas Mark 5 and bake for 30 minutes longer or until it is golden brown, and the bottom sounds hollow when tapped.

Mrs Rose decided to attempt *Challah* and chicken soup with saffron. She deliberately omitted mentioning the fact to her husband, who not only has a sensitive palate, but who had spent his childhood in eastern Europe. When he passed the kitchen he immediately remarked upon the wonderful aroma which kindled fond memories of his childhood.

Mrs Rose claims that one of the secrets of *Challah* is in the method of its twist, or plaiting. This is necessary because after the father's blessing, the bread is not cut, but broken and distributed. This same rich bread is baked for the new year, Rosh Hashana, but is round to symbolize the fullness of the coming year. On Yom Kippur, the day of atonement, the bread is baked in a ladder

Gilderne

Golden Chicken Soup

This rich, clear chicken soup is associated with Sabbaths and holidays in Jewish homes and is a must at wedding *anniversary meals, especially the 25th and 50th. Saffron is used to give it its golden colour.*

SERVES SIX TO EIGHT

1 x 4½–5 lb/2.3 kg chicken plus gizzard, heart and neck	1 ripe tomato
3½ pints/2 litres (8 cups) water	sprig of fresh parsley
1 large onion, peeled	2 teaspoons/10 ml salt
2 carrots, scraped and quartered	pinch of white pepper
2 stalks celery, including leaves	½ teaspoon/2.5 ml saffron threads, crumbled

Put the chicken with the gizzard, heart, neck and feet into a large saucepan or flameproof casserole. Add the water, and bring to the boil over a high heat. Skim carefully. Add all the remaining ingredients, bring back to the boil, lower the heat and simmer very gently either on top of the stove or in a preheated slow oven, 290°F, 140°C, Gas Mark 2, for 3 hours.

Strain the soup and serve garnished with cooked *lokshen* (vermicelli or egg noodles), *mandlen* or *knaidlach* (matzo balls). If preferred, the soup may be refrigerated as soon as it has cooled and the congealed fat removed the following day.

For additional flavouring, the cooked giblets and the carrots may be chopped and added to the soup.

shape to help prayers climb to heaven.

According to Mrs Rose, *Challah* has played a role in Jewish Sabbaths for nearly 3000 years. The recipe was developed by the bakers of the Macedonian King Perseus II.

> I love saffron and she loves me.
> They call me mellow yellow,
> they call me mellow yellow.
> DONOVAN, 1967

Oriental monks draped in saffron-coloured robes present a familiar image, but, in truth, saffron is a poor fabric dye. Not only is it water soluble requiring a chemical fixer, but it quickly fades in sunlight. Other substances are superior. Meadow safflower, for instance, has often passed for saffron. Today, there is no *safranschau* to put budding Johst Findekers in their place. It is best to buy the spice as 'hay' saffron, the dried stigmas themselves. Unfortunately, even this precaution is not altogether foolproof, for devious dealers have been known to infuse spent stigmas with ordinary yellow dye. Since so little saffron is needed in cooking, it would be a shame to have any but the real thing. So, please buy your saffron from a reliable source.

As for the unfortunate Johst Findeker, who was roasted with his phoney saffron, had he eaten rather than adulterated it, his end may have been much merrier. The famous seventeenth century herbalist, Nicholas Culpepper, wrote: '. . . The use of it ought to be moderate and seasonable; for when the dose is too large, it produces a heaviness in the head, and a sleepiness; some have fallen into an immoderate convulsive laughter, which ended in death.'

6
CHILLIES

It started down the way in old Terlingua. We had to move out because they had some mines out there and they had outhouses over the mines. A foreman said that you could go in one of those Terlingua outhouses, cup an ear, and hear the community singing in China. We were afraid that some patrons of the outhouses were going to fall in the mines, and they were always falling into dirty Woman Creek.

Frank Tolbert, big, healthy, seventy years old, shouts out from under his ten-gallon hat and still seems amazed at his own accomplishments. Terlingua squats in the dry brown vastness, of the West Texas desert about a day's pony ride to the Rio Grande and the Mexican border. It is 145 kilometres from the nearest town and so small, says Frank, that 'it didn't even have a village idiot'.

Yet, once a year, in November, people start arriving from everywhere, thousands of them, by car, truck, bus, even airplane. The only local inhabitants, the rattlesnakes, better lie low or else they could end up as part of the main course in what members of the gathering crowd would call 'a bowl of red'. This is it, Terlingua's annual Chilli Cook-Off, where *aficionados* vie with one another for America's coveted chilli con carne

The annual Chilli Cook-off at Terlingua in Texas where enthusiasts vie with one another for America's coveted chilli-con-carne crown.

Chilli con Carne

This is one of the many authentic Texan recipes. Some cooks prefer to serve the chilli or 'bowl of red' plain just accompanied by tortillas or cornbread. Others like to *add cooked red kidney or* pinto *beans during the last half hour of cooking. It is a matter of taste but make sure you cook the beans properly.*

SERVES SIX TO EIGHT	
2 ancho *chillies*	2 *bay leaves, crumbled*
or *2 tablespoons mild chilli powder, ground*	2 *lb/900 g tomatoes, peeled, seeded and chopped*
8 *dried hot red chillies, about 2 inches/5 cm long*	or *2 1-lb/450-g tins Italian plum tomatoes*
or *4 tablespoons ground hot chilli pepper*	*salt*
3 *lb/1.4 kg chuck steak, cut into ½-inch/1.5-cm cubes*	2 *tablespoons/30 ml yellow corn meal or masa harina*
3 *tablespoons/45 ml lard or vegetable oil*	1 *lb/450 g (2 cups) red kidney or* pinto *beans*
1 *lb/450 g onions, peeled and finely chopped*	**For the beans**
4 *cloves of garlic, peeled and minced*	1 *lb/450 g (2 cups) red kidney or* pinto *beans*
1 *teaspoon/5 ml ground cumin*	2½ *pints/1.5 litres (6 cups) water*
1 *teaspoon/5 ml crumbled oregano*	1 *teaspoon/5 ml salt*

To prepare the beans, pick over and wash them in cold running water. Pour the water into a large, heavy saucepan and bring to the boil. Add the beans and bring back to the boil over high heat. Simmer for 2 minutes, turn off the heat and let the beans soak for 1 hour. Add the salt and simmer the beans, covered, until they are tender, about 1 hour. It is essential when cooking kidney beans to bring them to the boil properly. Drain. There should not be a great deal of liquid. The beans are now ready to be added to the chilli.

To prepare the main ingredients, if using the whole chillies pull off the stems, shake out the seeds and cut the chillies into pieces. Put them to soak in warm water barely to cover. Soak for 30 minutes, turning from time to time. Drain, reserving the liquid. Purée the chillies in a blender or food processor, using a little of the soaking water if necessary. Set aside.

Pat the cubes of beef dry with kitchen paper. Heat the lard or vegetable oil in a heavy casserole or saucepan and sauté the beef, onions and garlic, over a moderate heat, stirring from time to time with a wooden spoon until the beef is lightly browned. Add the chilli paste, or the mild and hot chilli powder if using, stirring for a few minutes longer. Add the remaining soaking water, the cumin, oregano, bay leaves, tomatoes and salt. Bring to the boil, lower the heat and simmer, covered, for about 1½ hours until the meat is tender. Stirring constantly, pour in the cornmeal or *masa harina* in a slow stream, and simmer until the chilli has thickened slightly. If using beans, stir them in 30 minutes before the chilli is done.

crown. So popular is this dish, that cook-offs have sprouted throughout the United States, but Terlingua remains special, because, like chilli con carne itself, it is basic and rough.

Frank, one of the festival's originators claims that chilli con carne (he would simply call it chilli) really started just after the American Civil War in the 1860s. The North American Indians had used chilli peppers to preserve meat. When a form of chilli powder became available, 'chuck wagon cooks' on cattle drives mixed it with meat to feed the cowboys.

'We make it with the peppers themselves', declares Frank. 'It's laborious for the average housewife. It was even more laborious before you had food processors.'

Streets of chilli-makers sprout up as contestants set up stalls to serve passers-by. How about some 'Razorback's Revenge' or 'Devil's Red-Eye'? The judges sit at a long table shaded from the blazing sun by a large marquee and taste entry after entry from numbered styrofoam cups with little plastic spoons. The table is also littered with cans of beer used to remove the taste of the previous chilli. It is not the hottest chilli which will win, but the most subtle in flavour. Each contestant has a secret recipe which he or she would guard to the end. This is serious business. Throughout the contest, music blares from loudspeakers with one refrain repeated over and over '. . . if you know beans about chilli, you know that chilli has no beans . . .'. Well, the recipe for chilli con carne gives you an option. You can use beans if you wish, but be warned if you decide to enter the contest at Terlingua.

The festival boasts many side attractions, but certainly the most popular is the Wet-T-shirt Contest. With a crowd of cheering, hooting, beer-swigging chilli fanciers looking on, young women in T-shirts are paraded on a stage, and then one by one dowsed with water. To the delight of the crowd, the T-shirts cling to the women, revealing the full glory of their breasts. As the afternoon wears on, and the sun beats incessantly upon the beer and chilli-charged crowd, the formality of the T-shirts is dispensed with and hoots can be heard all the way to the Rio Grande, as the women bare all. It was suggested that next year's contest be between the men . . . but this is Texas where chilli is a man's food, and men are men, who would probably find the whole thing too threatening to their well-cultivated 'macho' images. Finally the Chilli Contest winner is announced and is presented with a large silver cup and a bottle of champagne. He shouts that he would rather be given the winner of the T-shirt Contest.

A proud Frank Tolbert looks forward to next year. 'Well, I think chilli pepper is a natural . . . humans kind of need them. There's a medical doctor in New Mexico who's been experimenting with old men who eat a lot of chilli peppers and they have no . . . I'm pretty healthy and I'm seventy!' Again the music seeps through. '. . . if you know beans about chilli, you know it didn't come from Mexico. Chilli is God's gift to Texas,

and that you really ought to know . . .'

Chilli con carne may be as American as the Fourth of July, but the chilli peppers upon which it is based, certainly reached Texas through Mexico. Chillies were unknown to the world outside the Americas until Christopher Columbus made landfall on the island of Hispaniola in 1492. The island, one of the Greater Antilles, lies across the Caribbean Sea from Venezuela and Colombia. The chillies that Columbus found growing there had been brought by the island's first settlers, the Arawaks and Caribs, who migrated there from the upper Orinoco river region of what is now Venezuela. They called the peppers *aji*.

By the time Columbus arrived, chillies had not only migrated into the Caribbean from their original home, Mexico, but all the way south to the tips of Chile and Argentina.

Everywhere in Latin America they played, and still play, a central role in the kitchen. They may be sweet, pungent or hot, green, yellow or red, large or small, smooth or wrinkled, and are used fresh, dried or pickled. They are found in soups or in sauces, with fish, shellfish, poultry, meat or vegetables, enlivening dishes with an exotic or with a richly mild flavour, or they may lend a touch of fire. There are a great many varieties, some authorities putting the number as high as a hundred in Mexico alone, others as low as sixty-one.

They are classified into two main groups of the genus *Capsicum*, *C. annum* and *C. frutescens* of the Solanaceae family to which the potato, tomato, eggplant and even tobacco all belong. *Capsicum*, *C. annum* is an annual and *C. frutescens* is perennial. It would be nice if all the hot chillies fell into one group and the mild into the other; however, nature is not so neat. Most of the large mild variety are *C. annum*, but some of the smallest and most pungent also belong to this group. It really does not matter as most of the world's chillies are cultivated by seeds planted annually. If the perennials are allowed to survive longer than one year, they become smaller and lose their pungency. In any event, if you approach your greengrocer and ask whether a particular capsicum is *C. annum* or *C. frutescens*, he will simply look you in the eye and say 'eh?'.

It is interesting to know that the word 'capsicum' probably comes from the same root as capsule, capsa, a box . . . which encloses seeds. There are some who claim the Greek word *capto* is also involved. It means 'I bite'! To avoid confusion, the small hot capsicums are often called 'chillies' while the larger, mild ones are 'sweet peppers' or just capsicums. In Mexico, all capsicums are called 'chillies' but sweet peppers are also called 'pimientos'. Of course, the sweet peppers are a favourite vegetable worldwide and in their dried and ground form become the mild spice, paprika.

Christopher Columbus and the Spanish *conquistadores* created half a millenium of confusion by naming all the spices they discovered pepper, pimiento. The Spanish could, perhaps, be forgiven their botanical ignorance had they not added to

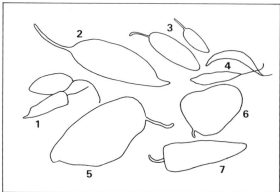

Left: Dried Mexican chillies, sweet, pungent and hot, are used widely in Mexican cooking. They include the following: **1.** Morita **2.** Guajillo **3.** Chipotle **4.** Chile de arbol **5.** Ancho **6.** Mulato **7.** Pasilla.
Right: Various kinds of fresh chillies including dark green *poblanos*, yellow *habaneros* and red, green and yellow sweet peppers.

the confusion by calling all the natives they met 'Indians'! There is a possible explanation for Columbus's confusion. When he first encountered chillies, he saw a little round green variety now called 'cascabels'. These had not yet reached their present size of 1.5 cm and may, indeed have resembled and even tasted like peppercorns. More likely, Columbus used the Queen of Spain's money to find pepper, but all he brought back were some silly red things. If they were called 'pepper', he at least could claim some success. In any event pepper (*Piper nigrum*) and chillies were now united by language and have remained together in the kitchen.

Archaeological records seem to confirm that chillies were eaten in the Valley of Mexico some 9000 years ago and were cultivated two thousand years later. This makes the spice one of the earliest plants known to be grown by the natives of America. Their original name in Nahuetl, the

language of ancient Mexico, was *chilli*, which the *conquistadores* converted into *chile*, pronounced almost identically. The name is still used in many parts of the world.

If you have been wondering whether the name of the country Chile is derived from a source common with the spice, the answer is, no. 'Chile' comes from an Aruacanian Indian word *Txile* whose meaning is unknown.

Members of the capsicum family are central to Mexican cooking. Take away the hot and the sweet peppers and the heart has gone out of the cuisine, yet, out of the enormous number of varieties that exist a Mexican cook can manage very comfortably with a mere dozen and get by with even fewer. Nearly all the Mexican peppers belong to the species *C. annum*, and from the cook's point of view they fall into two main categories, the red used dried and the green used fresh. They are as diverse in flavour and heat as they are in size, shape and colour. The names given here are standard but that is not to say that they will not vary from one region of Mexico to another. This just adds to the fun of finding out about them. Mexican food has the reputation of being incendiary, yet the most used of the dried red peppers is the *ancho*, large (about 10 cm long), wrinkled, deep red, mild and richly flavoured. It is used in the *adobos*, fish, chicken or pork, to make a heavy sauce, as well as in very simple dishes like *Pollo en Salsa de Chile Ancho* where it makes a different type of sauce. You will find it in the *pipianes* in combination with ground pumpkin or sesame seeds that thicken the sauce, and, after it has been soaked it may be stuffed.

Ancho is also used in combination with other dried peppers, notably *mulato*, a wrinkled pepper

Piles of chillies at Oaxaco City's Saturday market which sells not only food but also its famous black and green glazed pottery. Pictured here are dried *ancho*, *pasilla* and *guajillo* chillies as well as small, fresh, hot red chillies.

Pipian de Camarones

Prawns in Pumpkin Seed Sauce

Father Bernardino de Sahagun, the Spanish priest who arrived in Mexico before the Spanish Conquest was complete, records the culture of the ancient civilization in great detail in his monumental Historia General de las Cosas de la Nueva España. *He was a great frequenter, and admirer, of the magnificent markets of Tenochtitlán, the pre-Columbian capital, where he sampled many of the dishes that were on sale, bubbling*

away in great earthenware ollas *(pots) over charcoal fires. So keen was his relish and so accurate his description that it has been possible to reconstruct this pre-Columbian Mexican dish from his description. Concessions have, of course, been made to modern cooking equipment. If large raw prawns (shrimp) are not available, use cooked frozen ones.* Mexican *pepitas are dried pumpkin seeds.*

SERVES SIX

2 lb 3 oz/1 kg large raw prawns (jumbo shrimp)	3 sweet red peppers, seeded and chopped
6 oz/175 g (1 cup) Mexican pepitas	1 teaspoon/5 ml honey
6 dried hot red chilli peppers, crumbled	1 teaspoon/5 ml allspice
1 small onion, chopped	salt
2 cloves garlic, chopped	3 tablespoons/45 ml peanut oil
½ lb/225 g (2 medium) tomatoes, peeled and chopped	1 tablespoon/15 ml lemon juice

Peel the prawns (shrimp) and set them aside. Put the shells into a saucepan with water to cover and simmer for 15 minutes. Strain, measure the liquid, return it to the saucepan and reduce it to 8 fl oz/ 225 ml (1 cup). Set the stock aside.

Grind the pumpkin seeds and the dried chilli peppers as finely as possible in a blender, food processor or coffee grinder. Shake them through a sieve. Set aside. Combine the onion, garlic, tomatoes, sweet peppers, honey and allspice in a blender or food processor and reduce to a purée. Add salt

to taste. Stir in the pumpkin seed and chilli mixture.

Heat the oil in a heavy frying pan (skillet) and sauté the mixture for about 5 minutes, stirring constantly with a wooden spoon. Add the reserved stock and stir. The sauce should be the consistency of heavy cream. Stir in the lemon juice. Add the raw prawns (shrimp) and cook just long enough for them to turn pink, about 3 minutes. If using cooked prawns (shrimp), cook just long enough to heat them through. Do not overcook them or they will toughen. Serve immediately.

similar in size and shape but darker in colour, tapering, and pungent in flavour, and with *pasilla*, a long slender, very dark, wrinkled pepper sometimes called *chile negro* (black pepper), hot and richly flavoured. These are all used in the most famous of Mexican dishes, the *Mole Poblano de Guajolote* (Turkey in Chilli and Chocolate Sauce, Puebla-style). *Mole* (pronounced MOW-lay) is the Spanish version of the Nahautl word *molli* which means a sauce made with any of the peppers, sweet, pungent or hot. At the time of the Conquest there were hundreds of *mollis*, many of them on sale in great earthenware *ollas* (pots) in the markets of Tenochtitlán, the Aztec capital and now the site of modern Mexico City. Father Bernadino de Sahagun, a Spanish priest, arrived

in 1519, before the Conquest was consolidated. He described chillies in his marvellous work, *Historia General de las Cosas de Nueva España* which details every aspect of the ancient Mexican culture he found in the country. The *mole*, now Mexico's holiday dish which may be ordered in any Mexican restaurant serving traditional food, was once so royal that it is said to have been offered to Cortés by Emperor Moctezuma in the early days when they were still exchanging dinner invitations. Chocolate was permitted only to the Emperor, the merchant nobility, and the upper ranks of the priesthood and military. The *mole* has been described as 'the oldest surviving evolved recipe of cooked food of any system of cooking of any of the ancient civilizations in the world'.

The American author Richard Condon, an authority on Mexican food, who made the claim, believes that *mole* with chocolate is older than the Aztecs, going back to the earlier and more highly civilized Mayas. He believes the recipe could go back to the root of chilli cultivation, some 9000 years ago. Both Aztecs and Mayas raised the domesticated turkey; chocolate was first cultivated in what is now the Mexican state of Chiapas which was the northernmost part of the Maya Empire, site of one of its most beautiful cities, Palenque, whose ruins can still be visited. There was considerable cultural exchange between the Mayan and Aztec empires.

After the Conquest and the destruction of Tenochtitlán, the local cuisine fell into decline. Dishes like *Mole Poblano* would almost certainly have been lost but for the Spanish nuns who, in the many convents, kept the art of cooking alive. So many of the local ingredients were unfamiliar to the nuns, and so many of the new ingredients brought from Spain were unfamiliar to the Aztec young ladies who joined the religious communities that it is no wonder that a series of charming legends grew up around the origin of this dish. One is about Sor Andrea de la Asunción, a Dominican nun in the Convent of Santa Rosa in Puebla, City of the Angels. The good sister wished to thank both the Archbishop and the Viceroy for having had a convent constructed for her Order. When the two eminences visited the convent she was inspired to combine the foods of both Old and New Worlds in one dish and created *mole poblano* seen here below in the convent kitchen.

Mole Poblano de Pollo   *Chicken in Chilli and Chocolate Sauce*

The Aztecs had domesticated a great many birds but they adopted the domestic chicken introduced by Spain with enthusiasm and it has become a popular bird to use with mole *which becomes* Mole Poblano de Pollo *(Chicken in Chilli and Chocolate Sauce, Puebla-style). It is possible to buy* mole *powder or* mole *liquid in tins in speciality food shops but if it is at all possible to buy the correct dried chillies, then it is extremely* rewarding to make a molli *with chocolate as cooks did for the Emperor Moctezuma, but using modern cooking equipment and a modern stove. This is a simple, but entirely authentic recipe. If only* ancho *chilli is available, then use all* ancho *and add 2–3 very hot fresh chilli peppers, seeded and chopped, to the sauce to balance it. It will lack a little something but will be quite close to the true flavour.*

SERVES EIGHT
4 tablespoons/50 g lard
1 x 3½–4 lb/1.6–1.8 kg chicken, cut into 8 serving pieces
1 medium onion, peeled and chopped
2 cloves garlic, peeled and chopped
salt
For the sauce
6 ancho *chillies*
4 pasilla *chillies*
4 mulato *chillies*
4 oz/100 g blanched almonds
2 oz/50 g peanuts
2 oz/50 g pumpkin seeds

½ teaspoon/2.5 ml coriander seeds
¼ teaspoon/1.5 ml aniseed
2 cloves
1 x ½-inch/1.5-cm stick of cinnamon, broken up
2 medium onions, peeled and coarsely chopped
2 cloves garlic, peeled and chopped
1 lb/450 g tomatoes, peeled, seeded and chopped
3 oz/75 g (½ cup) raisins
lard
1½ oz/40 g unsweetened chocolate, broken in bits
salt
1 tablespoon/15 ml sugar (optional)
2 tablespoons/30 ml sesame seeds

Heat half the first amount of lard in a heavy frying pan (skillet) and sauté the chicken pieces, a few at a time, until lightly browned on both sides. As they are done, transfer them to a large casserole or heavy saucepan with the onion, garlic, and salt to taste and enough water barely to cover. Bring to the boil, reduce the heat and simmer, covered, for 45 minutes, or until the chicken is almost tender. Lift out the chicken pieces and set them aside. Strain and reserve the stock. Rinse out and dry the casserole and return the chicken pieces to it.

To make the sauce, remove the stems and seeds from the chillies and cut them into pieces. Put into a bowl with warm water barely to cover and leave to stand for 30 minutes, turning them from time to time. Meanwhile, grind the almonds, peanuts, pumpkin seeds, coriander seeds, aniseed, cloves and cinnamon to a fairly fine powder in a blender or food processor. Drain the chillies, reserving the water in which they have soaked. Put them into a blender or food processor with the onions, garlic, tomatoes and raisins and reduce to a heavy paste, using a little of the soaking water if needed. Add the nut mixture and a little more of the liquid and blend them together.

Measure the fat left in the frying pan and add enough lard to make up the quantity to 4 tablespoons/60 ml. Heat the lard, add the chilli paste and sauté over a moderate heat, stirring for 5 minutes. Stir in ¾ pint/425 ml (2 cups) of the reserved chicken stock, the chocolate, salt to taste and the sugar, if liked. Cook the mixture over a low heat, stirring, until the chocolate is melted and adding a little more stock if necessary to make the sauce of a coating consistency. Pour the sauce over the chicken pieces and simmer over very low heat for 20 minutes. Toast the sesame seeds in a small frying pan. Arrange the chicken pieces on a warmed serving dish and sprinkle with the sesame seeds. Serve with *tortillas* or plain, unstuffed *tamales*, white rice, beans and *guacamole* (avocado sauce).

If any sauce is left over, keep it to make *chilaquiles*, a delectable Mexican leftover dish made using fried *tortilla* strips, or use it as a sauce for cooked pork, or over fried eggs. It is very versatile and seems to go with almost anything except beef.

Sor Andrea and others in the convent undoubtedly discussed the problem of what to serve the Archbishop and the Viceroy. Probably, turkey would have been selected. The young Aztec girls would, naturally enough, equate the Viceroy with their Emperor and the Archbishop with their High Priest. What else but a *molli* containing chocolate, an ingredient forbidden to women and people of lower rank? It is natural that they would have reconstructed the recipe to the best of their ability. It is even more natural that instead of the alien spices of the New World, the Spanish nuns would have used cinnamon and cloves, and that they would have preferred Old World almonds or even walnuts to unfamiliar peanuts or pecans.

The blender and the food processor have taken the hard work out of making a *Mole Poblano*. It is no longer necessary for any cook to grind chillies on a *metate*, the flat, oblong, inclined grinding stone, or to grind chillies or spices in a *molcajete* (mortar) with a *tejolote*. Work that used to take three days can now be done in a morning.

In its 9000-year history, the chilli was cultivated to such a great extent that the various types found throughout the Americas are far too numerous to mention here. Such an important food naturally played a role in custom and ceremony. The Aztecs used chillies to punish wayward children by holding them over burning spice. Mothers controlled the sexual urges of their daughters with them. If a girl looked at a man, chilli was rubbed into her eyes. If she slept with him, the punishment was even nastier. If you think that people were more barbaric in bygone times, consider this

Making a *mole*, the national dish of Mexico, the hard, old-fashioned way using a *metate*, a flat, oblong grinding stone and a *tejolote* in the kitchen of the Convent of Santa Rosa in Puebla, Mexico.

newspaper report about events in Sri Lanka today: 'Human rights workers, Sri Lankan as well as Tamil, told me that the most favoured tortures are hanging prisoners upside down over heaps of burning chillies and inserting needles under their fingers.' *Plus ça change, plus c'est la même chose.*

Too often history is written from an Euro-centric point of view. The statement 'Columbus discovered America' can be challenged in a number of ways. The whole of the time he spent in the 'New' World, Columbus was hopelessly lost although the natives he 'discovered' knew precisely where *they* were. Columbus made a number of enormous miscalculations and went to his grave believing that he had found the Orient but had been just too unlucky to hit upon any of the large cities of India, China or Japan.

The European arrival in America was ultimately to change Europe and the 'Old' World as much as it changed America. Certainly food would never again be the same . . . mercifully. From the New World came maize (corn), tomatoes, potatoes, chocolate, vanilla, peanuts, turkeys and pineapples . . . a list so impressive that one has to wonder what Europeans ate before the sixteenth century. It is ironic that the Europeans came seeking one spice, pepper, and as a result, another spice, chilli, conquered the world. If you think that is claiming too much for chilli, consider this; today, in volume, chillies are the most grown and consumed of all the spices.

Early in the sixteenth century, chillies were planted in Spain and then in Portugal. They provided more heat than the tropical spices, would grow anywhere warm and a bit humid, and were cheap. They could also be dried and kept without losing their pungency. Soon chillies were being carried on Spanish and especially Portuguese ships making the long voyages around Africa to India and the East. The spice was also adopted by the Arabs who transported it backwards along trade routes from west to east towards the old centres of the pepper, cinnamon and clove trade.

When the first chilli arrived in India is unknown, but soon the subcontinent was being 'peppered' with them. Today, India produces many spices, but chillies are, by far, the most important. In fact, three-quarters of all spice-growing lands grow chillies. Since the spice provides most of the 'hot' taste in curries and Indian food in general, it is difficult to believe that it was unknown before the sixteenth century and in fact, the Indians still refuse to accept this. In an article in the January 1981 edition of the *India Magazine* we read:

> Western experts claim that this spice is a native of the New World and was discovered by the spice-searching Spaniards, but we doubt this belief. Once, many years ago, an Indian naval ship anchored near a deserted island in the Andamans (in the Indian Ocean off the coast of Burma). A few young officers went ashore hoping to bag some of the wild boar that infest many of the little, wooded, fastnesses. But their enthusiasm exceeded their skill and they returned to their ship empty-handed—or almost empty-handed. One of the midshipmen, with epicurean pretensions, brought back a handful of tiny chillies he had plucked somewhere in the depths of the island. These, with considerable flourish, he placed on the officers' dining table: tiny, green and innocent-looking. Most of the officers, starved of home cooking after many months on board, were eager to try something new. They ate two or three at a time and they gasped and spluttered and went red in the face, bellowing for water. For these apparently, were the famed Monkey Chillies of legendary and incandescent vigour! These were perhaps the original native chillies of India.

You may have noticed that the article gives no date for this amazing discovery. The story is at best unlikely; however, it is possible that the event described took place after the Portuguese had reached the Andamans which was sometime in the sixteenth century. In any event, chillies are absolutely fundamental to the cooking of India, yet are not mentioned in Indian literature, records or lore before the 1500s. Perhaps it is because the Portuguese were not finally expelled from the country until 1961 that the Indians refuse to acknowledge this important contribution to their culture. Pork Vindaloo, however, is a living reminder of Portuguese influence on the sub-continent.

By the middle of the sixteenth century, the Portuguese were also trading in Japan. The Japanese left the foreign traders on an island off Nagasaki, not allowing them to stay on the Japanese mainland, but this did not stop chillies from entering the country. Japanese cuisine is not known for its spiciness; however, today the pungent red plant is cultivated in large numbers in Japan and used in a variety of ways. Members of one very hot type of Japanese chilli are known as 'hawks' claws' because they are long and hooked. They are an ingredient of a seven-spice mixture which is widely used as a condiment for the very popular noodle soups, *soba* and *udon*.

The *daikon*, or white radish, provides the chilli with a more exotic or gourmet use. It is long and tapered. Chopsticks are used to poke holes along its length and dried, crumbled red chillies are pushed down the holes. The *daikon* is then grated. The mild *daikon* and pungent chillies form a tasty, wet, orange paste which is used to flavour fine soups.

If India is one of chilli's adopted spiritual homes, surely the Chinese province of Sichuan is another. The province lies in a basin surrounded by mountains at the very centre of China. The Yangtse river and its tributaries provide plenty of fertile valleys and terraced mountain slopes. Sichuan has been called remote; however, since it is twice the size of Great Britain and the home of over one hundred million people, that is a very Eurocentric claim. Sichuan is such an enormous rice-growing region that it has been dubbed 'the storehouse of heaven'. Everyone in Sichuan eats chillies, sometimes three times a day. The people are adamant that chillies arrived before the sixteenth century. Local historians claim that the chilli is indigenous

Right: Pork Vindaloo.

Pork Vindaloo   *Pork in a Hot, Spicy Sauce*

This is a dish from Goa, until recently a Portuguese colony in southern India adjoining the Indian Ocean.

SERVES FOUR	
1 lb/450 g lean pork cut into 2-inch/5-cm cubes	4 black peppercorns
salt	1 x 1-inch/2.5-cm stick of cinnamon
2 large dried hot red chillies	1 x ½-inch/1.5-cm slice of root ginger
1 teaspoon/5 ml cumin seeds	2 cloves garlic, peeled
1 teaspoon/5 ml coriander seeds	3 tablespoons/45 ml vinegar
2 cloves	3 tablespoons/45 ml vegetable oil
	2 medium onions, peeled and finely chopped

Put the pork into a saucepan with salt to taste and water to cover by about 1 inch/2.5 cm. Bring to the boil, reduce the heat to low and simmer, covered, until the meat is almost tender. This takes about 1 hour. Set aside.

Meanwhile, toast the chillies, cumin, coriander, cloves, peppercorns and stick of cinnamon in a heavy frying pan (skillet) for a few minutes. Let the spices cool slightly, then reduce to a paste in a blender or food processor with the ginger, garlic and vinegar. Set aside.

Heat the oil in the frying pan, add the onions and sauté until they are a rich golden brown. Add the ground spice mixture. Sauté for a few minutes, then drain the pork, reserving the liquid, and add. Stir to mix, cover and cook until the pork is tender. The mixture will be quite dry.

If the dish is preferred with sauce, add the stock in which the pork has simmered. There should be about ¾ pint/425 ml (2 cups). Add a little water to make up the quantity if necessary. Serve hot with boiled Basmati rice.

Today more land in India is under chilli cultivation than any other spice. This is especially surprising since chilli is a relatively recent arrival in the subcontinent, coming from the New World in the sixteenth century.

to the region and this time have records to support their case. The Chinese have experienced unbroken civilization for thousands of years and are meticulous record keepers.

There are many Chinese legends and stories of ancient contact with the Americas; of American natives coming to China and vice versa. There is some evidence for stories of a Chinese expedition landing in what is now southern California around the year AD 700. It is said that these Chinese Columbuses managed to make their way inland as far as the Grand Canyon in Arizona. If they had, they would have met natives who used chillies, and, indeed, they could have brought the spice back to China. But if so, why did the chilli not spread throughout Asia? Sichuan is remote, but not that remote. There are other 'hot' spices in the province like 'Sichuan pepper' a red, seed-like spice obtainable in Chinese grocery stores. Per-

haps, the records refer to them and when chillies arrived they simply assumed the roles of the new spice. Then, again, perhaps a hundred million Sichuanese cannot be wrong.

In any event, the chilli is in Sichuan to stay. The province produces a large proportion of China's chillies, and China has recently overtaken India as both the world's largest grower and exporter. Some experts estimate that the Chinese chilli crop is as high as a million tonnes per annum. Throughout history an important use of spices has been to flavour bland carbohydrates and use of chillies in Sichuan is no exception. A most interesting dish is *guoba*, the speciality of restaurants in the large city of Chengdu, one of China's culinary capitals. *Guoba* is the by-product of cooking rice. Rice is cooked in giant wok-like pans much wider than a person's reach. After it is cooked, the rice is scooped out into smaller containers, and the layer at the bottom of the pan has by this time become dry and thick. When the rest of the rice is removed this bottom layer can carefully be taken out in one piece. It is quite fantastic to see a chef holding high

The Chinese chilli crop is estimated to be as high as a million tonnes per annum, more than double the amount grown in India. The province of Sichuan produces most of China's chillies and it is renowned for its hot, spicy food which in recent years has become increasingly fashionable in Western capitals. It is much hotter than the more familiar Cantonese-style Chinese food and the extensive use of chillies is one of the main differences.

this enormous unbroken semi-sphere of baked rice. Later it is broken into smaller pieces and deep-fried to an even crispier texture. It is removed from the oil still sizzling and hot chilli sauce is poured on top. The whole thing snaps, pops and is hot enough to blow your head off! The Sichuanese have no reservations though, they eat hot chilli sauce *for breakfast, poured over noodles*.

More traditional Sichuan favourites are the Yui-Hsiang dishes; these consist of shredded fresh and dried chillies, stir-fried with shredded ginger, garlic and spring onion. *Mabu dofu*, chilli sauce on beancurd, is so popular that individual chefs never reveal their recipes until they retire and then only to their closest disciples. Another great favourite is *Huajiao Rajiao Pork* which is made with

Sichuan pepper (*Huajiao*) and chili (*Rajiao*) mixed together. Cabbage, celery and spring onion are fried together and then set aside. Chopped pork which has been dipped in eggwhite, cornflour and salt is fried and set aside. A mixture of chilli oil, chilli powder and Sichuan pepper is then heated in the wok. The pork is thrown back in and cooked. The hot mixture is then poured over the waiting vegetables. More Sichuan pepper is sprinkled on top and more hot chilli oil is poured over the whole thing. Wow!

The cooking of Sichuan is different from the rest of China. Instead of being soft and easily swallowed, it is hot and chewy. The heat is not supposed to drown out other tastes, on the contrary, it must enhance them. After the shock of the first taste, the palate settles and allows other more subtle tastes to filter through.

For people not used to chillies, they can be deceptive. The first bite or two will not taste too strong but, by the end of a meal, you may suddenly find that the cumulative effect leaves you feeling very uncomfortable. Chilli's pungency or heat is different from that of either black pepper or mustard. Chilli is felt deep at the back of the throat while black pepper affects mainly the top of the tongue. Mustard's pungency causes sensation throughout the whole of the mouth.

The pungency of capsicum is determined by its content of a chemical, capsaicin, which can be isolated and used in several chilli by-products. Cayenne pepper is a finely ground spice prepared from the small pungent chillies of East Africa, Japan or India. It does not come from Cayenne in French Guiana. Chilli powder is a blended and slightly milder product, consisting of ground chillies, cumin seed, oregano and garlic. Red pepper is a powder prepared from less pungent chillies. It is often found in sausages or other processed foods. The most pungent chilli is a small red variety from Uganda containing about one per cent of the chemical, capsaicin. By comparison, the strongest cayenne pepper would contain half that amount.

Chillies have always been the quintessential spice of hot, poor countries. Not only do they grow easily in hot, humid conditions, but these are places where bland carbohydrate diets predominate and what meat there is can go off quickly. Chilli's image has mostly been downmarket, but this is changing.

A genuine contender in the pungency sweepstakes comes from Louisiana, near the delta of the Mississippi river at a place called Avery Island. Part of the area is a lush, tropical bird and alligator sanctuary but nearby are grown fine-quality Tabasco chillies, for the world-famous Tabasco sauce. The industry sprang up in the aftermath of the American civil war in the 1860s. Edward McIlhenny had been a merchant banker who went bankrupt during the war. The fortune he left his family was greater than if he had remained a successful banker, all on account of chilli.

Ripe red peppers are brought each day to the factory where they are mixed with salt from local mines. Together they are ground into a mash, soaked in spirit vinegar and left in white-oak casks to age. Once fermentation starts the casks bubble and gurgle and exhale gas. The storage area smells

Top: Picking ripe, red Tabasco chillies in Louisiana to make the world famous hot chilli sauce of the same name.
Above: The Tabasco peppers are brought to the nearby factory where salt from the local mine is added. The salt restricts the fermentation to the desired fermenting agents and thus prevents the onset of mould.

Bloody Mary

Hot peppers are not only famous in food. One of the world's most popular drinks is the Bloody Mary enlivened with Tabasco or other hot pepper sauce. No one agrees on who first created the Bloody Mary. One story credits Fernand Petoit, an American working as a *bartender at Harry's New York bar in Paris, in the 1920s. It is also claimed by George Jessel and at least two other New York bartenders. Whoever was the inventor of this splendid drink deserves the world's thanks.*

SERVES ONE	
$1\frac{1}{2}$ fl oz/40 ml (3 tablespoons) vodka	dash Worcestershire sauce
3 fl oz/75 g (6 tablespoons) tomato juice	dash Tabasco, or more to taste
1 tablespoon/15 ml lemon juice	salt and freshly ground black pepper
	3–4 ice cubes

Combine all the ingredients in a cocktail shaker and shake vigorously. Strain into a glass with a cube or more of ice in it.

For a Bloody Marie: Reduce the lemon juice to 1 teaspoon/5 ml and add a dash of Pernod.

For a Bloody Maria: Use tequila instead of vodka.

For a Danish Mary: Use Akvavit instead of vodka and add a pinch of celery salt.

For Sake Mary: Use sake, the Japanese rice wine, instead of vodka.

---

like the air-conditioning system of hell, but three years later the object of the exercise is ready. Hot Louisiana chilli sauce is inserted into those familiar little bottles that let out a drop at a time.

According to legend, in 1920 Fernand Petoit, a bartender at Harry's New York Bar in Paris, conceived the idea of chillies in vodka and created the Bloody Mary.

New York City itself was the site of yet another dramatic chilli discovery. Years ago at the original Delmonico's restaurant, the fashionable place to eat, an ex-sea captain and dandy, Ben Wenberg, became popular for preparing food at the table. Wenberg's speciality was lobster cooked with cream, eggs and Madeira wine . . . and a special ingredient which the captain always pulled out of his pocket with a flourish, cayenne pepper, chilli. Delmonico was so impressed that he put this 'Lobster Wenberg' on the menu. Then Delmonico and Wenberg parted company but the restaurateur wanted to keep the popular dish on his menu. In an inspired fit of pique with his old friend, Delmonico reversed the first three letters of the name Wenberg and created 'Lobster Newberg'.

Today, chillies are not only eaten and drunk, but are used by the pharmaceutical industry in ointments. The hottest chillies are often found in those rubbed on aching muscles. Chillies are also used for curing stomach aches or flatulence. For years, the people of India have used chillies for stomach disorders and to arouse appetite, but then the people of India seem to eat chillies with everything.

Perhaps the chilli's most glorious medical moment came in 1937 when the Hungarian scientist Dr Albert von Szent-Gyocgyi was awarded the Nobel prize for isolating Vitamin C. Dr Szent-Gyorgyi's experiments were carried out on capsicums which proved to be rich in the vitamin. The hotter varieties of chillies were discovered to be equally blessed. Had Christopher Columbus only known! For centuries after his discoveries seafarers were plagued with the disease scurvy, which is caused by a vitamin C deficiency. From the chilli's point of view, it is hard to feel that knowledge would have made a great difference in the speed with which it became popular. From the time the chilli left America it only took it a century to become the world's most important spice.

7
ALLSPICE

Allspice, unlike many other spices, does not immediately conjure up a particular image. It is not surprising to learn that allspice owes its name to smelling and tasting like two, three or four other spices. Most people agree that it tastes a bit like cloves and a bit like cinnamon and some would say there was even a hint of nutmeg and black pepper in allspice. There are dissenters to this view. Elizabeth David, no less, has written that she cannot taste the cinnamon but concedes 'a touch of pepper'. Since she also writes that allspice is popular in the Middle East and the Levant, we also consulted Claudia Roden, an expert in food from that part of the world. In her *A Book of Middle Eastern Food*, she describes a popular spice mixture based on cinnamon, nutmeg, cloves and now ginger, named unimaginatively, 'the four spices' which is 'sometimes replaced by the one spice called allspice or Jamaican pepper, whose taste rather resembles that of all four together'. So, allspice tastes a bit like cloves and your own permutation of cinnamon, nutmeg, pepper and ginger; but, and this is the point, it is one spice.

You already know that sometimes it is called Jamaican pepper, so you will not be surprised to learn that most of the world's supply of allspice comes from Jamaica. You might, however, be mildly shocked to learn that if you went into a store in Jamaica and asked for allspice it would be likely that the shopkeeper would neither know what it is that you wanted, nor when you had explained to him what it was, would have any. In Jamaica, it literally grows on trees, and would be unprofitable on shop shelves; moreover, in the home of allspice, it is not called allspice.

Like chillies, prior to the voyages of Christopher Columbus, allspice was unknown in 'the old world'. It is possible that it was encountered by Christopher Columbus on his first voyage, in Cuba. He showed a group of natives a handful of pepper, *Piper nigrum*, which they instantly seemed to recognize. Possibly, it was allspice, which in its dried berry form resembles black pepper. On Columbus's second voyage, on one of the Leeward Islands, the ship's physician, Diego Chauca, wrote about examining a smooth, grey trunked evergreen whose leaves gave off the aroma of cinnamon, nutmeg and cloves, certainly either allspice or a closely related species. Forty years later, King Philip IV of Spain, upon hearing that 'pepper' grew wild in Jamaica, issued an order to investigate this Jamaican pepper, *la pimienta de Jamaica*. The name stuck, *pimienta* turned into *pimento*, the popular name for the spice. This was especially confusing since the Spanish had already called chillies *pimientos* and to this day they are known as *pimiento* or peppers. The Spanish could almost be forgiven for creating centuries of linguistic confusion had they not called all the natives they met 'Indians'.

In general, the dried berries, the spice of commerce are called allspice. In any other state it is called pimento. You would never say 'allspice tree' or 'allspice leaf oil', it would be pimento. Some pimento trees fruit by yielding clumps of small berries which hang like cherries. If they are left to ripen on the trees, they turn dark purple, but they are harvested when fully grown, but green. When these green berries are dried, they turn dark reddish brown and resemble large peppercorns. These are the allspice of commerce.

It is odd that when attempting to describe the flavour or aroma of cloves or cinnamon, nobody says that they resemble or have a hint of allspice.

It has been the fate of allspice to remain somewhat unknown, hidden and 'unglamourous'. Recently, at a well-stocked spice shop in London, where the spices are arranged on the shelves in alphabetical order, a bottle of ground spice on the top shelf was labelled 'Allspice' and a bottle of the whole berries on the bottom was marked 'Pimento'. The shop attendant was unaware that they were the same spice, one whole, one ground.

The name 'Jamaica' comes from *Xamayca* meaning 'land of wood and water' in the language of the island's pre-Spanish inhabitants, the Arawaks. The Arawaks died out shortly after the Spanish conquest, although a few Arawak genes probably still float in Jamaica's polyglot pool. These natives used allspice to help cure and preserve meats . . . sometimes the flesh of animals, sometimes of their enemies. The allspice cured meat was known in Arawak as *boucan* and so later Europeans who cured meat in the native way were called *boucaniers*, which was ultimately corrupted to buccaneers. Before they vanished, the Arawaks

The berries of the pimento tree are called allspice when they are fully grown but still green. When dried they turn dark reddish brown and resemble large peppercorns. If the berries are left to ripen on the trees they turn dark purple.

bequeathed upon us a host of words, including 'canoe', 'hurricane', 'hammock' and the indispensable 'barbecue'.

The Spanish identified pimento as a separate species by 1509; however, there was no mad rush of merchantmen from Spain seeking to make their fortunes. A few years earlier Christopher Columbus himself had gone to his deathbed, broken and despairing. He had sought pepper, real pepper, and all that he had found was pimento. In the early sixteenth century Magellan sailed from Spain around the world and suffered the most hideous horrors, for cloves! Allspice was not only much closer to Europe, but free. Allspice's neglect is one of the puzzles of spice history, because it is a good spice; no, it is a great spice, far better for most purposes than cloves and perhaps even better than cinnamon or nutmeg. The

Spanish used Jamaica only as a port of call *en route* to their real business, the search for gold, in Mexico and Peru. But that still does not explain why merchants of the sixteenth and seventeenth centuries insisted that spices had to be obtained from the Far East, the other side of the world.

In our own time we are very familiar with things having value only because people *think* they are valuable. Undoubtedly spice-conscious Europe of the sixteenth century was the same, with 'cinnamon', 'cloves' and 'nutmeg', all spices from the East, being the sought-after 'brand names' of the era. And what about chillies? They also came from the New World but were accepted instantly by the Old. In each area the chilli was taken, such as Spain, Africa, India and China, it was soon cultivated locally and so it became part of the local 'cuisine'. But allspice remained in Jamaica.

In fairness to the Spanish, it must be said that some of the spice was exported under their direction, but there is no record of any reaching as important a centre as London until 1601, and even then it went to pharmacists who treated it as a curiosity. In 1655, the English, themselves, did not so much conquer Jamaica as win it as a consolation prize. The English sent a fleet to wrest the neighbouring island of Hispaniola from Spain, but Spanish resistance proved too fierce. As nobody volunteered to return home to England and inform Oliver Cromwell of the defeat, the fleet attacked and took the relatively undefended adjoining island, Jamaica.

The English took their allspice responsibility a little more seriously than the Spanish and by 1737 regular shipments were being made back to England. Alas, Europe was losing its lust for spices while being seduced by more fashionable products of the New World. From Jamaica, the demand was for sugar and coffee and slaves were imported to harvest these important crops. A century or so later, the slaves were emancipated and in 1962 Jamaica joined the ranks of free nations. Even though she supplies the majority of the world's allspice, in all her history the spice has never accounted for more than 5 per cent of her total exports, and even that was during an allspice boomlet in the first decade of the twentieth century. Today pimento products account for less than 2 per cent of Jamaica's total exports.

Pimento grows on trees . . . beautiful trees . . . lovely trees . . . trees that stand in forests . . . trees which cling to cliffs overhanging the everpresent sea. The bark is smooth and grey. Primary branches branch from a central trunk a metre or two off the ground and then soar fifteen or twenty metres, all the while sending off secondary branches laden with clusters of oblong, eliptical, green leaves. These trees seem made for climbing.

Where a number of trees grow together, it is not called an orchard, but a 'walk' and once a year, usually in spring, when whole trees are blanketed by small, powder-white, aromatic flowers, one of nature's great sensual experiences is offered. The botanist Patrick Browne wrote in 1755:

> . . . nothing can be more delicious than the odour of these walks, when the trees are in bloom, as well as other times; the friction of the leaves and small branches even in a gentle breeze diffusing a most exhilarating scent.

In the old days, walks were created simply by allowing plots of land near existing walks to become overgrown with bush. After a few years everything was cleared away except for some pimento seedlings which were left standing at distances of no more than three metres apart. When these matured, it became a walk.

It could not have escaped notice that much of the story of spice is about the relationships between the 'developed' and 'underdeveloped' world. The tropical spices have been, and for the most part are still, cultivated and harvested in a most primitive manner using little, if any, of the technology developed over the last five hundred years. It is not rare to find a difference in the skin colours of plantation owners and workers. Today, a large proportion of tropical spices is used by food-processing, pharmaceutical and cosmetics industries.

It has been only recently that primary-producing nations have processed spices beyond the stages of elementary picking, cleaning and bagging. Most industrial processes performed on spices are carried out in the consuming countries of the industrial world. This is a difficult pattern to break, because spice processors work very closely with large food companies. Since spices are essential to so many manufactured foods, but represent only a fraction of the cost of production,

The pimento trees grow tall and graceful and in spring, when whole trees are blanketed by small, powder-white, aromatic flowers, a wonderful scent is given off.

the food industry wants reliability of supply and quality. The industry prefers to deal with experienced spice importer/processors who have the understanding and technological skills to provide what it wants, rather than trade with inexperienced agencies half-way across the world.

In recent years the cultivation, harvesting and primary processing of tropical spices has been moving towards a more scientific basis. The newly independent producing nations are striving for economic independence and a slice of the more

profitable action. Research into the life cycles and chemical compositions of spices is progressing throughout the tropics, but progress has been slow, very slow. The cultivation and harvesting of spices virtually everywhere throughout the tropics is still very primitive.

Problems of research are compounded by the fact that nature is never as neat as scientists would wish. After thousands of years of cultivation, much about tropical spices is still unknown.

In the case of pimento, certain fundamental processes are still not fully understood, for example, whether some trees are male and others female. It has long been known that some pimento trees will not bear fruit. Since in other respects these trees seem normal, it was a problem for the growers to identify them. Trees naturally fruit only after a wait of six or seven years from germination, so a substantial investment of time, effort and space was going into growing barren trees. In 1958 J. F. Ward, formerly horticulturalist for the Jamaican Ministry of Agriculture and Lands, wrote in his book *Pimento*:

> But perhaps the most outstanding variation in pimento is the existence of fruiting and non-fruiting or barren trees. This has given rise to the erroneous idea, which is still widely held, that there are 'male' and 'female' trees and that the presence of 'male' trees in pimento groves is a requisite for good cropping. Browne in 1755 disposed of this notion, but popular ideas take long in dying.

Since 1958, the Jamaican Ministry of Agriculture working with the Tropical Products Institute of Great Britain has developed a method of vegetative propagation for pimento. In essence, fruiting trees are cloned, by-passing the seed stage and the uncertainty of whether new plants will fruit. So it is now possible to plant and grow only fruit-bearing trees; but, are the barren trees necessary to pollinate them? The answer appears to be yes, at least in most cases. There is evidence to suggest that the barren trees which do not produce normal fruits (these are the 'male' trees) can pollinate up to ten 'female', ie fruiting, trees.

For most of botanical history the scientific name for pimento was *Pimento officinalis lindl* but for the past thirty or so years the name *Pimento dioica* (L), has predominated. This indicates a plant with defined sexes. The name, *Pimento officinalis* is still used and, to make matters more complicated, a number of trees are genuinely hermaphrodite.

Another old belief about pimento was that in order for its seeds to germinate, they had to pass through the innards of either birds or bats. Jamaica is full of both birds and bats, which love the abundant purple, ripe berries. It is also true that new pimento seedlings are most often found under mahogany or cedar branches or along hedgerows where the birds frequently perch. But, alas for romantic spirits, though passing through the innards of birds certainly does not prevent the pimento seeds from germinating, contrary to ancient belief, it is not strictly necessary.

There is yet another popular pimento belief, that the spice will only reproduce on the island of Jamaica. In fact, pimento grows wild but is harvested in parts of Mexico, Guatemala and Belize. The Central American berries are larger than the Jamaican but are generally considered less desirable. Pimento also grows in Grenada where the quality is high but quantity low. The history of the spice is full of stories of attempts to transplant pimento outside the Caribbean, all of which have failed. This is puzzling because pimento grows throughout Jamaica in a variety of soil and climatic conditions.

Here is an excerpt from a Jamaican Ministry of Agriculture bulletin called *Pimento, A Short Economic History* by D. W. Rodriguez:

> Early in the nineteenth century, pimento berries and seedlings were sent from Jamaica to Madras (India), Singapore, Ceylon, Fiji, Costa Rica, Haiti, Panama, Columbia, Honduras and Australia. Since then it has been taken to Malaya, Columbia, Venezuela, Grenada and other tropical areas, but with the exception of Grenada it has thrived and produced nowhere else as in Jamaica. Many theories have been advanced to explain this

striking behaviour of the pimento trees outside of Jamaica and Grenada, but so far they have been without scientific support.

In the botanical gardens of Brisbane (Australia), Ceylon and Singapore, the pimento tree flowers freely and profusely but never seems to set any berries. In Madras, India, the pimento tree seldom flowers and never bears. No doubt these may be all 'male' trees or perhaps the absence of critical environmental factors have combined to inhibit fruiting.

Contrast that to this excerpt about pimento from *Spices and Condiments* by J. S. Pruthi, published in 1976 by the National Book Trust, New Delhi, India. (The Indian version of its viability in the East differs widely from the Jamaican.)

It is also said to grow well and fruit heavily in Bangalore. It has been recommended for growing in the hilly districts of the Karnataka State along the river valleys. It is also found to grow in poor but well-drained soil, both in high ranges up to 1065 metres above sea level

Harvesting the pimento berries is a family affair in Jamaica. After the branches holding the berries have been picked, the berries are then stripped off. A good picker can harvest 30 kilograms of berries a day.

and in the plains of Kerala. It is further reported that though both the berries and leaves produced in the Wynad area of Kerala are highly flavoured, yet in the plains they were of inferior quality and need further investigation. There appears to be good scope for growing allspice in all house gardens for home consumption. However, commercial cultivation will be profitable only when there is simultaneous installation of distillation plants for the recovery of Pimenta berry and leaf oils which are in great demand all over the world.

Although you cannot believe everything you read about pimento, the Caribbean does supply one hundred per cent of the world's allspice *exports*, with Jamaica accounting for a majority of that.

Pimento grows everywhere in Jamaica. It grows wild; it grows on large plantations consisting of hundreds of acres and in small family plots. The main users of agricultural land are 'peasant cultivators' living on small patches in humble unpainted wood-frame dwellings. The first priority of small farmers is to feed themselves and their families; however, many inevitably enter the market economy and some surplus even goes for export. 'Intercropping', that is many different useful plants growing on a single plot, is common. Besides livestock, such as goats and pigs, a single smallholding could yield potatoes, yams, maize, sugar cane, bananas, coffee, cassava, gungo peas, avocado pears, coconuts and, of course, pimento. In Jamaica, where the seed drops, something grows.

Allspice is generally harvested in the most primitive manner possible. A youth climbs the tree, breaks off the brittle branches holding the green berries and drops them to the ground. Below, women, younger children and perhaps some men strip the fallen branches and put the berries into either tin cans or burlap sacks. These are not onerous tasks. It can be quite pleasant for a family to sit together in the shade of the tree and talk or even sing while stripping berries.

Pimento wood is extremely brittle and too

often whole branches are torn indiscriminately off the trees. Sometimes after harvesting, trees are so defoliated that they die of shock. Others suffer insect and fungi contamination through their open wounds. One nasty disease which kills trees with broken limbs is known locally as 'die-back'. Sometimes it takes trees suffering from harvest shock three or four years to recover, causing a sharp fluctuation in the annual production of berries.

On the plantations, contract pickers often harvest the berries. Owners try to ensure that trees endure only minimal harm through proper pruning. Clippers are used and leaves are cut off at their growing points. A good picker can harvest over thirty kilograms of berries a day.

Sacks of harvested berries are taken to a central point, a clearing in the bush, for weighing, using a scale which is often simply hung from a tree.

Berries are then allowed to 'sweat' for a few days before drying. During this process temperatures rise and they lose weight. They are then spread out to dry on a concrete platform called a 'barbeque'. Here they are turned frequently to ensure uniform drying. At night, or if rain threatens, the berries are swept into a small hut at the barbeque's corner. Drying takes from between five to ten days depending upon the weather.

The cleaning machine is a wooden barrel-like contraption set up on hobby-horse legs. One man pours berries in a hole at the barrel top while another turns a large handle to rotate the whole

thing. As berries pour out of the bottom, yet a third person removes by hand twigs and other debris missed by the machine.

Leaves are also harvested, but mainly from the non-bearing or 'male' trees. The eugenol content of these leaves is higher, perhaps because the trees do not have to put energy into fruiting. Since the 1920s more and more plantations have acquired distilleries where pimento leaves are turned into pimento leaf oil. The process is steam distillation with one hundred and forty parts leaf producing one part oil. Like clove and cinnamon leaf,

To dry the green berries, they are spread out on a large concrete platform called a 'barbeque'. During this process they lose nearly half their weight.

pimento leaf oil contains mostly eugenol and is found in ketchups, dill pickles, sauces, various flavourings, soaps and cosmetics. Jamaicans use it as an external rub for aches and pains and claim it brings relief to upset stomachs and asthma. Vanillin, an artificial substitute for vanilla came from eugenol, so the pimento tree contributed to vanilla ice-cream.

Once, pimento was sought for yet another purpose. In 1881 Mr Espent, the island botanist,

Pimento leaf oil is made by the method of steam distillation and many plantations have their own distilleries. It takes 140 parts leaf to produce one part oil.

wrote: 'Not long ago I brought to the notice of Government the destruction caused by uprooting of pimento saplings for export as walking sticks. I know a case in which some 200 acres of land were underwooded in order to allow the young pimento to grow and form a walk. The young plantation was practically destroyed by stick gatherers who uprooted thousands of young trees, many of which being found unsuitable for 'sticks' were left to rot on the ground.' Fortunately, the world's passion for pimento walking sticks disappeared with the depression of the 1930s, but many of the old sticks are still around.

Unlike some of the other tropical spices, allspice is used by the people who grow it. In Jamaica it is fundamental to cooking.

'Hurry it up, girl', prods Lynne Williamson at her teenage friend, Sylvie. They are both standing just outside their small woodframe house in the shade of a spreading tree. In front of them on a makeshift table are some onions, red peppers, shallots, cooking oil, spices and vinegar. About a half dozen fish of various sorts are hung by their gills on a nearby wire fence. On the ground by the table are two wood fires surrounded by rocks. One fire is covered with a frying pan containing

boiling oil and another frying pan sits on the ground. Sylvie has been taking the fish, one at a time, cleaning them, slitting their sides and rubbing them in a mixture of black pepper and cayenne. Lynne bends down and plops them into the boiling oil.

'A gold mullet,' explains Lynne. 'A nice fish, a beautiful fish.' And as she takes another, 'A jackfish, pretty colour, very nice.' In the meantime Sylvie has begun to cut the onions, shallots and red peppers into a salad. 'Hurry up, girl', prods Lynne again, 'I still want to go up to the bar and have a nice time.'

Lynne, who has been turning the frying fish, now puts the second frying pan on its fire and fills it with oil and a bit of vinegar. She throws in a handful of allspice, or as she would say 'pimento berries', and as they sizzle, she adds the onions and red peppers. 'Franklin and Malcolm are going to enjoy them a whole lot. Tonight, they are going to have a nice time, a nice dance, a lovely drink tonight.' Malcolm is Lynne's husband. He and Franklin are the fishermen who caught the fish.

Lynne has been frying a new batch of fish, this time parrot fish. They are multicoloured with mouths or beaks which do resemble parrots. Sylvie has arranged the fried fish on a platter. Lynne pours out the steaming contents of the vegetable pan over the fried fish. 'This makes a lovely salad,' she exclaims, 'lovely gravy, lovely dish, spicy and nice.' Lynne reaches up and pulls two leaves off the tree. It is a pimento tree. Sylvie washes them under the nearby outdoor tap. Lynne finally uses them to garnish the dish. It looks stunning.

The men are seated at another table on a wide, green lawn surrounded on three sides by lush and colourful tropical vegetation. The fourth side overlooks the cool, blue ocean. The women arrive with the cooked fish, bread and cans of famous Jamaican Red Stripe beer. This is paradise.

Malcolm and Franklin are about to enjoy what the Jamaicans call 'escovitch fish'. The name is a lingering reminder from the Spanish who prepared a pickled fish fried in oil and vinegar called 'Pescado en Escabeche'.

Left: Lynne and Sylvie prepare escovitch fish.

Escovitch Fish

Pickled Fish

The name escovitch or caveached fish is a corruption of the Spanish word for pickled, escabeche, in the Caribbean. This is a famous Jamaican recipe which is popular *for Sunday breakfast, and can be served either hot or cold. The gentle flavour of the spiced fish is complemented by sweet peppers.*

SERVES SIX

6 x 6 oz/175 g fillets any non-oily white fish	2 small carrots, scraped and thinly sliced
salt and freshly ground black pepper	3 fresh hot red chilli peppers, seeded and sliced
2 fl oz/50 ml (¼ cup) lime or lemon juice	12 allspice berries
2 fl oz/50 ml (¼ cup) olive or vegetable oil	1 bay leaf
2 medium onions, peeled and thinly sliced	8 fl oz/225 ml (1 cup) malt or cane vinegar

Season the fish with salt, pepper and the lime or lemon juice and marinate for 15 minutes. Lift out of the marinade and pat dry with kitchen paper. Heat half the oil in a frying pan (skillet) and sauté the fish until lightly browned on both sides. This takes about 8 minutes. Arrange the fish on a serving dish.

Put the onions, carrots, chilli peppers, allspice berries, bay leaf and vinegar in a saucepan. Season with salt and pepper and bring to the boil. Reduce the heat and simmer, covered, for 20 minutes. Stir in the remaining oil and pour over the fish. If the fish is to be served cold it can be kept, refrigerated, overnight.

The Jamaican motto is 'Out of Many, One People'. The British have also left their legacy, like the allspice Christmas pudding prepared by Mary-Jean Green, daughter of cookery expert Lady Mitchell. Their kitchen is part of a plantation mansion and is well-equipped and modern. It opens directly on to a delightful shady terrace set with comfortable wicker furniture and potted plants. This in turn gives way to a large, rolling green lawn surrounded by the most splendid of Jamaica's fabulous flora. It is a paradise of its own kind, of position, wealth and taste.

Mary-Jean explains that her father, Sir Harold Mitchell, grew up in Scotland and had an uncle who regularly brought him gifts from Jamaica, pimento, parrots and the like. Sir Harold, who grew to love things Jamaican, visited the island in 1936 and acquired the plantation which grows, amongst other things, pimento. Mary-Jean's mother, Lady Mitchell, became interested in adapting old Scottish recipes for Jamaican use. The Christmas pudding, which relies heavily on Jamaican sugar, rum and allspice, was one of her most successful creations.

'Traditionally we used to do this around about October,' explains Mary-Jean. 'It was usual for everyone in the house to give the Christmas pudding a stir and make a wish before it was put away until Christmas. It was always a great family event . . . The last ingredients are the coins. It is better not to put in so many that everyone gets one. Whoever gets a coin should feel very

Mrs Green preparing her Jamaican Christmas pudding.

Lady Mitchell's Christmas Pudding

Lady Mitchell's family came from the Borders of Scotland but she herself lived in Jamaica. This recipe has come down to her from her Scottish ancestors but has a Jamaican flavour to it.

MAKES ONE PUDDING

½ lb/225 g (2 cups) beef suet, finely chopped	2 oz/50 g (½ cup) chopped almonds
½ lb/225 g (2 cups) currants, chopped	4 oz/100 g (1 cup) plain (all-purpose) flour
½ lb/225 g (2 cups) seedless raisins, chopped	4 oz/100 g (2 cups) freshly made breadcrumbs
4 oz/100 g (1 cup) candied peel, chopped	7 oz/200 g (1 cup) dark brown sugar
grated peel of 3 limes or lemons	4 fl oz/100 ml (½ cup) dark rum
1 teaspoon/5 ml freshly ground nutmeg	4 large eggs, lightly beaten
½ teaspoon/2.5 ml ground allspice	2 fl oz/50 ml (¼ cup) milk

In a large bowl combine the beef suet, currants, raisins, candied peel, lime or lemon peel, nutmeg, allspice, and almonds and mix well. Add the flour, breadcrumbs and sugar, mixing again thoroughly. Add the rum. Combine the eggs and milk and stir into the fruit mixture. Butter a large pudding basin, add the batter, cover with greaseproof (wax) paper and a floured cloth, and steam for 1½ hours.

This pudding keeps for an indefinite period if covered tightly with greaseproof (wax) paper and is much improved if 2 tablespoons/30 ml rum are poured over the top of the pudding once a month. Steam the pudding for 2½ hours on the day of use and serve hot.

honoured on Christmas day. When mixing them in, they disappear and hopefully don't poke out, so make sure they are hidden in the pudding.'

Henry Morgan was the most famous of the pirates, cut-throats and buccaneers who used Jamaica as a base to raid Caribbean shipping. Ultimately, he rose to become governor of the island and the kitchen of his old residence still stands. Beside it is a large pimento tree. It is said of Morgan that when he felt rough from an upset tummy or too much rum, he calmed himself with a little liqueur known as 'pimento dram'. This is a bit strange because in Jamaica where male and female roles are clearly defined, pimento dram is known as a ladies' drink. It is made from rum, lime juice, sugar, cinnamon and ripe pimento berries.

The recipe is not given here because you would have difficulty in finding ripe pimento berries other than in Jamaica. Jamaicans swear by it, and the drink is something to look out for if ever you visit the island. In the meantime, Chartreuse and Benedictine are two more readily available liqueurs both containing allspice.

Perhaps the most majestic Jamaican use of allspice and pimento leaves is jerk pork. In recent years, this treat has become such a favourite with the millions of tourists visiting the island, it is difficult to know how much is real and how much is 'show biz'. Jerk pork is prepared everywhere and is wonderful.

Preparing jerk pork in Jamaica.

Jerk Pork

This is a very old dish going back to the days of the buccaneers. The rather odd name of Jerk Pork is a corruption of the Spanish, charquear, *which means to dry beef in the air.* Charqui *or* charque *is the name for sun-dried beef, not very far really from jerky or jerk even though the Jamaican meat is pork.*

Modern cooking equipment makes this recipe easy to do at home. In Jamaica it is a speciality of Port Antonio and the cooks who make it are known as 'jerk men'. It is a delicacy worth seeking in the market place where it has been made from suckling pig, or making at home with smaller cuts of pork.

SERVES EIGHT

2 oz/50 g ($\frac{1}{2}$ cup) allspice berries

6 spring onions (scallions), chopped

2–3 fresh hot red or green chilli peppers, chopped

$\frac{1}{2}$ teaspoon/2.5 ml ground cinnamon

1 teaspoon/5 ml freshly grated nutmeg

salt and freshly ground black pepper

4 lb/1.8 kg pork chops, or boneless loin

Pound the allspice, spring onions (scallions), chilli peppers, cinnamon, nutmeg, salt and pepper in a mortar with a pestle, or reduce in a blender or food processor. Spread the paste over the pork chops or

loin of pork and leave for at least 30 minutes.

Grill the meat slowly over charcoal or use a grill. In Jamaica the charcoal would be made from green pimento (allspice) wood, adding a special flavour.

First, you select a beauty spot on the sea or beside a lagoon. Jamaica certainly has an abundance of beauty spots. A ditch is dug which is covered with a framework of pimento poles. In the Taino language, which was spoken by the now-vanished Arawaks, such a framework was called a *barbacoa*, and, of course, now survives as barbecue. This is covered with palm leaves which form a bed for sides of pork which are then laid on it. These have been thoroughly rubbed with a spice mixture consisting of wild cinnamon, black pepper, onion, nutmeg, chillies, green pepper, salt, pimento leaves and allspice. The pork is covered first with pimento leaves and then long boards which are weighted to provide downward pressure. Burning coals from a nearby fire, fuelled with pimento logs, are shoved under the framework. As the whole thing cooks and smoke rises, the aroma is staggering. Crowds naturally gather round in eager anticipation. The whole scene is almost hypnotic, blue sky, lush tropical vegetation, a secret lagoon, perhaps the sea, a calypso band, puffs of smoke and the unbearably delicious smell. At last, the weights and boards are removed and leaves peeled away to reveal the steaming prize. It is literally torn apart and served on pieces

of brown paper. People wander, pork in one hand, a can of beer in the other. It is a culinary moment never to be forgotten.

Allspice now belongs to the world. In the Napoleonic war of 1812 Russian soldiers are said to have put it in their boots in order to keep their feet warm. They must have liked the barracks-room aroma because today the Soviet Union is one of the world's largest allspice consumers. Vast quantities are used in their fish-packing industries. Allspice is found everywhere where people pickle or preserve meat or fish.

Poland is another major consumer of allspice. There, it is used in the excellent pickle and meat-packing industries. The world's largest *per capita* allspice consumers are the Scandinavians. Here, it is used with fish such as the famous pickled herrings, roll mops. In a Swedish *smörgåsbord*, allspice is present in just about everything.

Pimento oil, which is important in the soap cosmetic industries, is usually associated with men's toiletries, especially with those products having the word 'spice' on the label. It is, however, in the food-processing industries that allspice is a virtual wonder spice. It is an 'all rounder' having equal value in meats, vegetable preserves and baking. Still, of all the major spices it seems the most misunderstood in domestic kitchens. In fact, only 5–10 per cent of its worldwide output is used for domestic purposes. Most of the rest is used by food industries with 70 per cent in ground spice form. This is surprising since industry generally prefers the essential oils.

Allspice accounts for 10 per cent of the flavour of pork sausages in the United Kingdom. For some reason, Americans prefer their sausages flavoured with ginger, sage and thyme. Allspice also provides 35 per cent of the flavour in British pork pies, 35 per cent in hamburger mix and a dramatic 50 per cent in canned spaghetti in meat sauce.

In Jamaica a pamphlet was recently published called *Ten Ways to Spice up Your Life with Jamaican Allspice*. It may give you ideas on how to use allspice.

(1) Drop allspice berries with dried rose petals in your bath water.

(2) Give your lover a rose with an allspice berry delicately implanted.

(3) Make jasmine, allspice (berries), and dried orange peel tea for your lover or special friend (hot or cold). It's an *Aphrodisiac*.

(4) Serve pimento/allspice liqueur over ice-cream and savour slowly the tantalizing taste.

(5) Put sachets of allspice in the drawer with your folded nightclothes.

(6) Have an allspice 'Snuff/Savour' party, provide berries for sniffing and hors d'oeuvres sprinkled with powdered allspice.

(7) Sprinkle allspice powder and lime juice over exotic tropical fruits and spoonfeed your lover or serve on toothpicks.

(8) Serve pimento/allspice liqueur with coffee or sprinkle powdered allspice over coffee with whipped cream.

(9) Use allspice indiscriminately, as a substitute for cinnamon, cloves or nutmeg (its flavour blend) and enjoy the aromatic pungence of this 'spice wonder'!

(10) Use allspice berries as a main fragrance ingredients in your dried flowers and herbs—Potpourri.

Surprisingly, there is one easy treat the pamphlet missed. Drop a few whole berries in your pepper grinder along with its normal black and white pepper. It enhances the pepper just slightly in all its uses, but do not tell anyone. Next time you cook, think allspice. You could do a lot worse than that useful spice which did not change the world.

8
MUSTARD

George Arsene is a big man in a big land and mustard is his life. He is Canadian, and Canada devotes about a quarter of a million acres annually to mustard cultivation and exports more seed than any other country. George operates from a small office in an industrial estate on the outskirts of the southern Alberta town of Lethbridge. During the harvest in September he is hardly ever there, but in his car clocking up miles on endless backroads through what seems like the middle of nowhere.· 'Well, we're approaching the Reservation right now,' shouts George 'Once we cross this bridge we're on the Indian Reserve. They've got about 367,000 acres of cultivated land in this area which is mostly farmed by the white man.'

In the distance a brown dust cloud shrouds a glass, steel and chromium apparition which finally materializes into an enormous Dodge truck-trailer combination. George waves and honks as it thunders by. He then reaches for his radio-telephone, calls the local grain storage elevator and ensures that they are ready to receive yet another giant load of mustard seed.

As an agent for a large grain company, George represents the moment when the world's demand for mustard meets the men who actually grow it. 'In this area I have about eight or ten farmers who grow mustard for us to a total of about thirty-thousand acres and they grow it every year. Most other crops just don't do too well for a drought crop and mustard is one of the heartiest. It produces well as long as it gets a good start . . . you get another two rains in the summertime and you've got it made.'

Mile after mile of low, brown, rolling hills pass by. The land is not quite as flat as in Saskatchewan, to the east, where even more mustard is grown.

There you can stand in a field and look at the horizon in every direction and see only mustard. But this too is big sky country with just the stubble of the Rocky Mountains rising far to the west.

There are basically two types of mustard, white and brown. These are broken into many sub-categories depending upon which botanist you choose to follow. All mustard belongs to the family Cruciferae, so called because the four petals on the flowers form a cross. No one has yet found any poisonous members of this large family which embraces turnips, radishes and horseradish.

It is generally agreed that both white and brown mustard belong to a sub-classification, *Brassica*. This is the cabbage and cress group. White mustard, just to confuse matters, is sometimes known as 'yellow mustard'. It goes by the botanical names *Brassica alba*, *Brassica hirta* or

The large seeds of the white mustard variety, *Brassica alba*. White mustard seed is used to make the prepared mustards, the hot dog and hamburger mustards so loved in North America and also found in English made mustards.

Sinapis alba. Sinapis is the ancient Greek word for mustard. About half of all the mustard grown in Canada is this variety. Most of it is exported across the border into the United States, but it is also the local favourite.

George Arsene, a grain agent, on the right, evaluating a farmer's mustard seed crop in Alberta, Canada. It is vital to harvest at just the right moment when the seeds are mature but before the pods burst, spreading seeds everywhere.

If George and the boys go up to Calgary to watch the Stampeders play football they might buy a hot dog. Nearby will be one of those large glass bottles filled with yellow mush. A few presses on the plastic pump and out it squirts. *That* is *Brassica alba*, white mustard, mixed with starch, vinegar, yellow food colouring and perhaps another spice or two. It is the hot dog and hamburger mustard so loved in North America.

Brown mustard is not so simple. A variety called *Brassica nigra* was once used throughout Europe. It was extremely tasty and pungent and was known as 'black' or 'true' mustard. It is a tall plant with rather unstable seed pods. Since it does not lend itself to mechanized harvesting, today it grows only in remote areas where it can be cut and collected by hand.

Hand-harvesting is not going to get anyone very far on the Canadian prairie, so here they grow another variety called *Brassica juncea*. This is divided into two sub-types, oriental, sometimes called yellow, and brown. Confusion reigns because these two sub-types are also variously referred to as 'Indian' and 'Black'! It hardly matters, because it takes an expert, like George, to tell them apart.

You will not be surprised to learn that the oriental variety is preferred by the Japanese. Japan is not often thought of as a great spice-using nation, but it does purchase considerable quantities of Canadian mustard. Used exotically, it is stuffed into holes in large *renkon* or lotus roots and coated with tempura batter, fried and eaten as a vegetable. More simply, the Japanese mix it with water for use as a condiment.

Most of the brown variety of *Brassica juncea* is shipped to Europe, to such legendary mustard capitals as Dijon, Bordeaux and Düsseldorf. Ironically, some finds its way back to shop shelves in newly affluent Alberta, which also is the home of wheat, beef, oil and computers. 'Gourmet' mustards are the rage of a climbing social class.

Mustard was hardly grown in Canada before World War II. Farmers turned to it when the principal crop of the area, wheat, became heavily controlled by government regulatory agencies. Mustard is a cash crop with payment on delivery.

Traditionally, half the Canadian crop was *Brassica alba* and the other half *juncea*, divided equally between oriental and brown, but in recent years the proportion of oriental has been growing.

George's job is to ensure that the correct amount of the right type of mustard seed arrives at storage elevators in good condition ready for shipment out by rail. Nobody grows mustard on speculation. Not only are farmers instructed to grow certain numbers of acres, but they are given the right kind and amount of seed, and are supervised. George likes to tell of the farmer who seeded several thousand acres, but the plants sprouted unevenly. George recommended that he plough the whole crop in and start anew. This cost four days of backbreaking day and night labour, but the man's final profit was doubled.

Nobody else has a fieldman who's in charge of any of the crops. They first say here it is, grow it, do what you want. We see that the farmer does it right. He knows that we care about him and his crops, which we do, you know, we're involved. The more pounds he gets per acre, the more pounds we get to sell and it's all sold. Now, if he gets a crop failure, then I've got a crop failure, and I haven't the product to sell.

George arrives at Henry's land. Henry had already taken the crop off another field, but it contained seeds of a weed, cow cockle, and could therefore be downgraded, fetching a lower price. Henry needs to know two things; could he average the prior crop with that of this field to improve the grade, and is the field ready for harvest?

Together Henry and George wade into the shoulder-high mass of fully grown plants. The mustard seeds themselves are in long pods hanging from the spiny stalks. There are millions of them,

billions! If the harvest is left too late, the pods will burst, spreading seeds everywhere. The crop will not only be lost, but mustard is so prolific, it will be a weed for years to come. If the crop is harvested too early, the seeds may not be fully mature and will be downgraded. Worse, seeds having too high a moisture content could cause heat and fermentation in the storage elevators. There is one right moment, and George knows it.

This one is starting to turn, see. You see once they've got this little brown spot on them, right there, then it's going to mature—and that takes ten days. No, another day sure wouldn't hurt it—we'll leave it one more day, then come back.

Henry's field is uneven. There are low spots which are less ripe than others, so George recommends swathing before combining. In a few days, rows of green and red tractors lugging sets of long blades will lay these fields flat. The cut crop will lie on the ground for over a week to allow uniform ripening and drying. Then another row of giant combine harvesters will follow the first, blowing the harvested seed into the cavernous holds of accompanying truck trailers. The roar of machinery will be heard for miles and the air waves will crackle with Citizen's Band and radio-telephone. The spices of the tropics are still harvested as they have been for centuries. Mustard is different. It is as old as any of them, yet it is the spice of the twentieth century and big business.

George breaks a few pods and spreads the seeds on the fender of a nearby truck. 'My God, you know, it's clean. It hasn't got any cow cockle in it, Henry, I don't think we'll have any trouble with it at all. I'm sure that if we mix this with the other, you know, it'll upgrade everything'. Henry sighs with relief and replies: 'I think I'm getting beat on the price, I think I should get more money.' 'I can't see you getting any more money though,' says George, 'that's about the best we can do.'

The very essence which makes mustard, mustard, is not even contained in the seeds. The seeds do contain a fixed oil, which is odourless, and when removed has the property of an ordinary vegetable oil. Indeed, some of the less expensive brands of vegetable oil on the market will likely contain mustard oil. It is *the* cooking oil in parts of India and elsewhere in the Third World. Some writers claim that it is important to local cuisine and the cooking oil of choice; however, its wide use is more probably the result of its low price. Brown seeds are smaller than white but richer in fixed oils. Brown mustard, *Brassica juncea*, is closely related to canola or rape which is cultivated specifically for its oil, but, you cannot make mustard from rape.

Brown and white mustard seeds contain both a special enzyme and a chemical substance related to sugar called a glucoside. When a crushed seed comes into contact with water, the enzyme attacks the glucoside breaking it up into sugar and the light volatile essential oils. These oils which give

Harvesting brown mustard seed in Alberta. Canada grows about a quarter of a million acres of mustard annually. It is a cash crop with payment on delivery and the most modern machinery is used. Most of this crop will be exported to Europe or to Japan.

mustard its characteristic, sharp aroma and pungency, do not form except in the presence of water. In the traditional method of preparing hot English mustard the mustard powder is mixed with cold water and allowed to stand anywhere from ten minutes to an hour depending upon the quality of the mustard and individual taste. The waiting period is necessary to permit the chemical reaction to happen, but, if the preparation is left too long, the light volatile oils disappear into the air. If hot rather than cold water is used, the oils disappear that much quicker. This is why mustard used in cooking is usually added at the very last minute.

For millennia, human beings have mixed mustard with just about every liquid substance they themselves eat or drink. These include vinegar, wine, beer, fruit juices and even milk, all containing water. Vinegar is an ancient favourite because it is about 10 per cent acetic acid and 90 per cent water. The acetic acid acts as a sort of fixer, slowing down the chemical reaction to produce

mustard which is not only milder but holds its potency longer.

The word 'mustard' itself is derived from the name of one of the liquid mixers. 'Mustum' is newly fermented grape juice on its way to becoming wine. *Ardere* is the Latin verb 'to burn'. So 'mustard' was 'hot must', not a bad description, but certainly medieval. The Greeks and the Romans, great fanciers of the aromatic seed, both called the spice *sinapis*, a name still remembered in the Italian *senape* and the German *senf*. Mustard is much more ancient than classical antiquity, being one of those spices used long before the advent of civilization. Seeds have been discovered in prehistoric caves both in Europe and China.

In the fifth century BC, Hippocrates was prescribing white mustard both as an internal medicine and as an exterior poultice. In the twentieth century, the 'mustard plaster' or poultice still is considered effective for relieving bronchitis and rheumatism, yet modern medical science remains, at best, neutral in the matter. It is, however, hard to believe that no factual basis exists for thousands of years of continuous human experience.

Black mustard, *Brassica nigra*, was so cherished as a medicine by the ancient Greeks that they thought it had been invented by Aesculapius, the god of medicine. History makes it difficult to tell whether mustard was considered more a medicine or a food. The Greeks simply ate whole seeds along with their meat, but the Romans blended them into a variety of sophisticated sauces not unlike modern cuisine. One Roman recipe for mustard as a table condiment calls for the seeds to be washed, ground with fresh pine kernels and almonds, and then mixed carefully with vinegar. This preparation would not be too out of place on a modern grocer's shelf. The Romans were addicted to a taste which has survived unabated the rise and fall of civilizations . . . mustard on sausages.

Mustard became *the* medieval spice. Everywhere, it grew locally with little difficulty and was esteemed as an inexpensive cure-all. The people of medieval Europe ate more meat than

It was a mighty moment in food history when mustard met the sausage. The tradition began with the Romans but for centuries has been practised with passion in Germany. This could be breakfast, lunch, tea, dinner or just a snack.

the Romans yet had a more limited access to the tropical spices. Mustard was used to cover the taste of bland, and yes, putrid meat. There hardly exist any medieval writings about food which fail to extol mustard's virtues.

Le Ménagier de Paris is a work written in 1393 by an elderly husband instructing his teenaged orphan wife on what could best be described as 'domestic science'. Mustard is mentioned frequently. He advises her to purchase from the saucemaker a quart of cameline for dinner and two quarts of mustard for supper. He explains the preparation of dried cod or stockfish to her. Before it is edible it must be pounded with a mallet for an hour and soaked in water for two hours more. Mustard, of course, is the condiment essential to make it palatable. Finally he details the selection of mustard seed and its preparation:

Item: if you would make good mustard and at leisure, set the mustard seed to soak for a night in good vinegar, then grind it with a mill and then moisten it little by little with vinegar; and if you have any spices left over . . . let them be ground with it and afterwards prepare it well.

Kings and popes all had their sauce cooks and mustard makers. In Tudor England, being appointed carver of the meat in a large household meant gaining a position of great responsibility. The occupant of the office was required to know the correct sauce for every possible meal. Mustard was favoured with brawn, beef and salted mutton while a ginger sauce was served with kid, lamb or piglet. At the beginning of the fifteenth century, mustard could be purchased for less than a farthing a pound and was used in enormous quantities.

Several writers describe a picnic or banquet held in the year 1336, to which the Duke of Burgundy invited King Philip the Fair of France to sample local produce. It is said that a *poinçon*, or over sixty gallons, of mustard was consumed. Depending upon which version you read, the mustard was either consumed by the entire party at one meal, by Philip at one meal, or by Philip over the period of a week. Sadly, the story is apocryphal because Philip the Fair died in 1314.

The point is that the picnic was supposed to have happened in Dijon and, of course, throughout history Dijon and mustard have been inseparable. Some of the tales told in the town may not exactly ring with veracity, but it is true that for centuries the French have said: '*Il n'est moutarde qu'à Dijon.*'

Another story concerns a later Duke of Burgundy, Philip the Good, who tried to restore heraldic tradition to his duchy by establishing a new order of chivalry, the Toison d'Or, or Golden Fleece. In 1430 he married the King of Portugal's daughter Isobel, who, apparently was appalled at the state of French cuisine. It is said that it was through her efforts that the lavish use of mustard was introduced into the court giving a boost to the mustard-makers of Dijon. As far as the food was concerned, she may have had a point. A detailed description of her wedding feast lists such 'dishes' as men dressed up as savages or wild beasts riding on roasted pigs and a giant pie containing live sheep dyed blue with gilded horns.

Today, the Toison d'Or is a restaurant which sits on the very site where Philip met his Knights. Not only does the restaurant prepare the great mustard-based sauce of Dijon, but it probably cooks up a legend or two also.

Anyone really interested in the literature of mustard should not miss the essay by the novelist and keen gastronome, Alexandre Dumas. An excerpt in English is published in the invaluable

Mustard Sauce for Ham

Mustard changes a simple slice of boiled ham into a delectable meal for two in this recipe. The sauce is also very good served with grilled herrings. The recipe for béchamel sauce is given on page 23.

SERVES TWO	
½ lb/225 g slice of cold boiled ham	2 tablespoons/30 ml Dijon mustard
4 fl oz/100 ml (½ cup) béchamel sauce	3 tablespoons/45 ml grated Parmesan cheese
	2–3 tablespoons/30–45 ml double (heavy) cream

In a saucepan combine the béchamel sauce, mustard, 1 tablespoon/15 ml of the Parmesan cheese and the cream. Stir to mix, and heat through. Arrange the ham in a flameproof serving dish and spread the sauce over it.

Sprinkle with the remaining cheese and put under a grill (broiler) until the cheese is lightly browned. Serve with plain boiled potatoes, tossed in butter and finely chopped parsley, and a green vegetable of your choice.

Poulet à dijonnaise

Dijon-style Chicken

Properly speaking, this would be called Poulet Mme Gaston Gèrard after the wife of a former mayor of Dijon, who created it in honour of a visit by Curnonsky, who was crowned Prince of Gastronomes by the French in *1927. The dish is now a popular speciality in the region and this recipe is the the one used by chef Daniel Broyer at Le Toison D'Or in Dijon. It is equally good with loin of pork.*

SERVES TWO

3 lb/1.4 kg chicken	2 fl oz/50 ml dry white wine
salt and freshly ground black pepper	¼ pt/150 ml double (heavy) cream
2 oz/50 g butter	1 tablespoon/15 ml Dijon mustard
1 bay leaf	6 oz/175 g Gruyère cheese, grated
¼ teaspoon/2.5 ml thyme	1 oz/25 g freshly made breadcrumbs

Cut the chicken in half lengthwise and reserve the other half for another use. Cut away the backbone and separate the chicken into breast and leg portions. Pat dry with kitchen paper (paper towels). Season with salt and pepper. Heat half the butter in a casserole and add the chicken pieces, the bay leaf and thyme. Sauté over moderate heat, turning from time to time until the chicken pieces are browned all over, about 15 minutes. Cover the casserole, reduce the heat to low and cook until the chicken is tender, about 10 minutes. If the leg needs longer cooking, remove the breast and keep it warm. Cook the leg for 5–10 minutes longer. Lift out and keep warm with the breast.

Pour off the fat in the casserole. Add the rest of the butter to the casserole with the white wine and cream and reduce over high heat to half its volume. Lower the heat, stir in the mustard and 5 oz/150 g of the cheese and cook, stirring, for about 1 minute or until the cheese has melted into a smooth sauce. Do not overcook as the sauce will go stringy. Pour the sauce over the chicken, sprinkle with the breadcrumbs and the remaining 1 oz/25 g cheese and put under the grill (broiler) to brown.

book, *Dumas on Food*, translated by Alan and Jane Davidson. Dumas informs us that mustard-making had always been kept alive in Dijon, which the Romans called 'Divio'. In the thirteenth century, one Etienne Boileau, who was the Provost of Paris under Saint-Louis, granted to the vinegar-makers, the right to make mustard. An early street cry was:

> *Vinaigre qui est beau et bon!*
> *Vinaigre de moutarde.*

Mustard use declined in the sixteenth century with the arrival of quantities of tropical spices from the East. This is somewhat ironic, because much of the responsibility for the age of discovery, with its easier access to spices, rests upon the Portuguese Prince Henry the Navigator who was the brother of Isobel, wife of Philip the Good of Burgundy.

In 1634 new statutes were passed in Dijon elevating mustard makers or *moutardiers* to the status of a guild and regulating the quality and labelling of the product. Twenty-three *moutardiers* endorsed the regulations including one named Naigeon whose grandson Dumas considered an inspired genius. Jean Naigeon substituted the traditional wine vinegar with verjuice and created a new taste in mustard which became the rage of France.

Dijon sits at the centre of one of the world's great wine-making regions, Burgundy. Often, after the grape harvest, it was found that some of the larger grapes had not fully ripened. These were pressed separately producing a highly acidic liquid, verjuice, from *vert-jus*, green or sour juice.

'The result of this', claimed Dumas, 'was that mustard no longer contained any sugar or acetic acid, but only tartaric, citric and malic acids.'

Small mustard factories or workshops sprouted up in Dijon. The mustard seeds (always black, *Brassica nigra*, or brown, *Brassica juncea*; *never* white, *Brassica alba*) were ground between large circular stones not unlike those used by millers. Verjuice was mixed with the crushed seeds at the centre of the grinder and the resulting thick paste was spooned into wooden troughs and passed through horsehair sieves. This last operation removed the husks or the seed's hard outside cover.

Wooden casks were fumigated with brimstone, or 'sulphured' and filled with the mustard paste which was left to ferment from eight to ten days. The mustard was then vigorously beaten and bottled for distribution.

Dumas goes on to describe a France where style and social acceptability depended upon knowing the latest mustard. Manufacturers introduced new tastes such as capers and anchovy essence, and Paris itself began to rival Dijon. Every kind of wine was tried and new vinegars developed.

A gentleman called Maille, who claimed to be the vinegar-maker to the Kings of France and

Mustard Sauce for Steak or Pork Chops

SERVES TWO	*1 tablespoon/15 ml shallots, peeled and chopped*
steak or pork chops for two	*2 oz/50 g (4 tablespoons) butter, cut into bits*
8 fl oz/225 ml (1 cup) dry white wine	*salt and freshly ground black pepper*
2 tablespoons/30 ml Dijon mustard	*chopped parsley or chervil*

Cook the steak or chops in a frying pan (skillet), remove to a warm serving dish and keep warm.

Pour away the fat from the pan. Add the wine, and over a high heat stir to scrape up any brown bits. Let the wine reduce to half its volume. Lower the heat, stir in the mustard and shallots and cook for 1 minute longer. Remove from the heat and beat in the butter, a bit at a time, until it is incorporated into the sauce. Season to taste with salt and freshly ground black pepper. Pour the sauce over the steak or chops, sprinkle with parsley or chervil and serve immediately.

Emperors of Russia and Germany, invented ninety-two vinegars and twenty-four mustards. There were separate mustards for men and women and presumably children. Serving last month's 'in' mustard was strictly *déclassé*. By 1812, according to Dumas, France had no less than eighty-four distinct kinds of mustard.

Today in Dijon, or for that matter anywhere in France, it is possible to buy virtually every combination and permutation of mustard . . . some are ground with vinegar, wine, verjuice or all three; some are coarse, others fine; and some are flavoured with capers, anchovies, tarragon, capsicum, various herbs or combinations of all of them.

For centuries the French city of Dijon has been the mustard capital of the world and by 1812, the novelist and gastronome, Alexandre Dumas claimed that there were eighty-four distinct kinds of mustard in France alone. Even today, the mustard shops of Dijon draw visitors from all over the world.

The only sweeping statement that can be made is that virtually all European mustards are made from brown seeds, *Brassica juncea*.

There are four basic methods of grinding the seeds. The first to grind them finely to, or almost to, a powder. The second is to grind coarsely, just cracking the seeds. The third is to pre-soak the seeds, wet grind the paste and filter out the outer husks. The fourth is the same as the third, but the husks are kept. Many methods have been used to grind mustard seed. Two particularly 'macho' ones reflect the pungency of the spice . . . the rolling of a round iron bullet in a bowl and smashing with a pistol handle.

Traditional Dijon mustard is a result of the third method . . . presoak, wet-grind and filter. Bordeaux mustard was usually a result of the fourth. The husks were left in, but the grind was slightly finer. The fourth method also produced many of the German mustards where sugar was commonly added.

The English, however, have enjoyed a very different mustard philosophy and tradition. Shakespeare's Falstaff says of his crony Poins '. . . his wit is as thick as Tewkesbury mustard'. Wild mustard seed was crushed with pease flour, wetted and shaped into balls which were left to dry. Ultimately they were mixed with a liquid of the user's choice. Only coarsely ground mustard of varying quality and cleanliness was produced in England until about 1720.

The problem lay in the fixed oils; the more the seed was ground, the more it turned into an oily wet paste. The story goes that in 1720, an old woman, Mrs Clements, of Durham, developed a process of grinding mustard into a fine powder. Her method was kept secret, but it involved a milling process similar to that used with wheat. Apparently, Mrs Clements was her own best salesman, travelling throughout the land selling what came to be known as 'Durham' mustard.

The powder caught on. It kept indefinitely and when mixed with water proved sharp and pungent, much superior to the coarsely ground vinegar-based product. In 1742 a gentleman named Keen built a mustard factory in London on Garlick Hill. He manufactured the English powder there for over a hundred and fifty years until the firm was bought by Colmans.

If Dijon is the most memorable name in the history of mustard, Colmans has to be its only rival. It seems that for the past century and a half or so, the Colman company has been blessed with that unbeatable combination, good fortune and talent. Like the Hebrews of old, the firm started with the three great patriarchs and to this day, company history and tradition is important in the manufacture of its product. If you visit the mustard factory at Carrow near the English city of Norwich, you might find hanging on the large mixing hoppers, signs reading 'MANAGEMENT IN'. This, of course, does not mean that directors of the company have jumped into the vat but something quite different.

The Colmans were millers, and mustard was only one of a number of products they milled. Powdered mustard seed is extremely strong and pungent, so from the earliest times, the company modified it by adding various amounts of wheat flour. The Colmans, not anxious that the public learn this fact, even tried to keep it from their own employees. A tunnel with a locked door linked their flour and mustard mills. Daily, flour workers

Mustard Cream Sauce

This sauce is good with hot or cold fish, shellfish, meats and poultry.

SERVES FOUR TO SIX

1 hardboiled egg yolk	*1 tablespoon/15 ml white wine vinegar*
1 raw egg yolk	*salt and freshly ground black pepper*
1 tablespoon/15 ml Dijon mustard	*8 fl oz/225 ml (1 cup) double (heavy) cream*

Mash the hardboiled egg yolk in a medium-sized bowl. Lightly beat the raw egg yolk and mix it into the mashed yolk. Add the mustard, wine vinegar, salt and pepper and mix to a smooth paste. Beat the cream until it stands in peaks, and then fold it into the egg yolk mixture, gently but thoroughly.

would take unmarked sacks through the tunnel and leave them by the door. At an appointed time the mustard workers would retrieve the sacks and empty their contents into the mixing bins. A little turmeric was also added to give the powder its famous yellow 'mustard' look. The additives were euphemistically called 'Management' and although modern labelling laws have rendered the ruse unnecessary, the name still persists. The seed used in the famous English powder is a mixture of white and brown and is mostly home grown.

Only the third patriarch, Jeremiah James Colman, was alive in 1854 when the business moved to its present site at Carrow in order to take advantage of the local mustard fields, the adjacent canal and most especially, the new railway. For forty years, he and his family lived on the Carrow site and were personally involved not only in Colman business, but in that of Norfolk. Jeremiah James served both as mayor of the city and for a long time was the local member of parliament. He transformed the firm from a mere company to an empire by three acts of brilliance. First, he bought out virtually all his competitors. Secondly, he developed a type of company-employee relationship at Carrow, almost unheard of in Victorian times. The works had a school for the children of employees, a highly subsidized cafeteria and a dispensary. A trained nurse, Miss Flowerday, made history by becoming the first industrial nurse in Britain. This might not seem impressive today, but the goodwill created survives in the community to the present time. Finally, Jeremiah James and his staff virtually created the concept of mass marketing and applied it to mustard.

The familiar red and yellow packages with the bull's head, almost unchanged for over a century, worked their way first into the consciousness of a nation and then the world. The name and symbol were not only plastered on wrappers, cardboard boxes, cartons, hoardings, iron plates and the sides of vans, but on any number of those little personal things which people like to keep. Children were especially targeted as potential clientele. The company built cabinets in school classrooms, naturally bearing the donor's name, and supplied wall charts and illustrated booklets. Comic books with the Colman version of fairy tales were often the only Christmas presents poor children received.

In 1898, at the height of the Klondike gold rush, the company commissioned the artist, John Hassell, to commemorate the event with a series of posters which today are considered classics of advertising art.

Eighteen ninety-eight was also the year of Jeremiah James's death. His funeral was unlike anything ever seen before in Norfolk. An eye-witness remembered, '. . . a column of great J & J Colman wagons, drawn by the firm's matchless horses, loaded high with wreaths and tributes of every size and description from every conceivable source. There must have been thousands of them. Behind that came walking some twelve hundred of the workpeople of Carrow.'

Mass-marketing techniques carried well on into the twentieth century, perhaps reaching a zenith in 1926 with 'The Mustard Club'. Even though the name Colman was everywhere, mustard is essentially dull stuff and the firm's image was considered old-fashioned. Oswald Greene of the Benson's advertising agency thought up the idea of the Mustard Club and Dorothy L. Sayers, the detective story writer, was one of the copywriters. The club was modelled on the Pickwick Club in Dickens' *Pickwick Papers*. The campaign started simply with posters on London buses reading, 'Has Father joined the Mustard Club?' Something very deep in the British national consciousness was touched and the campaign took off beyond the dreams of its perpetrators. Mustard club songs, films, games, memberships and mottoes like 'Mustard makyth Methuselahs' proliferated. It was only the Great Depression five years later which brought the campaign to an end. When it was all over, an assessment revealed that probably the campaign had not sold any more

At the end of the nineteenth century Colmans was famous for its advertising posters.

mustard than usual, but it had been good fun and mustard awareness was at an all time high.

Today Colmans is part of the giant international conglomerate Reckitt & Colman, which makes everything from baby foods to boot polish. They own a substantial proportion of the American mustard market through their brand name 'French's' and their head office is in Rochester, New York, at Number One Mustard Street.

Wiltshire, the English county, has been called 'The Kingdom of the Pig'. In the eighteenth century, before the railway, pigs from Ireland and the west were driven through the county on the way to market in London. The little Wiltshire town of Calne had special significance. It was close enough to London so that if the pigs were slaughtered there, the pork could arrive relatively fresh at market. It was also sufficiently distant to permit horse-drawn carts of pork to arrive well before the pigs driven on foot. So a slaughtering industry began in Calne, especially in Butcher's Row. In 1847 one butcher, John Harris, learned in America of a new technique for curing pork all year round and brought it back to Wiltshire. Harris on Butcher's Row became one of Britain's largest meat packers.

Today, Butcher's Row is called Church Street and the old Harris plant has ceased to operate, but the old town is becoming newly famous as the location of one of Britain's smallest and most appreciated mustard-makers, Wiltshire Tracklements.

'I started to experiment with mustard because I was a sausage salesman,' explains William Tullberg, the firm's founder, owner, chief mustard-maker and bottle-packer. 'I used to visit two or three sausage factories every week and they would give me some of their latest product to take home and try. Twelve years ago, there was only standard English mustard on the market and the French Moutarde de Meaux and I really didn't care for what was available so I started making my own.

'I experimented with various mixes just using a small coffee mill with slightly adjusted grinders. Then I started manufacturing in a very, very tiny

way just for myself. Every Saturday morning I said to all my friends to come and eat sausages, and they came. One fine day, one of them said to me, "Hey Bill, this mustard of yours is superb—won't you make me a jar next time you're making it?"

'So, next time I was making, I made an extra couple of jars and put funny labels on them. I said, "Michael, here's your mustard." He took it home with him, called in at the pub to pick up some cigarettes, and the landlord asked, "What's that?" He had a little taste and a sniff and the next time I went into the village pub, the landlord said to me, "You couldn't make me a dozen of those mustards

Facing page: The ingredients for Wiltshire Tracklements's Urchfont Full Strength Mustard: white mustard seed, allspice, dried red chillies, peppercorns and cider vinegar with a little addition of wine vinegar. White mustard seed used alone is very pungent. When mixed with brown seed, the resulting mustard is more aromatic. North American hot dog mustard is also made from the white seed but mixed with wheat flour to reduce the sharpness.
Below: William Tullberg, the founder of Wiltshire Tracklements, in his shop at Calne.

to sell could you?" I said, "Why not?" and so I made a dozen mustards.'

The rest is history. Bill Tullberg spent more and more time making mustard and less and less time selling sausages. Today the various types of Wiltshire Tracklements mustards are available in speciality shops in the United Kingdom and abroad.

Bill Tullberg sees himself as very much reviving ancient traditions. He considers the white seeds to have more strength and the brown more aroma. He often uses both, but here he describes making a mustard using white only:

We take white mustard seed, allspice, chillies, peppercorns and we grind them all up

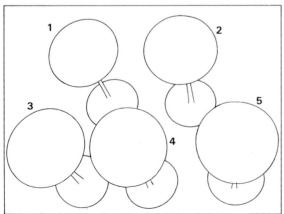

Some mustards and their ingredients:
1. *English made:* Brown and white seeds mixed, fine ground, husks removed, added wheat flour, salt, sugar, extra spice and colouring. Mixed in cold water.
2. *Dijon:* Brown seeds, fine ground, husks removed, wine vinegar, verjuice and a small amount of added spices.
3. *Urchfont Black (Tullberg's):* Brown and white seeds mixed, coarse ground, wine vinegar, black pepper, allspice and chillies.
4. *Bordeaux:* Brown seeds, ground with some husk, fine ground, wine vinegar, anchovies and capers.
5. *Urchfont Full Strength (Tullberg's):* White seeds, coarse ground, cider vinegar, wine vinegar, black pepper, allspice and chillies.

Boeuf Miroton with Mustard

Mustard, called the 'spice of nations' as every country has its favourite, has a marvellous way of enlivening leftover meat. Use a Dijon-type mustard or coarse-ground Moutarde de Meaux.

SERVES TWO TO THREE

1½ oz/40 g (3 tablespoons) butter	6 fl oz/175 ml (¾ cup) beef stock
3 medium onions, peeled and finely chopped	freshly ground black pepper
2 teaspoons/10 ml flour	1 tablespoon/15 ml Dijon or Meaux mustard
4 fl oz/100 ml (½ cup) dry white wine	1 lb/450 g thinly sliced cold roast beef

In a heavy frying pan (skillet), heat the butter and sauté the onions over a moderate heat until they are soft. Stir in the flour and cook for 2 minutes longer. Stir in the wine and the beef stock and simmer gently for 5 minutes until the sauce is smooth and well blended. Season to taste with pepper, stir in the mustard and simmer for 1–2 minutes longer.

Arrange the sliced beef on a warm dish and pour the hot sauce over it. Serve immediately. The sauce will warm the slices of beef through but will not toughen them.

simultaneously. This is very important because it keeps the essential oils all in together so that they absorb together. Then, very quickly we mix in cider vinegar and just a little wine vinegar as well. After five to seven days we check the liquid solid content again to make sure the consistency is the kind of thing you people want to see on your plates, then we pot it.

I think that the finest spicing for mustard is a combination of flavours—not just any one. It's a question of taking a careful balance. I think the fire of chillies, the triple subtlety of allspice and the aromatic sensation of black peppercorns all ground together with the *Brassica alba*, bring out just that bit of power that makes mustard sing.

Bill Tullberg feels that people should experiment with mustards to find the one that tastes best for them with different foods. He considers a particular blend of wine and cider vinegars essential for mustards prepared to draw out the special tastes of sausages. 'I don't think of mustard primarily as a spice,' he remarks, 'Mustard as a spice is splendid in cooking but made mustard which is what we make here, I think of as a tracklement—in other words a meat accompaniment.'

So, from a gigantic corporate empire to a small successful cottage industry, mustard still plays its part. People have been using mustard in more or less the same way since the beginning of time, and probably always will so long as they eat. Bill Tullberg has the last word:

The whole question of which mustard anybody prefers with any particular food is terribly individual. I'm not averse to having two or three different mustards available so that I can try to see which one I really prefer. Of course, I often end up thinking that they are all very good. They say that one of the world's largest mustard manufacturers made his money out of what people left on the side of their plates. Well, on that basis I'm going to end up a poor man. People seem to eat all of mine!

9
GARLIC

The fact that garlic no longer can grow on its own from seed shows that it is dependent on human beings. In fact, when you think about it, human beings and garlic have been co-evolving together for thousands of years. They are really part of us, as we are part of them. To me, this gives a clue to understanding people who say they don't like the smell of garlic . . . They aren't people.

CHARLES PERRY, at the Garlic Summit, Truckee, California

Truckee sits in the mountains of northern California just two hundred and fifty kilometres from San Francisco, but it takes all day in the train to get there. The train itself is one of the world's most modern and comfortable, but the track was laid at a time when Indian ambush was still a potential hazard. No one complains about the gentle pace, indeed it is one of the attractions. There are many others, including the young, blond, female conductor who, with a cheery smile, invites passengers to have a terrific time and to do just whatever they please. The passengers themselves are a slice of America, Indians, Chicanos and carloads of tourists on their annual pilgrimage to the roulette tables of Reno, Nevada, the stop after Truckee.

As the train pulls out of the station, the skyline of San Francisco and the Golden Gate bridge are seen clearly across the wide, blue bay. The train glides by inlets, bays, sprouting subdivisions and flat farmland and into the dusty suburbs of California's capital, Sacramento. It then begins a slow, dignified ascent into the lonely mountains. By contrast the train's insides hum with conviviality. From the piano bar, the glass observation lounge and the snack area come the sounds of laughter and conversation. Whiffs of snow start appearing in the passing forests. The train pulls into the little mountain town of Colfax, a truck parked by the station bears a large sign reading "ORANGES . . . 12 LB/$2.00".

The climb steepens; heavy snow bends branches; forests burst into wide valleys, some lined with silver lakes. Passengers react with appropriate awe to the purple-red sunset on the left. At first, only the valleys are dark but climbing shadows soon bring night. Below, in the distance, lights can be seen. The train descends and pulls to a stop. Only a few passengers step out into the brisk night air. Truckee, Truckee? Tomorrow, Truckee would be to garlic what Paris is to fashion. The garlic summit would commence.

Facing page: Garlic on sale in a Mexican market. Garlic has always been the food and medicine of the common people everywhere. Recently it has been gaining slow acceptance in more aristocratic circles.
Below: Garlic is one of the oldest foods to be recorded in history and is even mentioned in the Bible and in ancient Egyptian writings. Of all the plants, garlic is the one that inspires most passion for and against its use both as a medicine and as a food.

The hotels of Truckee could easily double as the set for *High Noon*, but instead of Gary Coopers, they are packed with eager, early-rising skiers. The town is not one of the world's culinary capitals, but for visitors from afar, breakfast can be an event. The coffee shop on the main street is a large warm sanctuary from the morning cold. A cup of steaming coffee and the breakfast menu magically appears. Simple orders become pleasing rituals:

'Eggs and toast please.'
'How'd you like the eggs? Up, over, scrambled, poached or boiled?'
'Over, please.'
'Will that be easy, medium or hard?'
'Um, easy.'
'Just a minute.'

And so they arrive, exactly as ordered. Oh, America, some things should never change.

Across the tracks, past the Speedway 76 station in front of the bridge over the Truckee river squats La Vieille Maison, the old house. Two stories, wood frame, dark brown stain, small porch, modest wood sign, yet, soon, this old house would be the focus of the garlic world. Robert Charles (French pronunciation for both names) operated a number of famous San Franciscan restaurants before coming, with his wife Amora, to Truckee. The idea was to lead a simple life, serving the food they love. Today, the world comes to them.

Amora, a native of Brazil, once danced in the capitals of Europe, but now she runs the dining-room with the informal good cheer and hospitality of the old west. Robert, long hair, beard and chef's uniform all white, is master of the kitchen. He does make forays to the dining-room where he works hard at cultivating his chosen image of a gallant but suave Frenchman. It is absolutely not true that the wine glass is grafted to his right hand. It was his idea to run a restaurant where garlic, in large doses, is an ingredient of every course. Every course? Yes, every course.

On the morning of the great summit the summiteers started to arrive. Charles Perry, noted 'gastrojournalist' came by plane. Charles is an associate editor of *Rolling Stone* magazine and unexpectedly an eminent scholar of Medieval Arabic. He is an expert in ancient Middle Eastern cookery. To fly to Truckee, he stifled a cold and interrupted work on his new book, a history of the hippies in San Francisco's Haight-Ashbury district. Film-makers Les Blank and Maureen Gosling drove to the summit. The finale of their recent film *Garlic is as Good as Ten Mothers* is a glorious scene depicting Robert massaging a naked lady with aïoli. (The recipe is set out further on—for aïoli, that is!) Bruce Aidells' chef at Berkeley's 'Poulet' arrived by train. He brought with him a yard of his special garlic sausage which was to be devoured with special mustard, especially flown in for this event from Wiltshire Tracklements in England.

The group waited. Only the chairman had still to come. The restaurant is what used to be the living-room, dining-room and centre hallway of the old house. Graffitti completely covers the walls save for a series of paintings depicting the lore of garlic. 'Garlic takes your breath away'; 'make love, eat garlic'; 'after eating at Vieille Maison, you really know who your friends are!' About half the slogans refer in one way or another to garlic's reputation as an aphrodisiac . . . 'Eat garlic and you'll get it tonight!' is hardly subtle. If either Oscar Wilde or Dorothy Parker ever ate at Vieille Maison, obviously they did not put their pens to the wall.

The room is intimate but not oppressive. Garlic braids hang everywhere. A giant picture of Charlie Chaplin commemorates the use of the house by the cast during the filming of *The Gold Rush*. Robert's claim that the building was once Truckee's finest bordello seems reasonable.

The chairman is about to enter. John Harris (formerly Lloyd J. Harris) has been called the 'Head Garlic-head' of Lovers of the Stinking Rose (LSR), an organization of fanatical aliophiles. His newsletter, *The Garlic Times*, is the allium world's chief organ. His book, the subject's most comprehensive and funny, is called unastonishingly *The Book of Garlic*.

The following is the official minutes, including the complete transcript, of the Truckee Garlic summit.

JOHN HARRIS: Well, I'd like to call to odour the official summit of the Lovers of the Stinking Rose, and I'll put on my ceremonial garlic turban and call a toast.
(Struggles to keep cermonial garlic turban on his head.)
CHARLES PERRY (CHARLIE): A garlic toast?
JOHN HARRIS (JOHN): A garlic toast! And a prayer. May the Gods of garlic breathe upon us . . . And if we can survive that, we can survive anything.
(Chorus of cheers. Clinking glasses.)
JOHN: Now let's have the first course.
(Amora arrives with a large crock of Aïoli.)
Well, it looks like a really great *Aïoli*. Do you want to pass a plate or shall we pass the crock?
LES BLANK: Let's pass the crock.
JOHN: The *Aïoli* is always passed to the left.
BRUCE AIDELLS *(Holds up glass.)*: To Amora and Robert . . .
JOHN: . . . and their fine garlic establishment . . .
(Glasses clink.) . . the old house.

A garlic toast at the Garlic Summit at Truckee in California, 1981. The chairman, John Lloyd Harris, is wearing his ceremonial garlic turban.

CHARLIE: If you really want to talk about 'old', that's garlic. I've found that every place civilized for a long time has a lot of garlic in it. The ancient Egyptians had many words for garlic. All the semitic languages have words for garlic and the Sumerians borrowed their's from them. In ancient China it was called *Suan* (Phonetic) and has been the word for thousands

Aïoli

This is the garlic mayonnaise that is traditionally served in Provence with poached salt cod, potatoes, carrots, green beans, artichokes, chickpeas, beets, snails and hardboiled eggs. It is a great favourite for Friday lunch in Provence, and a favourite at any time among garlic lovers. It is magnificent with boiled lobster or

SERVES SIX TO EIGHT
12–16 large cloves garlic
$\frac{1}{2}$ teaspoon/2.5 ml salt

Peel the garlic cloves and place them in a mortar. Pound them until smooth, or crush them in a garlic press and place them in a mortar. Add the salt and mix well. Add the egg yolks and pound into the garlic until the mixture is smooth. Then beat in the lemon juice. Start adding the oil, a drop at a time while continuing to pound or beat the

Provençal Garlic Mayonnaise

giant prawns (shrimp). For a robust aïoli *estimate roughly 2 large cloves of garlic per person. It is possible to use a garlic press for crushing the garlic to speed things up a little in making the mayonnaise, but making it in a blender is not satisfactory. Making the* aïoli *by hand achieves a better result.*

3 egg yolks
2 tablespoons/30 ml lemon juice
16 fl oz/450 ml (2 cups) olive oil

mixture. When the mixture becomes thick it is possible to add the oil in a thin stream, beating constantly, as for any mayonnaise. Never add more oil than can be immediately absorbed. If the finished sauce is too thick, thin with a little tepid water or chicken stock. Serve with fish, meat, vegetables or salads.

of years. In northwest India there was an old Indus valley culture which I think was pretty garlicky. It was obliterated by the Indo-Europeans, who didn't have a word for garlic. They *did* have a word for 'leek' which became the Sanskrit word for 'garlic', I think they must have found a lot of garlic but no leeks.

[It is generally accepted that the English word 'garlic' is derived from the old Scandinavian *gar* for spear and *leac* meaning herbs. It is obviously descriptive of garlic's spearlike leaves. In French, garlic is *ail*, from the Latin *allium*. The German is *knoblauch*; Italian, *aglio*; Russian, *chesnok*; Japanese, *nin-niku*; Arabic, *tum*; Indian, *lashuna*.]

The word for garlic spread out from the ancient civilized areas. Its history goes back to the peoples who learned how to cultivate the plants and raise their own. In fact, I think of it as one of the mainsprings of civilization. The garlic is dependent on us, and we are dependent upon it . . . a true symbiosis. It's part of the human metabolism and, I think, the human being is really part and parcel of the garlic plan.

JOHN: It sounds like we're getting into the religious significance of garlic and its companionship with mankind throughout time.

CHARLIE: I know you have studied the Tibetan myth of garlic's invention.

JOHN: The Gods in heaven had a fight and the evil god was killed by the good gods. His body fell to earth in thousands of pieces and from each, sprung garlic.

CHARLIE: What does it mean?

JOHN: It means that garlic incorporates some of the divine essence of the gods themselves and that's why we find ourselves today celebrating garlic . . . which reminds me: to garlic!

(Glasses clink.)

[In Moslem mythology, when the triumphant Satan left the garden of Eden, onions sprang up from his right footprint and garlic from the left.]

CHARLIE: There is a festival in Egypt as ancient as the Pharaohs. It's called 'Sniffing of the Breezes', an interesting name for a festival featuring garlic so prominently. It is the first day of spring. Dressed in their new clothes, everybody goes down to the banks of the Nile. They set off fireworks, eat garlic and wear garlic. They then smash garlic over their doorframes, put it in their beds and all over their houses. It cleanses.

JOHN: This seems connected to a whole range of traditions like hanging garlic in windows or protecting newborn children by putting garlic under their pillows and hanging it over their cribs. It's a protection against outside evil influences. There is also the ritual of keeping bride and groom separate before a wedding. Garlic is hung in the bride's room to ensure that no malicious influences interrupt the ceremony.

BRUCE: Charlie, when do you think garlic first started appearing in cuisine?

CHARLIE: As soon as there was a cuisine . . . even before that, garlic is one of the basic foods.

[There is some evidence that the plant originated in what is now the Soviet Republic of Kirgizskaya, which lies on the border between the USSR and the most westerly reaches of the People's Republic of China. The ancient silk route passed through the area on its way to nearby Tashkent and Samarkand.]

JOHN: Garlic goes back six thousand years or more, beyond reported history, for sure. In the Bible, it is mentioned as one of the foods the Hebrews missed when they were wandering in the desert.

[NUMBERS Chapter 11: 4,5. And the mixt multitude that was among them fell a lusting; and the children of Israel also wept again, and said, who shall give us flesh to eat? We remember the fish, which we did eat in Egypt freely; the cucumbers, and the melons, and the leeks, and the onions, and the garlick:]

You have to remember that thousands of years ago there wasn't a separation between cuisine and medicine. We are sort of a fallen people. We divide our medicine from our food. To the ancients, natural substances growing indigenously in the soil were both food and medicine. Diet was a very sophisticated set of principles balancing nutrition and the prevention and cure of disease. Garlic was very much part of the combination from the beginning.

CHARLIE: That's one of the reasons why there's so much garlic in the Egyptian tombs.

MAUREEN: Isn't that where garlic was responsible for the first strike in history?

CHARLIE: Right, in the time of the Pharaohs, the workers on the pyramids went on strike.

JOHN: They wouldn't go back to work because their ration of garlic, leeks and onions was cut. This is recorded in the pyramids and in ancient historical writings.

CHARLIE: All they were getting to eat besides plants like garlic were bread and beer. It's interesting that they didn't strike for either bread or beer!

JOHN: By the way, this *Aïoli* we are enjoying right now is an ancient dish. *Aïoli*, which is simply garlic, eggs and olive oil, gives its name to a series of ritualistic festivals celebrated in the south of France and throughout the Mediterranean.

CHARLIE: In one city in this country, *Aïoli* is a traditional condiment. That's Mobile, Alabama! However, since they no longer speak French, they call it high holy sauce!

(General uproar. Robert enters, flirts with the one woman diner and then itemizes the rest of the menu . . . A special soup; baked garlic cloves on mushrooms; California game hen stuffed with forty cloves of garlic; goat cheese incensed with garlic; and garlic sorbet.)

BRUCE: A fantastic menu! Of course we can only eat so much, but some of the best use of garlic is with fish or other sea foods.

Escargots Bourguignonne is the classic dish: snail in its shell stuffed with garlic, chopped parsley and butter. It is then sizzled and comes to the table with such a fantastic aroma you immediately begin to salivate.

Robert Charles, the *patron* of La Vieille Maison, who has fulfilled his dream of opening a restaurant where every course is based on garlic, including dessert and wines.

Spaghetti Vongole comes from Italy. You take very thin spaghetti and blanch it to the point of *al dente*. Simply sauté garlic in olive oil with parsley and quickly add little baby clams. In the last second, toss the noddles in, throw in your cheese and it's wonderful.

JOHN: The smell of garlic wafting from a restaurant in New York created a neighbourhood scandal. The local residents tried to have the place closed. The case actually got to the Supreme Court of New York. The judge ruled that the odour of garlic and other cooking smells were beneficial to civilization. The neighbours couldn't close the restaurant.

[Would-be lawyers can find the case cited as *Sourian vs Saleh*; New York Law Journal, 2 January, 1975.]

(Enter Amora: chorus of oohs and aahs.)

AMORA: Soup John Lloyd Harris!

(Slurp, slurp.)

BRUCE: John, take a bow. You should be extremly fortunate to have this fantastic soup named after you. It's absolutely delicious!

CHARLIE: It looks beautiful.

JOHN: It's really a variation of *soupe à l'oignon*, the classic onion soup of France, which Robert has changed to include garlic, a large quantity of garlic. *(Sips.)* This looks like . . . crust of bread and cheese on top . . .

BRUCE: No . . . It's not a crust on top . . . It's cheese and egg cooked just like a soufflé or custard . . . There's no bread in it whatsoever . . . It's really light . . . It's a beautiful idea . . .

[In a short discussion of aliophobes (garlic haters) John Harris explained that in every century and culture garlic was adored by the masses and shunned by the clergy and aristocracy. In certain class-conscious societies, like Britain, garlic taboos are only just now in the process of being broken. In his book, John Harris goes so far as to speculate whether the eating of garlic by the pyramid builders was the original cause of anti-Semitism. In New York, there is an old Yiddish saying, which translates, 'Three nickles will get you into the subway, but only one knoble (garlic) will get you a seat.']

(Amora enters.)

BRUCE: Now, what do we have here?

JOHN: Champignons.

BRUCE: Wonderful, mmm, your favourite, John. Baked garlic with a sauce of garlic sprinkled on top with chopped garlic!

(Laughter.)

And I notice this version is garnished with

Soupe 'Lloyd Harris'

Onion and Garlic Soup

SERVES FOUR	salt and freshly ground black pepper
4 oz/100 g (¼ cup) butter	½ teaspoon/2.5 ml crumbled thyme
6 large onions, peeled and finely chopped	1¾ pints/1 litre (4 cups) chicken stock
4–6 large cloves garlic, peeled and minced	4 large eggs
1 teaspoon/5 ml plain (all-purpose) flour	4 oz/100 g (1 cup) Gruyère or Emmenthal cheese, grated
16 fl oz/450 ml (2 cups) dry white wine (Chablis)	4 fl oz/100 ml (½ cup) whipping cream

Heat the butter in a heavy flameproof casserole. Add the onions and garlic and sauté until the onions are a light, golden brown. Stir in the flour and sauté for 1–2 minutes longer. Add the wine, salt, pepper and thyme and simmer, uncovered, over a low heat for 30 minutes, stirring from time to time. Add the chicken stock, bring back to the boil, cover and cook in a preheated moderate oven, 350°F, 180°C, Gas Mark 4, for 2 hours.

Serve the soup in 4 small ovenproof soup bowls. Beat the eggs separately and add one to each serving, stirring it into the soup to mix well. Sprinkle with the Gruyère or Emmenthal cheese and cook in the oven for 10 minutes longer. Add 1 fl oz/25 ml (2 tablespoons) whipping cream to each serving. Serve straight away.

mushrooms, little mushrooms.

AMORA: And, to go with that I have a bottle of Stevenot Zinfandel with a clove of garlic . . . would you believe, bottled just for us.

(Chorus, of Oh's, wonderful, etc.)

JOHN *(sips)*: Mmm, it has a bulbous nose. It has an undertone of alium. Delicious, very drinkable, palatable and potable.

AMORA: You must realize, in the bottom of this bottle is a clove of garlic.

JOHN: The ritual is that the one who gets the clove is the lucky person for the evening.

AMORA: Right!

JOHN: Garlic has always been called a cure-all. One Roman naturalist prescribed sixty-one

A common sight in India, separating the cloves of garlic using a large sieve and the wind to remove the loose outer skins. It is not widely known that garlic is an essential part of much of Indian cooking but it is almost always eaten cooked not raw.

garlic remedies for sixty-one separate illnesses. Contemporary research seems to validate the use of garlic for so many things; like lowering blood cholesterol, dilating the arteries, killing intestinal bacteria and invigorating hormonal secretions.

Garlic was on the verge of being accepted as a valid antibiotic before the development of synthetic antibiotics in the 1940s. Because of dangerous side effects in some of the synthetics, people are looking again at garlic. One researcher I know in India is attempting to show that a clove a day will reduce the chances of arterial sclerosis and other heart-related diseases. Right now, his research is being duplicated at both Georgetown University and the University of Minnesota. They have shown that on rabbits fed a rich diet of fats, garlic cuts down the accumulation of cholesterol in the blood and dilates the arteries preventing the formation of clots. In terms of curing everything from cancer to the common cold, there is as yet no

definite proof . . . but there are indications. The Chinese have just published the results of a study undertaken in two adjoining provinces. One province had a high incidence of bowel cancer and low consumption of garlic. The neighbouring province, just the opposite, high garlic consumption and a low incidence of bowel cancer. The research seems to show that garlic enters the colon itself and breaks down cancer-inducing products.

LES: In Peru I ate one or two cloves a day chopped in fresh orange juice. I didn't get any of the intestinal parasites others did.

JOHN: The Japanese are conducting research to show that garlic cuts down certain industrial pollutants. They even have a clinic devoted to garlic remedies. Garlic is sprayed from a shower-like apparatus onto people suffering everything from hepatitis to frostbite; it's really amazing.

[John is referring to Yoshio Kato's Oyama Garlic Laboratory in Amagasaki, Japan.]

Katsuo No Tataki   *Grilled Bonito*

Bonito, *a member of the mackerel family, and related to tuna, is found on both sides of the Atlantic. The striped* bonito *or skipjack is found in the warmer parts* *of all the oceans so that it should be possible to get the right fish for this delicious Japanese dish in which garlic plays an important part.*

SERVES FOUR TO SIX	
2 lb/900 g bonito *fillets with skin left on*	*2 tablespoons/30 ml spring onions (scallions), chopped*
1 tablespoon crushed garlic	*2 tablespoons/30 ml finely grated* daikon *(white radish)*
2 tablespoons/30 ml grated fresh ginger root	*1 tablespoon/15 ml* shiso *(beefsteak leaves), chopped*
2 tablespoons/30 ml shallots, peeled and finely chopped	*3 fl oz/75 ml ($\frac{1}{3}$ cup)* ponzu *(citrus vinegar)*
	3 fl oz/75 ml ($\frac{1}{3}$ cup) soy sauce

Cut the fish fillets into rectangles, 4–5 inches/ 10–12 cm by 2 inches/5 cm. Grill the fish quickly over charcoal just long enough to cook the skin side, and the flesh side without browning it. Quickly drop the fish into a bowl of cold water and ice cubes to stop the cooking process. Lift the fish out immediately. It should remain in the water for only about 30 seconds. Pat the fish dry with kitchen paper, then cut into $\frac{1}{2}$-inch/1.5-cm slices. Arrange the fish on a large serving dish.

In a bowl mix together the garlic, ginger, shallots, spring onions, radish, *shiso, ponzu* and soy

to make a sauce. Using hands or a pastry brush, coat the fish with the sauce. Serve the rest of the sauce in small bowls as a dipping sauce with the fish.

In Japan the dish would be garnished with fresh seaweeds. These may be available in Japanese shops. *Shiso* (beefsteak leaves) are often available in markets selling Japanese foods. They are worth looking out for. *Ponzu,* Japanese citrus vinegar, is always available in bottled form in Japanese markets. If it is not obtainable, use a very light white wine vinegar mixed in equal proportions with lemon juice.

The common denominator in all of these potential cures is garlic's sulphur content. Garlic is rich in various sulphur compounds. These are responsible not only for the odour but for garlic's ability to reduce bacteria and cholesterol.

[The ancient Egyptians used garlic to test for pregnancy. A clove of garlic was inserted 'in the womb' and left overnight. In the morning, if there was a garlicky taste in the mouth, the woman was supposed to be pregnant. It is now claimed that this test, based on the stimulation of the clove by pregnancy urine, has some validity.

The fact still remains that no garlic 'cure' has been fully accepted by modern medical science. Still, history, literature and legend, from every period of human experience abound with such stories and claims.]

BRUCE: Garlic is an interesting vegetable, surprisingly, it's a member of the lily family . . . Latin name, *Allium sativum*. The seeds are sterile on the domestic garlic, which means for its cultivation, it's dependent upon humans. It is cultivated in a 'vegetative' manner; simply take a clove and stick it in the ground.

CHARLIE: That's evidence of how long people have been raising garlic. They live in a symbiotic relationship with us. They are part of us . . . that is the real human beings among us.

I've often thought that there is only one way to understand the prejudice against the smell of garlic. Garlic doesn't smell like bad breath; bad breath smells like illness or not brushing your teeth. Garlic smells like food. The only explanation is that the prejudice is political. The vendetta benefits only one class of person, I use the term loosely, the kind of person who sleeps in a coffin!

(Nervous laughter.)

I mean vampires! and their dupes and running dogs! I've noticed a lot of inroads they have been making in our culture. Recently, we've been having revisionist vampire movies. Vampires are portrayed as young, cute and sensitive. They even suffer! Well, I never go abroad without a bulb. None of the streets are safe.

MAUREEN: Charlie, have you ever been attacked by a vampire?

CHARLIE: No, it works!

[Here is an excerpt from *The Natural History of the Vampire*, by Anthony Masters:

PROTECTION AGAINST RUMANIAN VAMPIRES

It was essential that in all circumstances heavy precautions should be taken at burials of suspected vampires. These were roughly the same as those of the rest of Eastern Europe, as follows:

(1) At one blow a stake must be driven through the heart or navel.

(2) Small stones or grains of incense must be placed in all the extremities so that the vampire would have something to nibble on awakening — thus diverting his attention from more succulent fare.

(3) Garlic must be stuffed in his mouth.

(4) As another delaying factor, millet must be scattered over the vampire's body, as the vampire delays his exit from the tomb until each grain of millet has been eaten or counted.

(5) The corpse has to be buried face downwards.

(6) Wild, thorny roses must be strung around the outside of the coffin in order to impede the vampire's progress out of the tomb.

These, however, were only the minimum general precautions and more intricate preventions differed from district to district.]

BRUCE: Robert, you're bringing us dinner . . . The *pièce de résistance*!

(Robert enters carrying a tray.)

JOHN: My God!

(Chorus of aaahs!)

(Robert hands the tray to Amora and commences to kiss Maureen's hand . . . her arm . . . her shoulder.)

ROBERT: I am a Frenchman.

MAUREEN: I know!

ROBERT: See, this is a clove of garlic. Now, I want you to close your eyes and remember . . . garlic is love.

(Murmurs of contentment.)

You're going with me from now on?

BRUCE: I'd like to toast a dirty old Frenchman.

(Laughter.)

May the world continue to produce them in vast quantities.

(Glasses clink. Amora has been serving.)

JOHN: This is *Poulet Ali avec Forty-Eight Cloves of Garlic.*

CHARLIE: Chicken with forty cloves of garlic goes back an awful long time. I've seen it written in Arabic in a thirteenth-century recipe from Spain. It was called 'Four Oukiers (phonetic) of Garlic'. An oukier weighed about an ounce. Four per chicken meant a quarter pound or about forty cloves. The recipe was identical to this, except they mashed the garlic and added some spices and almonds. They sealed the chicken with a flour paste. The recipe ends by saying that when it is served and the top removed a wonderful aroma fills the entire room.

JOHN: Until recently, no one but Charlie had ever heard of forty cloves of garlic in one dish. Even French *haute cuisine* recipes call for cloves of garlic to be removed before serving. Only in the south of France did you actually eat the garlic itself.

MAUREEN: But when it's cooked like this, the garlic is the best part.

JOHN: Our taste buds are so used to extensive amounts of garlic, we wouldn't even taste a stew with one clove that has been removed. But, for the delicate palates of the nobility, maybe that was a lot.

MAUREEN: Don't you think that garlic is becoming acceptable now to the . . . rich . . . the upper crust?

JOHN: Well, it's like Amora says, 'It's chic to reek.'

(Amora enters with yet another tray.)

AMORA: This is really going to tell . . .

(Gasps.)

JOHN: The garlic lovers . . .

AMORA: From the garlic lovers . . .

JOHN: This is a garlic *boursin*, a French-style goat cheese with walnuts on the outside and infused with garlic. You eat it with pears and raisins . . .

Poulet aux quarante gousses d'ail   *Forty-clove Chicken*

This is a version of the famous Provençal dish Poulet aux quarante gousses d'ail, *chicken with forty cloves of garlic. As the author of this version of the dish says, 'Don't let the amount of garlic scare you; the garlic after prolonged cooking has a mild nutty flavour.' Anyone who has cooked this dish, or its companion dish cooked with a leg of lamb, can testify that forty cloves of garlic are more than forty times better than one!*

SERVES FOUR

4 fl oz/100 ml (½ cup) olive oil	nutmeg, freshly grated
4 sticks celery, chopped	40 cloves garlic, peeled
1 tablespoon/15 ml parsley, finely chopped	2 fl oz/50 ml (¼ cup) Cognac
1 tablespoon/15 ml tarragon, fresh if possible, chopped	3 oz/75 g (¾ cup) plain (all-purpose) flour
1 x 3–3½ lb/1.4–1.5 kg chicken, cut into quarters	water
salt and freshly ground black pepper	toast

Heat the oil in a large, heavy casserole. Add the celery, parsley and tarragon and sauté them lightly for 2–3 minutes. Season the chicken pieces with salt, pepper and nutmeg. Add the chicken to the casserole and sauté it briefly, turning it once or twice. Add the garlic cloves and the Cognac.

Mix the flour with enough water in a bowl to make a stiff paste. Cover the casserole with its lid, then seal the lid with the flour and water paste, pressing the paste firmly round the rim. Bake the chicken in a preheated, moderate oven, 375°F, 190°C, Gas Mark 5, for 1½ hours. Take out of the oven and remove the pastry seal when you are ready to serve the chicken.

Serve with toast on which the garlic, which will have cooked to a purée, can be spread.

Garlic *grappes* on sale at a market in southern France where the plant has always been an important part of the local Provençal cooking. Southern France produces some of the world's finest garlic, and the pinkish tinge, caused by the soil conditions is highly desirable.

BRUCE: Robert made this himself from cream cheese, some Swiss cheese, sour cream and a load of garlic.

JOHN: Eat the pear with it because the pear cuts the . . .

CHARLIE: Isn't that cheating?

JOHN: No, that's treating garlic as a science. We are not so crass as to think raw garlic or garlic straight is all we like.

(Another tray arrives. It is loaded with tall frosty dessert glasses filled with a bright emerald green substance.)

JOHN: This meal needs as fitting conclusion, a fruity sweet garlicky dessert.

(Howls of approval.)

   Sorbet à garlic.

AMORA: Sebet, there is no 'r'.

BRUCE: Oh! Green garlic . . . you read my mind.

CHARLIE: Wow!

LES: God!

(It is impossible adequately to describe the atmosphere in the dining-room. The air hangs heavy, dense with layer upon layer of garlic essence. Every corner, crease, fold, pore reeks, yet the diners sit numb, unaware. They are beyond taste. Garlic has penetrated even to that inner tiny spot which is pure self, the swelling place of the soul. They now glide upon planes of pure consciousness so lofty, that if the authorities found out, garlic would be made illegal.)

JOHN: You guys, this has been a meal that will go down in history as one of the great stinking rose summits.

(Murmurs of yes, oh God, what an honour.)

CHARLIE: How can we top this next year?

BRUCE: The next meal will have to be on Everest.

(It's night. As they stumble down the old wooden steps even Truckee's frosty mountain air cannot remove the glaze from their eyes. The town sits silent, deserted, yet visible. The railway tracks, the gas station, the main street all sleep in a raw unearthly light. A distant dog howls at the cold full moon which hangs above La Vieille Maison. The garlic eaters notice, but tonight of all nights, they will not be afraid of the forces of darkness.)

Garlic has become a cult food. Garlic junkies from all over America flock to the small Californian town of Gilroy for its annual festival. 'Garlic-heads' make and eat tons of garlic soups, breads, stews, soufflés and even puddings and wines. The event now attracts tens of thousands of people, proving that it is 'chic to reek'.

10
CURRY

. . . the very asking of certain questions in India makes them dissolve into something and then something else.

E. M. FORSTER *A Passage to India*

Curry powder has a bad press. No modern cookery writer, whether Indian or otherwise, seems to have a good thing to say about it. Even the word 'curry' is anathema to all but those heretics who write 'curry' cookery books. The Indian cookery expert Madhur Jaffrey has said: 'To me the word "curry" is as degrading to India's great cuisine as the term "chop suey" was to China's . . .' and she imagined curry's origin:

A British officer in full uniform (possibly a young David Niven) is standing under a palm tree looking fondly at his bungalow as Indian servants go back and forth carrying heavy trunks from the house into a waiting carriage. When the carriage is loaded, the servants line up on the verandah with tears in their eyes. The officer himself, overcome with emotion, turns to Khansamah (cook):

OFFICER: How I shall miss your delicious cooking. My good man, why don't you mix me a box of those wonderful spices that you have been using. I will carry it back with me to Surrey, and there, whenever I feel nostalgic about India, I will take out this box and sprinkle some of your aromatic spice mixture into my bubbling pot.

KHANSAMAH: Yes, Sa'ab, as you say, Sa'ab. (Runs off into kitchen.)

Scene changes to kitchen, where cook is seen hastily throwing spices into the box. He runs back with it to officer.

KHANSAMAH: Here is the box, Sa'ab. Sa'ab, if your friends also like, for a sum of two rupees each, I can make more boxes for them as well . . .

Several years later: former cook is now successful exporter. He is seen filling boxes marked 'Best curry powder'. When the boxes are filled, he puts them in a large crate and stamps them in black: '*For Export Only*'.

What so infuriates cookery writers is that while curry is so strongly linked to Indian food, it represents the very antithesis of the philosophy of Indian cuisine. India is a very large country. In geographical area, population and cultural diversity it exceeds Western Europe. The range of culinary tastes, styles and taboos is so vast that most generalizations are rendered meaningless, yet, from the meat-loving Muslims of northern Punjab to the strictly vegetarian Hindus of southern Kerala there seems to be an inherent understanding of spices. Unlike the West, there are no written recipes. Dishes, identified by their ingredients and methods of cooking, are brought to life and made distinct by the skilful use of spices. The same dish cooked by two different chefs will taste different, yet, both will be 'correct'. This system, or non-system, has firm roots in Indian philosophy.

Traditionally, seasoning depended upon circumstance; was it hot or cold outside? What time of day will the dish be eaten? Is the diner in good spirits? Is the sun shining? Cooks finely adjusted their ratios of spices to a series of physical and metaphysical queries. (The English, on the other hand, only put such questions when playing the game of cricket, which is, perhaps, why the Indians are so taken by it.)

A map of India showing
dishes from various parts of
the subcontinent.
Traditionally, the staple
food of the south was rice
and of the north,
unleavened bread. Highly
spiced sauces flavoured
these bland carbohydrates.
These sauces were the
forerunners of modern
curry. In the foreground
are some of the dishes of
southern India: Kerala
prawns, ripe papaya and
grapefruit, shahi tukra,
mutton korma, idli,
sambar and dosa.

Spices and food in general were an integral part of the Indian system of well-being known as Ayurvedic thought. Unlike medicine, which is often obsessed with symptoms, Ayurveda is a holistic arrangement of subtle balances designed to nourish and maintain good health. Every food has a temperature, not a physical temperature, but an effect upon the body system which is expressed as hot or cold. Nuts, tea and meat are warming, while coffee, tomatoes, and fish are cooling. Ancient texts set out the many rules in minute detail. The point is that sensitive cooks, when seasoning, took into consideration the general health and immediate needs of those who were to eat the food.

Chefs are also artists. The array of spices set before the cook can be compared to the paints on a painter's palette. In the lavish courts of India's Mogul rulers, chefs were highly honoured and rewarded, often taking great pains to ensure their secrets remained concealed even from others in the same kitchen.

Today in India, as always, most spices are purchased in the market from spice merchants whose relationships with customers and their families has often lasted for generations. In the past, an assistant, sent by the merchant to the purchaser's residence, ground the spices in a large circular stone mortar. The preparation of just one kilogram of ground spice could occupy the better part of a day. Now, most of the vast collection of spices available in the markets is prepared by grinders at the merchants' stalls. Everything is available all the year round, but generally people prepare enough spice in advance to last over the two months of the humid summer monsoons when grinding is more difficult.

A few years ago, one of London's famous Promenade concerts was devoted entirely to the music of India. It started at 11 pm and ended at 7 am the following morning. The reason for this unusual time was to permit the audience to hear, at the appropriate hour, *ragas*, or Indian musical pieces, composed for the night and early morning hours. The musicians would only play a '3-am raga' at 3 am. They would not even permit it to be

Above: A professional spice grinder, a sight less frequent in India today. The spice grinder visits homes in the city, grinding both fresh and dried spices required by the household. Here she is preparing a wet masala from chillies, coriander, garlic, onions and ginger.
Facing page above: The spice market in Delhi is one of the largest in the world. Spices in India are usually bought whole and then ground at home according to need.
Facing page below: Commercially ground chilli in Delhi.

recorded and re-broadcast at any other time. The Raga is an improvisation around a central structure wherein the spirit of place, time and the players' own inner feelings all influence and change the music.

So it is with the Indian chef, each creation is unique. It is nonsense to think that Western chefs and musicians are not affected by the same considerations. Of course they are. But often, the training in the East is designed to bring ambient factors more directly into the realm of consciousness, thus lessening the separation between the artist and the immediate environment. Can you imagine an Indian cook going into a supermarket and picking off the shelf a can of spice mixed at some factory, and then using that same mixture in each dish cooked? Of course not. The vast majority of the people of India, who also represent

a sizeable proportion of the earth's population, has never even heard the word 'curry' and would not know what it meant if they did. 'Curry' is an English word. That it is so associated with India is what makes Indian cookery writers cross, but, does that in itself mean that curry powder is a bad thing?

Curry powder is a seasoning, and a seasoning is anything added to food to improve its flavour. Flavour is a complex appreciation of the total sensations perceived whenever food or drink is consumed. It is an ironic trick of nature that the most staple of human foods have the least flavour. Raw meats, cereals, milk, fish and most root vegetables can be categorized as being low in flavour. They are also the most nutritious and vital of foods. To this group can be added water, which while low in flavour and nutrition is essential to human survival. Next, there is a class of foods possessing moderate nutritional value and a medium flavour . . . fruits, nuts and some aromatic vegetables. The final group has little or no nutritional value but is extremely high in flavour . . . herbs, spices, vanilla, cacao and so on. The essence of cuisine has always been to blend artfully the products in the latter two groups, to enhance the flavour of the essential life-sustaining foods in the first group. A constant theme of this book is

---

Hyderabadi Katchi Biriyani — *Lamb Biriyani*

This dish is from Uttar Pradesh in the north of India where lamb is a large part of the local cuisine.

SERVES SIX

2 lb/900 g lean, boned lamb cut into 1½-inch/4-cm cubes	1 x 2-inch/5-cm stick of cinnamon, broken into 2–3 pieces
8 oz/225 g (1 cup) ghee	1 teaspoon/5 ml black cumin seeds
3 medium onions, peeled and finely chopped	1 oz/25 g (½ cup) fresh mint leaves, finely chopped
4 oz/100 g (½ cup) plain yogurt	1 oz/25 g (½ cup) fresh coriander leaves, finely chopped
2 fresh hot green chilli peppers	8 fl oz/225 ml (1 cup) lemon juice
1 x 4-inch/10-cm fresh root of ginger	salt
4 cloves garlic	2 lb/900 g Basmati rice
6 green cardamom pods	3 oz/75 g (¾ cup) plain (all-purpose) flour
6 cloves	water

Put the lamb pieces into a bowl with cold water to cover and let them soak for 1 hour. Then, thoroughly drain the lamb and prick the pieces with a fork. Heat the ghee in a heavy frying pan (skillet) and sauté the onions until they are a rich golden brown. Put the yogurt into a bowl and stir in the onion mixture. Reduce the chillies, ginger and garlic to a paste in a blender or food processor.

Add the lamb pieces to the paste, mixing well. Prick the lamb again with a fork. Cover and set aside for 30 minutes, then add to the yogurt mixture. Remove the cardamom seeds from the pods and lightly crush them. Add to the yogurt and meat. Add the cloves, cinnamon, cumin seeds, mint and coriander leaves. Stir in the lemon juice and season to taste with salt. Stir to mix and then leave in a cool place to marinate for 4–5 hours.

Thoroughly wash the rice in several changes of water. Drain well. Put the meat mixture into a heavy saucepan and add the rice. Stir well to mix. Cover with a tight-fitting lid, then seal with a flour and water paste. To do this, mix the flour with enough water to make a stiff paste and press this firmly round the rim.

Bake in a preheated moderate oven, 400°F, 200°C, Gas Mark 6, for 15 minutes. Reduce the heat to 275°F, 130°C, Gas Mark 1 and cook for 25–30 minutes longer or until the meat is tender and all the liquid absorbed. Remove the pastry seal and open the saucepan, standing back to avoid the steam. Leave uncovered for a few minutes, then fluff the rice with a fork and serve immediately.

that the seemingly simple human craving for flavour was, and perhaps still is, the force behind some of the most important geo-political events in history. One of these events occurred in 1608 when Sir Thomas Roe, of the East India Company, obtained permission for Britain to trade in India from the Mogul Emperor. Sir Thomas's secretary, later the Reverend Edward Terry, described a banquet given by the Emperor:

The Asaph Chan entertained my Lord Ambassador in a very spacious and a beautiful tent. The tent was kept full of a very pleasant perfume; in which scents the King and Grandees there take very much delight. The floor of the tent was first covered all over with very rich and large carpets . . . and these were covered again with pure white and fine Callico cloths, and all these covered with very many dishes of silver, but for the greater part of those silver dishes they were not larger than our largest trencher-plates, the brims of them all gilt.

We sat in that large room as it were in a triangle: the Ambassador on Asaph Chan's right hand a good distance from him, and myself below; all of us in the ground as they there all do when they eat, with our faces looking each to the other, and every one of us had his several mess. The Ambassador had more dishes by ten and I less by ten, than our entertainer had, yet, for my part I had fifty dishes.

They were all set before us at once, and little paths left betwixt them, that our entertainer's servants might come and reach them to us one after another and so they did so that I tasted of all set before me, and of most did but taste, though all of them tasted very well.

Now, of the provision itself, for our large dishes, they were filled with rice dressed. And this rice was presented to us, some of it white, in its own proper colour, some of it yellow, with saffron, and some of it was made green, and some of it put in purple colour . . . And with rice thus ordered, several of our dishes were furnished; and very many more of them with flesh of several kinds, and with hens and

When the Mogul emperors came to northern India they continued the local tradition of elaborately spicing the food and brought Indian food to a magnificent new height.

with other sorts of foul cut in pieces, as before observed in their Indian Cookery. To these we had many jellie and Culices; Rice ground to flour and then boyled and after sweetened with sugar, candy and rosewater to be eaten cold. The flower of rice mingled with sweet almonds, made as small as they could, and with some of the most fleshy parts hens, stewed with it and after, the flesh beaten to pieces, that it could not be discerned, all made sweet with rose-water and sugar candy, and scented with amber-greece which was another of our dishes, and a most lucious one, with the Portuguls call "Manger Real", food for a king.

Edward Terry was one of the first Englishmen to taste the delights of India. He experienced at first hand Mogul cookery at the height of its magnificence. He also observed something else:

> For the boiling of flesh in water, or baking or roasting any flesh, are pieces of cookery (if I observed well) they know not; but they stew all their flesh as their kid and other venison cut into snippets or slices or little parts, to which they put onions and herbs and roots and ginger (which they take green out of the earth) and other spices, with some butter which ingredients when as they are well proportioned, make a food that is exceedingly pleasing to all palates, at their first tasting thereof most savoury meat, happily that very dish which Jacob made for his father Isaac, when he got the blessing.

Whether or not the dish was the one Jacob made for Isaac, Edward Terry had seen what later Englishmen would call a 'curry'.

Curry is more of a mystical concept than a thing, and therein lies its problem of definition. Most writers claim the word 'curry' is derived from the Tamil (South India) *Kari*, but they differ on the meaning of even that! Some say that the original *Kari* meant 'bazaar' or 'marketplace'. Others claim that no curry is authentic unless prepared with yogurt, which is the real meaning of *Kari*. The arbiters of colonial language were Colonel Henry Yule and A. C. Burnell, who, together in the nineteenth century, wrote *A Glossary of Colloquial Anglo-Indian Words or Phrases*, known as 'Hobson-Jobson'. This excerpt is taken from the entry on curry:

> In the East the staple food consists of some cereal, either (as in North India) in the form of flour-baked into unleavened cakes, or boiled in the grain, as rice is. Such food having little taste, some small quantity of a much more savoury preparation is added as a relish, or kitchen, to use the phrase of our forefathers. And this is in fact the proper office of *curry* in native diet. It consists of meat, fish, fruit, or vegetables, cooked with a quantity of bruised spices and turmeric, and a little of this gives a flavour to a large mass of rice!

Note, the rice or bread is the central food, the curry is a flavouring or condiment. As British influence in India grew, so did the number of troops under their command. The original curry was the ideal food to feed an army, especially one as religiously diverse as that in India. There were massive amounts of basically nutritious breads and rice seasoned by small quantities of spicy sauces which could be adjusted to suit the religious needs of the troops. The Muslims ate no pork. Some Hindus ate pork but no beef, others were vegetarians. To be a Christian simply meant that you would eat anything. Hobson-Jobson points out that when curry was transported back to England, the sauce, not the bread or rice became dominant, but first it examines the origin of the name 'curry'.

> The word is Tamil. *Kari* ie: 'Sauce': the Canarese for *Karil* was that adopted by the Portuguese, and is still in use in Goa. It is remarkable in how many countries a similar dish is habitual.
>
> In England, the proportions of rice and 'Kitchen' are usually reversed, so that the latter is made to constitute the bulk of the dish.
>
> It is possible . . . that a kind of 'curry' used by Europeans and Mohammedans is not of purely Indian origin, but has come down from the spiced cookery of Medieval Europe and Western Asia. The Medieval spiced dishes in question were even coloured like curry. Turmeric, indeed, called by Garcia de Orta, Indian saffron, was yet unknown in Europe, but it was represented by saffron and sandalwood.

Hobson-Jobson makes an essential point in the understanding of the origins of curry; when Europeans first arrived in India, the food they found there was remarkably like their own, only more so. The heavily spiced stews of late medieval Europe were served on 'trenchers' or slabs of stale

bread and were scooped up to the mouth with handheld bread sops. This was identical to the eating habits of the Indians who called their breads 'the third hand'. In the south, Indians ate, and still eat, rice and sauces by hand. In Europe the fork did not appear outside of Italy until late in the seventeenth century.

It was the Indian custom after meals then as now, to eat a mixture of spices and betel leaves called *pa'an*. It is sometimes possible to forget the leaves and eat a mixture of anise seed, cardamom seed, cloves and almonds. The idea is to relax the diner and aid digestion. Late medieval Europeans practised an identical custom called a *voidée*. Here is the Oxford Dictionary definition:

A collation consisting of wine with spices, comfits, or the like, partaken of before retiring to rest or before the departure of guests; a repast of this nature following upon a feast or fuller meal; a parting dish.

An artist's impression of Portuguese women eating a meal in sixteenth-century India. The region of Goa in the southwest was a Portuguese colony until as recently as 1956 and Goanese food is today a blend of Portuguese and southern Indian influences.

It is reported that the spices and wines of the *voidée* were served on the most magnificent gold and silver trays, as were the makings of the *pa'an* in the Mogul Court.

Even Edward Terry's banquet with the great Khan or Chan would not have seemed too remarkable as the princes of Europe certainly knew how to present lavish feasts. Today, people think of Indian food as hot, yet it should be noted that the European Terry omitted even a mention of the banquet's heat. Could it be that pungent, hot chillies had only recently arrived in India themselves, and had not yet infiltrated the whole culinary system? In any event, contrary to popular belief, Indian food does not have to burn the tongue off. There was, however, one thing Terry did miss, which the English just had to import.

> At this entertainment we sat long and much longer than we could with ease crosslegged . . . My Lord Ambassador observed not that uneasy way of sitting at his meat, but in his own house had tables and chayres . . .

From the seventeenth century on, European food fell under the sway of a new flavouring agent, sugar, and with the introduction of cutlery, stoves and new methods of preservation, gradually it grew into the culinary system we enjoy today. Perhaps, when Europeans eat curry, they are tasting a bit of their own lost past. Still, this style of cooking was known in India from ancient times. Hobson-Jobson continues:

> The earliest precise mention of *curry* is in the Mahavanso (c AD 477) where it is said of Kassapo that 'he partook of rice, dressed in butter, with its full accompaniment of curries'.
> A recipe for curry (*caril*) is given . . . in the Portuguese *Arte de Cazinlia*. This must be of the seventeenth century. It should be added that *kari* was, among the people of South India, the name of only one form of 'kitchen' for rice, viz of that in consistency resembling broth. Europeans have applied it to all the savoury concoctions of spicy character eaten with rice.

As travel between east and west increased, and food styles diverged, a western interest in eastern food grew. By 1781, a famous English cookery writer Hannah Glasse had even published a recipe for curry. Another recipe for curry powder appeared in Williamsburg, Virginia in 1831:

> One ounce turmeric, one Do coriander seed, one Do cummin seed, one Do white ginger, one of nutmeg, one of mace, and one of cayenne pepper; pound all together, and pass them through a fine sieve; bottle and cork it well— one teaspoonful is sufficient to season any made dish.

There are literally thousands of spice combinations, employing virtually every spice in India, which at one time or another have been labelled as 'curry powder'. Over the years, certain combinations have become more 'standard' than others. Today, most curry powders will be dominated in volume by coriander seed and will contain black pepper, cumin seed, cardamom, fenugreek and the obligatory turmeric and chillies. It is not unusual to find these mixed with various combinations of cloves, cinnamon, ginger, mace, mustard seed, poppy seed and to confuse matters thoroughly, a southern Indian herb known as 'curry leaves'.

To the question of how this particular mixture of spices developed, the answer is . . . nobody really knows. Perhaps the story at the beginning of this chapter contains more than just a grain of truth. But there are other possibilities. The Indians themselves, especially in the north, have long used a mixture of prepared spices called 'Garam Masala'. Like everything else related to Indian cooking, there is no official garam masala as each family would grind or have ground a quantity to suit their own particular tastes. The mixture was kept bottled in a shelf available for constant use.

Tom Stobart in his book *Herbs, Spices and Flavourings* says, 'the nearest the average Indian household gets to curry powder is in the garam masala which means literally 'hot mixture'.

The Europeans who arrived in India must have observed cooks using and extending this mixture, and from it they could have developed curry powder. Here we are on dangerous ground. Knowledgeable experts in Indian cooking go out of their way to deny the connection between garam masala and curry powder. One of the very best books on the subject is *Indian Regional Cookery*, by Meera Taneja. Here is what she has to say about garam masala:

> Garam Masala is one of the most versatile of a combination of spices. It has many uses, both in the process of cooking and for adding to the food after it has been cooked for extra fragrance. As a combination of spices produces a very strong flavour when ground, it is advisable to use a small quantity. Garam Masala can be made

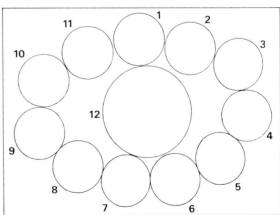

Top: The major spices used to make a commercial curry powder. **1.** Turmeric **2.** Coriander **3.** Ginger **4.** Chilli **5.** Black pepper **6.** Brown mustard **7.** Cloves **8.** Fennel **9.** Nigella **10.** Cumin **11.** Green cardamom **12.** Commercial curry powder.
Above left: Coriander seed. When ground, this forms the basis of most commercial curry powders.

at home and stored in airtight containers. The best result is achieved by buying whole spices, cleaning and then grinding them. An electric coffee grinder can be used very satisfactorily. Garam Masala is not a curry powder and should never be used as such.

    3 tbsp whole black pepper
    2 tbsp whole black cummin seeds
    1–2 inch stick of cinnamon
    2 tbsp cloves
    8 black cardamoms
    6 bay leaves
    1 tbsp mace

Forgive us Meera, but it must be pointed out that if you took that very mixture and added a substantial quantity of coriander seeds, a bit of fenugreek, some turmeric to colour it yellow and chillies to make it hot, the result would be what most people would call 'curry powder'.

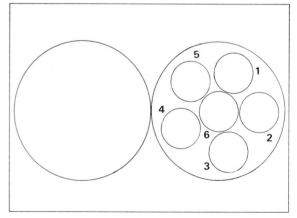

A garam masala is a mixture of ground warming spices. There is no one standard garam masala recipe and Indian families grind their own mixture of spices. Unlike curry powder garam masala is usually added towards the end of cooking to garnish a dish.
The illustration shows (left) a selection of whole spices which Indians often use in a garam masala and (right) in their ground form.
1. White cumin **2.** Cloves **3.** Black cardamoms **4.** Green cardamoms **5.** Black peppercorns **6.** Cinnamon.

The British in India must have spent considerable time observing the Indians using these spices. In fact they had so much time to do so that it became fashionable to write books. Mostly, the books were guides to others intent upon journeying to the colonies and inevitably they contained advice about curries. The title of one written in 1865 is: *The Englishwoman in India containing information for the use of ladies proceeding to, or residing in, the East Indies, on the subject of their OUTFIT, FURNITURE, HOUSEKEEPING, THE REARING OF CHILDREN, duties and wages of servants, management of the stables and arrangements for travelling to which are added receipts for Indian Cookery by a Lady Resident.*

One section entitled 'What Is Needed By Ladies of Modest Means' proffers the following information:

In a real comfortable household consisting of master, mistress and several children, where any visitors are received, it will be found necessary to keep a good many servants, certainly the following will be found rather below than above its requirements:

1 Head Boy	10 rupees a month
1 Maty	7 ,, ,, ,,
1 Under Maty	5 ,, ,, ,,
1 Chokera, or Dog Boy	3 ,, ,, ,,
1 Cook	8 ,, ,, ,,
1 Tanniketch	4 ,, ,, ,,
1 Dhirzee	8 ,, ,, ,,
1 Dhobie	9 ,, ,, ,,
1 Ayah	12 ,, ,, ,,
1 Under Ayah	7 ,, ,, ,,
1 Metranee	4 ,, ,, ,,
2 Ghorawallahs	14 ,, ,, ,,
2 Grasscutters	7 ,, ,, ,,
1 Waterman	5 ,, ,, ,,

This does not include mahlee and punkah-wallahs: it can be increased to any amount when required or decreased where there is no family, but it will be found a fair average for the generality of officers and civilians establishments on moderate pay.

[A Maty is a footman; a Chokera a dressing boy; a Tanniketch a scullerymaid; a Dhirzee a tailor; a Dhobie an ironing man; a Ghorawallah a housekeeper; an Ayah a lady's attendant; a Metranee a sweeper.]

The 'Authoress' as she calls herself, comments extensively on curries. 'Every native knows how to make these', she exclaims and then sets out several recipes for curry powders and pastes.

Curry literature exploded when Englishmen and women returned home and yearned for the aromas and comforts they had left behind in India. In 1895, Henrietta Harvey of Hammersmith wrote: *Anglo-Indian Cookery At Home, A Short Treatise For Returned Exiles by The Wife of a Retired Indian Officer.* Here is an excerpt on how to make Madras curry powder.

Take three pounds coriander seeds, three quarter pound saffron, three quarter pound dry chillies, three quarter pound pepper, three quarter pound mustard seed, six ounces dry ginger, four ounces 'medium', three quarter pound salt, three quarter pound sugar, six ounces cumin seed, quarter pound poppy seed, quarter pound mixed spices, one pound dried 'ea flour. Clean, dry, pound and sift the whole and keep in well corked bottles.

The mouth puckers at the thought! On today's market, the price of the saffron alone could purchase a small colour television set. Of course, Mrs Harvey did more than her fair share to plant the flag of curry on Hammersmith's green and pleasant fields. 'Our English servant, I find *is* open to instruction. Ours a raw country Essex girl, has learnt to boil rice as well as any old *Thunnikurchi* or cook-boy out there, and I am hopeful of being able to entrust her with curries at no very distant date. Patience is a virtue and everything.'

One returnee, John Loudoun Shand, not only brought his trusted servant back to England with him, but the servant, Daniel Santiago wrote a book whose full title in the second edition in 1889 was *The Curry Cook's Assistant or Curries, How To Make Them In England In Their Original Style by Daniel Santiago, General Servant, SON OF FRANCIS*

DANIEL, BUTLER AND FIDDLER, TRICHINOPOLY, MADRAS, INDIA AND COLOMBO, CEYLON, Servant to John Loudoun Shand, 24 Rood Lane, EC.

The author writes; 'My intention in publishing this second edition is that I have given too little recipes and information in my first book for sixpence each a copy.'

One of his new recipes, mushrooms curried and served on toast, sounds quite delightful:

Pick out half-pound of fresh and good mushrooms; sprinkle with a little pepper and salt. Now prepare curry sauce . . . fry the mushrooms in a dessertspoon of butter, and add to the curry sauce; let it simmer gently for five minutes, then serve on hot toast. A nice dish for lunch or supper. When eating, a dash of cayenne and mushroom ketchup may be a nice taste. Try the above.

John Loudoun Shand actually roused himself to write an introduction for his faithful servant in which he states:

All human nature requires to be occasionally stimulated, and a mild curry acts upon the torpid liver, reacts upon the digestive organs, and provides the necessary stimulant without injurious consequences. It is a remarkable fact that nearly all curry eating nations are abstainers from strong drink.

As curry was establishing itself firmly in England, it seems that back in India and Ceylon, English influence was damaging ancient skills. Laments Daniel Santiago, 'At present there are too many cooks in Ceylon; almost every butler, appoo, second servant, kitchen mate, groom, etc, knows how to cook an English dinner!!!.' An

Chicken and Pineapple Curry

SERVES SIX TO EIGHT

1 x ½-inch/1.5-cm fresh root of ginger	1 large onion, peeled and finely chopped
1 clove garlic, or more to taste, peeled	1 sweet green pepper, seeded and chopped
2 tablespoons/30 ml coriander seeds	1 sweet red pepper, seeded and chopped
1 tablespoon/15 ml cumin seeds	1 lb/450 g ripe tomatoes, peeled, chopped and puréed
2 teaspoons/10 ml paprika	or 1 lb/450 g Italian plum tomatoes, with juice, sieved
1 teaspoon/5 ml ground cloves	½ lb/225 g fresh pineapple, peeled and cubed, with juice
1 teaspoon/5 ml ground cinnamon	or 1 x ½-lb/225-g tin pineapple chunks in natural juice
1 teaspoon/5 ml freshly ground black pepper	2 teaspoons/10 ml salt
1 x 4-lb/1.8-kg chicken, jointed	1 tablespoon/15 ml wine vinegar (optional)
	3 tablespoons/45 ml lemon juice (optional)
vegetable oil for frying	pineapple slices for garnish

Pound the ginger and garlic in a mortar. Add the coriander and cumin seeds and pound to a paste. Add the paprika, cloves, cinnamon and black pepper and mix thoroughly, or reduce the spices to a paste in a blender. Rub the spice mixture into the chicken pieces, coating them thoroughly. Set the chicken pieces aside on a dish.

In a large, heavy frying pan (skillet) heat 3 tablespoons/45 ml of vegetable oil and sauté the onion until it is golden and soft. Add the chicken pieces with the spice mixture and sauté over moderate heat until golden on both sides. Add a little more oil

if necessary to prevent the chicken pieces from sticking. Reduce the heat to low and add the peppers, tomatoes and pineapple and sauté for a few minutes longer. Add half the pineapple juice (you do not need the remaining juice), season to taste with salt and stir in the vinegar and lemon juice, if using. They will give a sweet-sour taste to the curry. Transfer the contents of the frying pan to a heavy, lidded casserole and bake the curry in a preheated moderate oven, 350°F, 180°C, Gas Mark 4, for 45 minutes, or until the chicken is tender. Serve garnished with pineapple slices.

Coronation Chicken Curry

SERVES SIX

4 fl oz/100 ml (½ cup) single (light) cream

4 fl oz/100 ml (½ cup) plain yogurt

4 fl oz/100 ml (½ cup) mayonnaise

4 oz/100 g (1 cup) apples, peeled, cored and chopped

2 medium stalks (about 4 oz/100 g) celery, chopped

2 teaspoons/10 ml chopped onion

2 oz/50 g (½ cup) toasted, flaked (slivered) almonds

1 x 3–4 lb/1.4–1.8 kg chicken, cooked

For the curry powder

1 tablespoon/15 ml ground coriander seeds

½ teaspoon/2.5 ml ground mustard seeds

½ teaspoon/2.5 ml ground cumin seeds

½ teaspoon/2.5 ml ground turmeric

¼ teaspoon/1.5 ml ground ginger

1 teaspoon/5 ml ground dried hot red chillies

To make the curry powder, combine the coriander, mustard, cumin, turmeric, ginger and chillies in a bowl, mixing thoroughly. Transfer to a screwtop jar and store in a cool place.

In a large bowl, combine the cream, yogurt and mayonnaise. Stir in 2 teaspoons/10 ml of the curry powder and reserve the rest for another use. Add all the remaining ingredients. Cut the cooked chicken into boneless bite-size pieces and fold into the curry mixture, gently. Serve lightly chilled.

Chicken and pineapple curry (top left) and Coronation chicken curry (below right).

Englishman writing under the pseudonym 'Wyvern' in 1878 agreed. He complained:

We are often told by men of old time, whose long connection with the country entitles them to speak with the confidence of 'fellows who know, don't you know', that inverse proportion, as it were, to the steady advance of civilisation in India, the sublime art of curry-making has gradually passed away from the native cook. Elders at Madras . . . while the acknowledged head-centre of the craft – shake their heads and say 'Ichabod!' and if encouraged to do so, paint beautiful mouth-watering 'pictures in words' of succulent morsels cunningly dressed with all the savoury spices and condiments of India, the like of which we ne'er shall look upon again.

Curries now-a-days are only licensed to be eaten at breakfast, at luncheon, and perhaps at the little home dinner, when they may, for a change, occasionally form the *pièces de résistance* of that cosy meal. Having thus lost 'caste', so to

speak, it ought hardly to surprise me that curries have deteriorated in quality. The old cooks, who studied the art, and were encouraged in its cultivation, have passed away to their happy hunting grounds; and the sons and grandsons who now reign in their stead have been taught to devote themselves to more fashionable dishes.

Wyvern was by far the best and most interesting of all the 'curry authors'. He was, in reality,

Colonel Kenny-Herbett, who later made important contributions to British food writing. In his *Culinary Jottings For Madras* it is clear that he wanted to arrest the slide of curry culture by publishing the absolute and definitive recipe on the subject. He approached his task with military directness and precision.

The actual cooking of a curry presents no special difficulty. A cook who is adept with the stewpan and who has mastered the art of slow, and very

Facing page and above: A Hindu birthday feast in Bali. A Balinese speciality, hot smoked duck called *bebek tutu* uses Indian spices as an essential flavour. Over twenty different spices are rubbed into the duck which is then wrapped in banana leaves and cooked on a fire of coconut husks.

gentle simmering, will, whether a Frenchman, an Englishman, or a mild Hindu, soon become familiar with the treatment of this particular dish.

The knotty points are these: first the powder or paste, next the accessories, and lastly the order in which the various component parts should be added.

Concerning powders, it behoves us to proceed with caution, or we shall soon lose ourselves in a maze of recipes. Speaking of them generally, however, it is not, I think, commonly known that curry powders improve by keeping it carefully bottled.

Even today that last statement might raise a few eyebrows, but, the Colonel is right. When spices are first ground and mixed they are 'raw', but when they sit for a time in an airtight container, simple chemical compounds interact with one another to form more complex and pleasing combinations. The trick is an airtight container away from light, but be warned, if kept too long, spice mixtures can go mouldy.

The Colonel is not averse to purchasing prepared curry powder, provided the ingredients are of excellent quality, unadulterated and not too old. The difficulty is that all the dishes will taste the same. He does give the following recipe for a standard curry powder; which, he says, if faithfully followed will be found most trustworthy:

4 lbs of turmeric
8 lbs of coriander seed
2 lbs of cumin seed
1 lb of poppy seed
2 lbs of fenugreek
1 lb of dry ginger
$\frac{1}{2}$ lb of mustard seed
1 lb of dried chillies
1 lb of black peppercorns

'Do not be alarmed at the quantity', says the Colonel, who had a whole regiment at his command to grind and use the stuff. Of course, smaller

Making a crab curry in Sri Lanka. The crabs are always used fresh and are ripped apart while still alive. The traditional cooking pot of unglazed clay can be seen on the left.

quantities can be used, but it does not pay to roast and grind too little. Each ingredient should be roasted in an ordinary frying pan until fragrant and the mixture ground in an electric grinder, which is then committed solely to spices. The powder should pass through a fine sieve, be bottled and left.

The Colonel then describes four essential ingredients for all good curries. The first is butter, the second an ingredient needed to produce 'that suspicion of sweet-acid which it will be remembered, forms a salient feature of a superior curry'. He mentions that the natives in the south use tamarind and that it is possible to use chopped mango, apple or sweetish chutney and vinegar, but he simply prefers a little redcurrant jelly. For the third essential, coconut milk, he gives a recipe, but today it can be purchased tinned at good grocers. The fourth ingredient is a cupful and a

Travelling within their extensive empire in the Far East, the English soon acquired a taste for curried food; the famous Raffles Hotel in Singapore still serves a buffet curry luncheon on Sundays to satisfy the demands of its mainly European clientele.

half of good stock or gravy. This, he suggests, makes some curries eaten in England far better than those of India.

We may now work out, step by step, the process to be followed in cooking a chicken curry. Choose a nice young chicken—and here let me point out that large chickens nearly full grown ought never to be used in curries—and having cut it up neatly as for a fricassee place the pieces aside, and dredge over them a little flour. Next take all the trimmings . . . and cast them into a saucepan with an onion sliced, a carrot sliced, half a dozen peppercorns, a bit of celery, a pinch of salt and one of sugar, cover them with cold water and make the best broth you can. When ready, strain the contents of the saucepan into a bowl, and skim it clean. A good breakfast-cupful of weak stock should thus be obtained. Lastly, make a breakfast-cupful of milk of coconut or almond.

Now take your stewpan and having sliced up six good shallots, or two small white onions, cast the rings into it, with two ounces of butter;

add a finely-minced clove of garlic and fry till the onions turn a nice yellow brown.

Then add two tablespoonfuls of the stock powder, cook the curry-stuff with the onions and butter for a minute or two, slowly, adding by degrees a wine-glassful of the coconut milk, and then also by degrees the breakfast cupful of broth.

The effect of this when simmered for a quarter of an hour will be a rich, thick curry gravy, or sauce. The stewpan should then be placed *en bain-marie* while we proceed to prepare the chicken.

Take a frying pan: melt in it an ounce of butter, or clarified beef suet, add a shallot cut up small, and fry for a couple of minutes. Next put the pieces of chicken into the sauté pan, and lightly fry them. As soon as slightly coloured, the pieces of chicken should be transferred to the stewpan in which they should rest for at least half an hour, marinating, as it were, in the curry gravy. After that, the stewpan should be placed over a gentle fire, and if the liquid be found insufficient to cover the pieces of chicken, stock, if available, or water, should be added.

The Colonel then asks for a gentle simmering and the addition of a bayleaf, some chutney and the sweet acid of choice, perhaps the redcurrant jelly. Some pounded almond, coconut and grated green ginger should all be added to taste:

As soon as the pieces of chicken have become tender, thoroughly stewed, that is to say, a coffee-cupful of coconut 'milk' should be stirred in, and in three minutes the operation will be complete.

If a semi-dry or dry curry be required, the gravy must be still further reduced by simmering with the lid off, the pieces of meat being continually stirred about with a wooden spoon to prevent their catching at the bottom of the pan. When the proper amount of absorption has been attained, remove the pan and serve.

Now, those to whom the slipshod method of curry-making ordinarily followed by native cooks, is familiar, will, perhaps, think that the process I have recommended is needlessly troublesome . . .

I am, however, perfectly confident that in order to produce a dish of superior class we must be prepared to take all this trouble, bringing an enlightened system of cookery to bear upon the condiments and ingredients, which, so to speak, provide the curry flavour . . .

If a gravy curry be kept during the night in a china curry dish, and be resuscitated the next morning with some fresh butter, onions and a little gravy, it ought, if anything, to be found better than on the previous night, since the meat has become thoroughly flavoured by the curry gravy, while the latter has become reduced and so strengthened by the second simmering. The directions will be found practicable with most ordinary meat curries. Those made of fresh fish, prawns and shellfish require a somewhat different process . . .

No one has said it better before or since. To curry's detractors it can be demonstrated that this dish has a history and culture as rich as any, even if it is not entirely 'authentic', whatever that means. That bad curries and curry powders exist, which is undeniable, does not necessarily mean that it is impossible to have good ones.

Curry's difficulty of definition has proven an advantage, for, as it reached country after country it was quickly adapted and incorporated into local cuisines. For example, curried goat is the great delicacy and natural dish of Jamaica.

In 1957 the United States imported just over one million tonnes of coriander seed, by volume the largest component in curry powder. By 1980 that amount had almost tripled, but there is an even more astounding statistic. In 1957 Japan imported less than 200,000 tonnes of the seed, but by 1980 the figure had grown to two million tonnes, or ten times the 1957 amount. Today the average Japanese family eats curry and rice at least once every week and often more. Curry just keeps marching on.

People have always made mixtures of spices, herbs, salt, sugar, honey and other substances in an

Curried Goat

Jamaicans call this curried goat but kid (baby goat) is more usually used. Kid is available in speciality markets *but may be hard to get so use lamb or mutton instead. Allspice is the famous local Jamaican spice.*

SERVES SIX	
3 lb/1.4 kg kid (baby goat)	½ teaspoon/2.5 ml allspice
3 tablespoons/45 ml dripping or vegetable shortening	1 bay leaf
2 large onions, peeled and finely chopped	8 fl oz/225 ml coconut milk
1 fresh hot red chilli pepper, seeded and chopped	16 fl oz/450 ml (2 cups) beef or chicken stock
3 tablespoons/45 ml curry powder	salt and freshly ground black pepper
	2 tablespoons/30 ml lime or lemon juice

Cut the meat into 1-inch/2.5-cm pieces. Heat the dripping or vegetable shortening in a large, heavy frying pan (skillet) and brown the meat all over. Transfer the meat to a large saucepan or heavy casserole. In the fat remaining in the pan, adding a little more if necessary, sauté the onion and the chilli pepper until the onion is soft.

Stir in the curry powder and the allspice and sauté, stirring, for 2–3 minutes. Add the mixture to the casserole with the bay leaf and the coconut milk. Add enough stock to cover the meat, bring to a simmer and cook, covered, over a low heat until the meat is tender, about 2 hours. Stir in the lime juice and simmer for 1–2 minutes longer.

attempt to improve the flavour of their foods. Trial and error along with cook's intuition have generally been the main paths of development. Yet, some mixtures and blends proved so successful that the final product produced somehow seems greater than the sum of its individual parts. Even though the sensations of flavour are highly subjective, and their manufacture is undoubtedly an art, the question arises . . . is it also a science?

Henry Heath has spent a large part of his life addressing just that question. In the years he spent as a British officer in India during World War II, he acquired a love for the tastes of the subcontinent which drove him to seek a greater understanding of them. No one is more aware of the subjective nature of flavour than he, yet, if a science is to progress, a common ground of understanding with the universal principles must be found. Henry Heath writes:

A seasoning may be considered to have four main flavouring contributions:

(a) Light, sweet herbaceous or aromatic notes which give instant odour impact when the food is served and when being placed in the mouth.

(b) Medium aromatic herbs and spices selected to bring out the finer notes present in the main food components eg: the sweetness of pork, the delicate flavour in chicken etc.

(c) Heavy, full-bodied spicy notes which add richness and full flavour character to the dish.

(d) Pungency or piquancy which in the case of ginger and pepper is accompanied by a characteristic flavour, whereas with chillies the additional flavour is minimal so that one can achieve pungency without affecting any delicate flavours present.

That not all spices have the same flavouring power or impact becomes obvious if one considers, say, one kilogram of chillies and one kilogram of sage. Through years of analysis and testing Henry Heath and his colleagues have now been able to compile a 'flavour index' or approximate measure of the power of each spice.

For those who wish to delve deeper into the art of blending herbs and spices the subject has been

treated more scientifically in a separate section at the end of this book on page 184.

So, if spices are to work, they must satisfy the original four requirements and contain correct proportions of component spices. One blend which time has proven proper is curry powder. Here are Henry Heath's comments:

NOTES ON SPICES IN CURRY POWDER
Typical formulation:

Cumin	10
Coriander	37
Fenugreek	7
Turmeric	14.5
Black Pepper	7
Cardamom	2.5
Chillies	8

Small green cardamoms. The glossy ones are ripe cardamoms. These are then dried for twenty-four hours in hot furnaces and the outer skins shrivel up. This is how they are sold commercially. Cardamoms are difficult to cultivate and have a complicated process of drying; hence, they are expensive to buy and are used often only in elaborate dishes.

CUMIN—gives to the curry powder a strongly penetrating aromatic character but also a warm overall spiciness. Because of its almost universal use in curry mixtures this spice is often described as being 'curry like'.

CORIANDER—although predominating in quantity present, does not have anything like the impact. Its flavour is fruity and warmly sweet with a slightly floral background which makes it blend well with other spices.

FENUGREEK—is more pleasant to smell than to taste having a very tenacious flavour which is somewhat similar to that of celery but with a very bitter backnote. It is rich in protein and hence contributes to the food value of the mix. In India the fresh green herb is often used in curry products (but not in curry powder, obviously).

TURMERIC—is present in the mix to give it the characteristic deep yellow colour but it also has a warm, spicy flavour which if used at too high a level can make the product somewhat earthy.

BLACK PEPPER—contributes both a pleasingly fresh aroma which is slightly lemony in character but principally it is used for its sharp pungency on the tongue, unlike . . .

CHILLIES—which give to the curry powder a heavy piquancy which is experienced deep in the throat and also makes one sweat. Indians would use this at higher levels than would be tolerated by most Europeans.

CARDAMOM—has a warmly spicy yet light camphoraceous character (such as one gets by using bay leaves which are sometimes used in curry as being a cheaper spice). It gives to the mixture a pleasing, fruity sweetness with a slight astringency. Its use is somewhat restricted as too high levels can make the product perfumed and 'soapy'.

Of course, curry powder, like all mixtures, can and should be adjusted or tuned to the demands of the ingredients being flavoured.

11 HERBS

'I favour very much clutching to herbs that grow in our own gardens. If you knew just six herbs very well, their medicinal value and their cooking value, I think you could call yourself a herbalist.' Jill Davies would be too modest to say so, but by her own definition she is a herbalist many times over. A glance from her kitchen window reveals a glorious scene. Jill and her husband Nick have spent the past few years restoring a seventeenth-century herb garden. It is, in fact, made up of several gardens. Side by side are planted an astrological garden, a bee and butterfly garden, a vegetable and pot herbs garden, a wild coloured garden and, perhaps most significant of all, a medieval knot garden.

Jill is a qualified horticulturist who trained at the famous gardens of Kew and Wisley in south England. When the chance came to restore the

Above and right: Jill Davies, a twentieth-century herbalist, in her magnificent herb garden in Suffolk.

rundown gardens of Lord Henniker's rambling but beautiful Suffolk estates, Jill jumped at it. At first, she lived in a caravan and broke the earth herself. The locals dubbed her 'the Gypsy'. Today she and her family live in modest comfort in a converted potting shed surrounded by splendid shapes, scents and inflorescences. Herbs influence most aspects of their lives.

Just outside the kitchen window are, naturally, the culinary herbs including gold marjoram, rosemary, thyme, dill, sage, parsley, blue borage and so on. Before lunch on every summer's day Jill picks a basketful. They not only flavour the tomato soup, but form the makings of a salad which looks good, tastes good and does good. Distinctions between food and medicine are deliberately blurred. Jill and Nick make up tisanes, which are infusions of leaves and flowers,

and sell them, together with herbs fresh or dried, from a tiny shop on the premises. They also have a small laboratory where they test and experiment with made up potions and lotions. First of all Jill is a teacher and this year she is involved with an unique product.

For a period of two weeks, two hundred children a day will be transported for twenty-four hours at a time back to the fourteenth century. The time machine is Orford Castle, built in the twelfth century, and Jill will be on hand to identify the herbs growing wild in the area, and more. 'There will be no let up', she declares, 'I mean if they cut themselves, it's herbs they'll be restored with. There's no tea or coffee; if they're thirsty, they'll have to drink herb tea. If they want to eat, they'll have to strangle a chicken . . . It's completely as it was.'

Jill Davies's herb salad based on an everyday seventeenth-century recipe. The recipe uses at least thirty-five ingredients, a few for flavour, some for health and many for decoration.

Jill is one of a new breed of herbalists who actively mine the past seeking lost values which may help us to survive in the future. She believes that a familiarity with herbs, knowing what they are, where they grow, how they taste and how they blend with and gently influence human physiology, can bring people in close touch with themselves and their surroundings. There is a quiet urgency about the work. Ours is the first generation ever to be cut off completely from such knowledge, and of all times, we live in the most precarious time.

'Sadly,' says Jill, 'modern children know very little about herbs. I even find there's absolutely no difference between children living in the country and those in London. Those in London have often never seen a herb, whereas Suffolk children see them every day, but don't know what they are.'

Scientists believe that human beings have walked the face of this planet for some two million plus years. Just five thousand or so years ago, human beings underwent a change of lifestyle. They, our ancestors, became 'civilized'. Yet, despite all our knowledge and 'civilization', we have brought things to a state where the very survival of our species is in doubt. Perhaps it is time to seek new ideas and restore values from the past. A knowledge of herbs may help us to understand the past, and in so doing, ourselves.

What, then, are herbs? Some say they are the green leafy parts of aromatic plants which grow in temperate climates and die each year. By contrast, spices are the aromatic parts of tropical plants. This definition fits for, say, pepper which everyone knows is a spice and marjoram, clearly a herb, but what about mustard or coriander where both seeds and leaves are used? Some people have tried to construct a third category, 'aromatic seeds', but this fails to solve the problem of plants like garlic, and, in any event, few herbalists would consider themselves bound by such narrow definitions.

The most general definition of herbs is that they are any plant that is beneficial or useful to humans. Aside from being a rather 'homocentric' definition, it is difficult to think of even one plant which has never been of any use to a human being. The definition is simply too general to be meaningful. Nature can be very frustrating. Time and again she refuses to order herself for the convenience of human academic neatness. The terms 'herb' and 'spice' are more matters of intuition and semantics than science, but that does not mean the words are meaningless. If a definition of herbs is absolutely necessary, one proffered by the distinguished food expert, Alan Davidson, is better than most. He says that herbs are green plants used for flavouring and decoration rather than for sustenance.

Herbs are different from spices. The latter are tiny explosive packages of tropical fury while the former are more gentle and subtle. Until the last few hundred years, spices were inaccessible, for most of the world's people. Cloves, for example, were known at first only to the inhabitants of the Moluccan Islands. Herbs, on the other hand, have always been known and used by ordinary people everywhere. They were just outside the kitchen door.

The history of spice is, if you will excuse the pun, peppered with the names of men of action: Christopher Columbus, Vasco Da Gama, Ferdinand Magellan, Jan Pieterzoon Coen, Pierre Poivre, Jonathan Carnes . . . whose adventures are related in other chapters of this book. If there is such a thing as a history of herbs it would boast such names as . . . Theophrastus, Dioscorides, Gerard, Culpeper and Mrs Grieve, a different lot altogether; botanists, healers and thinkers.

Five hundred years ago, European men set out on a furious quest for spices, the effects of which were felt or suffered throughout the world. Not only did those adventurers and businessmen create the concept of geopolitics, they opened wounds still unhealed to this day. We can only speculate on what would be the state of the world had the driving passion been for gentle herbs instead of burning spices. As for the women of Europe who sought knowledge of herbs, many paid for their efforts by being burned at the stake as witches.

It would be far too simple to claim male characteristics for spices and female for herbs. Of course, many herbalists were male, and Isabella of Spain and Elizabeth I of England played their roles in the great spice age of discovery and conquest. The point is that the conquest of the world through the search for spices could only have happened in what anthropologists call a male-dominated patriarchal society. Matriarchal societies, where females and female characteristics dominated, flourished prior to the advent of 'civilization'. These societies were unaware of spices but used many herbs.

Bouquet garni

Herbs play an important role in the everyday flavouring of dishes. An example is the bouquet garni *used to flavour sauces and stews. It consists of a bunch of mixed herbs, preferably fresh though dried may be used, tied together with cotton, or tied in a small square of cheesecloth. Classically, this consists of a bay leaf, thyme and parsley, but other flavourings can be added according to the dish. In Provence a strip of dried orange peel is often included, especially in the* daubes, *which are the braised beef dishes of the region. A stalk (rib) of celery may be added, or if a stronger flavour is liked, a sprig of lovage.*

No distinctions were made between food, magic, religion and medicine, there was simply an organic whole. People thought of themselves as part of and not distinct from the natural forces around them. Members of such societies never sailed around Africa, never conquered the Moluccas, never read a book, never wrote the ninth symphony, never walked on the moon or saw the rings of Saturn and never had to contend with the hydrogen bomb. But, they did survive, not only for millions of years, but long enough to breed us.

Herbs were there from the start. Through aeons of trial and error every available plant was tried for every conceivable purpose. People came to know which tasted good, which were useful for colourings or dyes, which were poisonous, which caused hypnotic states, and which helped cure disease. Information passed from generation to generation by word of mouth, song, myth and tribal custom. Naturally, plants and animals became the subject matter of legends, superstitions and tales and symbols of every kind.

When the written word finally arrived, the lore of plants and herbs was amongst the very first things recorded. Almost 5000 years ago, the Chinese Emperor Chin Nong is said to have written a herbal, or a list of herbs and their properties. Sumerian herbals from Mesopotamia go back 4500 years and the Egyptians were composing their own 4000 years ago. By the time the Greeks and Romans came along, herbal literature was already massive. In the third century BC Theophrastus, a disciple of Aristotle, was the first person to attempt a scientific classification of plants. In essence, he became the founder of the science of botany. Almost three hundred years later, another Greek, Dioscorides, wrote *De Materia Medica*, which not only listed plants and their properties, but their medicinal uses as well. *De Materia Medica* became the model upon which virtually all future herbals were based. In the first and second centuries AD the Roman authors Pliny and Galen both wrote extensively about herbs and their medicinal uses. Pliny is always good for an amusing quotation, but Galen is considered far more accurate.

From the many centuries of plant observation and comment, only a trickle of knowledge has been passed on to our time. One can only imagine the store of knowledge which must have been housed in the great library of Alexandria before its devastation in the fourth century AD and final destruction in the seventh century.

During the European Dark Ages the monasteries took over as protectors of ancient knowledge and were ideally suited to the task. The monks both ministered to the sick and obtained their herbs by planting gardens. It was, however, through Spain and Islam that much of the ancient learning, along with Islamic modification, reached Western Europe. By the fourteenth century, Europeans were again composing herbals in earnest. William Turner and John Gerard were English herbalists of the sixteenth century whose works, benefiting from the invention of printing, were circulated to a far greater extent than any of their predecessors.

As always, the herbals were mixtures of observation, lore and superstition. It is not surprising that the philosophy of herbs should have been influenced by the new-found spices. In the sixteenth century human beings overcame previously insurmountable natural barriers with confidence. By inventing the compass and learning to read the sun, stars, winds and ocean currents, sailors travelled to the ends of the earth. It seemed as if the universe contained a series of messages which would work to the benefit of any who could read or understand them. It was logical that the kingdom of plants should be impressed with such signs.

Theophrastus Bombastus von Hohenheim was born in 1493, the year after Columbus's first journey to America, and he would have been a mature adult when Magellan's crew completed its circumnavigation. He contributed to the history of knowledge by being the first alchemist to proclaim that the purpose of the ancient art was not to transmute base metals into gold, but to

The south of France is a 'herb factory' as the climate is ideal for growing herbs on a commercial scale.

produce from plants, medicines that heal. He lived up to his name 'Bombastus' by leading a rowdy and quarrelsome existence and he is far better known by his adopted nickname 'Paracelsus' which means 'better than Celsus'. Celsus was a patrician Roman physician of the first century. More than anyone, Paracelsus popularized 'The Doctrine of Signatures', the idea that God has impressed upon the form of every herb an instruction for its use. The key to understanding these instructions or signatures was 'treat like with like'. If a person was suffering from jaundice, yellow turmeric would be the treatment. Liverwort, with leaves shaped like a liver would be the perfect treatment for ailments of that organ. The idea quickly caught on and as years passed, signatures grew wilder and wilder . . . Walnuts were used to treat maladies of the brain because a halved walnut looks like a brain. Roots with forked tips were applied for snakebite; red roses for nosebleed and so on.

One of the most famous herbal authors is Nicholas Culpeper who lived from 1616 to 1654. Like everyone else, he was influenced by the 'Doctrine of Signatures'. However, he was never fully comfortable with it. To him something was missing. Signatures could not account for the complete nature of plants. So, he re-introduced ancient astrological concepts. Herbs and different parts of the body were under the various influences of the sun, the moon and the five planets. Almost immediately Culpeper's critics cried foul. They maintained that not only was it irrational to believe that plants were governed by the lights in the firmament, but such a notion violated the declared word of God. You see, they argued, according to the Bible, grass and herb-yielding seed were created on the third day while the stars, planets, sun and moon were all created on the fourth day. Surely the very essence of a thing could not be controlled by a force arising after the thing itself.

Soon the various disciplines which are now considered as modern medicine split away from the mainstream of herbal thought, perhaps with some justification. In time, in the consciousness of the general public, medicine came to be regarded as pure, rational and beneficial, while

---

Omelette aux fines herbes

Omelette with fresh herbs

Herbs play a vital culinary role in the mixture of fresh herbs known as fines herbes *and used mostly in salads and in omelettes. The mixture always includes finely chopped parsley and the most usual herbs, apart from parsley, are chives, chervil and tarragon, but other condiments may be added if a recipe specifies them. It is hardly an exaggeration to say, when cooking with herbs, that combinations are without limits.*

SERVES TWO

4 eggs

salt and freshly ground black pepper

2 tablespoons/30 ml finely chopped mixed fresh herbs

2 tablespoons/25 g butter

Break the eggs into a bowl, season with salt and pepper and the herbs and beat lightly with a fork just to mix the whites and yolks together. Warm an 8-inch/20-cm omelette pan briefly over a high heat. Add the butter and when the foam begins to subside, but before the butter starts to brown, pour in the eggs. Stir the mixture with the flat of a fork to reach all over the bottom of the pan for about 4 seconds. At this stage the omelette will look like scrambled eggs. Then cook 20 seconds longer without stirring any further.

If there is any uncooked egg, lift the edge of the omelette with a fork and tilt the pan so that the uncooked egg runs underneath and sets. To roll the omelette, tilt the pan and with the fork fold the omelette away from you into the centre. Then roll it over towards the edge of the pan and slide it on to a warmed plate. Rub the top of the omelette with a little butter, sprinkle with more chopped herbs, cut it in half and serve immediately.

herbalism represented ignorance and superstition. The schism was tragic, because in fact, there was both wisdom and rationality, ignorance and superstition on both sides. Nobody can deny the benefits brought forth by modern medicine, yet, there are people living now who were treated for fever by being bled by trained physicians. The point is, that for all its rationality, modern medicine has skeletons in its own closet, both figuratively and literally. At one time their 'wonder drugs' were the deadly poisons, mercury and arsenic. Even the greatest miracles sometimes turn into nightmares. Antibiotics were heralded as the most important medical advance of all time and for a generation or two did effect impressive cures. They also accounted for the development of 'super-bugs' resistant to all attempts to destroy them. Today, antibiotic research is a frantic race to keep ahead of new and powerful strains of bacteria. We are still not sure whether 'wonder drugs' are worth the risk.

In some respects, modern scientists are not unlike the spice seekers of the age of discovery. Doctors are always seeking the next miracle cure over the next horizon. If there is a growing distrust of medicine it is because people see doctors not as healers helping them overcome their problems, but as impersonal diagnosticians and drug dispensers. The medical profession can arrest symptoms, but they are losing their ability to heal, and the people know.

Modern herbalists are a varied lot, but they seem to agree on certain basic principles. The first is that all food is medicine and vice versa. In other words, by far the greater effect should go to keeping people well instead of waiting until they are ill and then effecting cures. The second is that natural substances and chemicals unrefined in their original plant form are superior to synthetics, even when chemical compositions are identical. Herbs do contain powerful ingredients and often form the basis of extracted medicines. The medical profession generally prefers refined chemical substances because their strengths are standardised and purity unquestioned. Herbalists counter that people have lived with the natural substances for

Mixtures of dried herbs on sale in a Dijon market. The revival of interest in natural treatments is international. The medieval characters depicted on the labels suggest a reaction against modern medicine and pharmacology.

aeons and they are less likely to have unwanted side effects. Finally and most important of all, the herbalists claim that they treat people, not symptoms. Disease symptoms are not what is wrong with the patient. In fact, the symptom is only the body's way of fighting the real malady. A healer must have sympathy and empathy and the patient must be treated as a whole, unique person.

Enlightened herbalists do not dispute the worth of medicine, quite the contrary. They do point out, however, that unless there is an adherence to the basic principles of healing, many of the great benefits of medicine are wasted. In an article in the *Herbal Review*, 'The Ancient Roots of Herbal Medicine', the author, Ann Warren-Davis tries to explain why this obvious idea is so difficult to put across. She writes: 'Why this antipathy? Why this great gulf? Why this antagonism in healing methods?"

In attempting to find an answer to her question, Ann Warren-Davis discovered that medicine, like all other institutions in our society, is governed by the ethic of a power-seeking patriarchal society. In contrast, she traces a direct line of influence from the customs of North American native Indians to herbalist thinking. She concludes:

> The wheel is turning: it is having to as the Egyptians predicted. Man is about to exterminate himself unless he appreciates this in time. The cerebral sciences of cosmobiology, biochemistry and geomagnetic fields demonstrate more and more clearly that the observations of early peoples were absolutely correct. What is essential for health and happiness is the balancing of man to his environment with understanding and not its thoughtless domination. Nature's powers should be used in accordance with the forces and laws of the cosmos and not by their attempted domination, for nature and the cosmos will always hit back in the end. The roots of herbal medicine sprang from the careful observation of nature and her needs, her pains and discomforts are only cries for aid and understanding, physical, mental or spiritual: not their suppression with drugs thoughtlessly used.

Sitting in Jill Davies's garden is pleasant. There is no need to worry about religion, politics, superstition or magic. Jill herself seems to pay precious little attention to them. It seems quite remarkable that these gentle plants inspire such passion, that groups of people walk under the banner of their name. Perhaps it is their intimate connection with us. We eat herbs, we have strewn them on floors of our dwellings, we dye our clothes with them and sometimes even our bodies. We have used them to transport us to altered states of consciousness and to maintain us and to heal us. For each individual, understanding herbs can give an insight into the inner workings of themselves. As a society, perhaps we can go about the age-old task of well being able to enjoy the full benefit of the work of modern science, but in the spirit of Jill Davies's garden. The herbs are here and waiting. In 1982, The Prince of Wales said the

A luscious North American Indian herb garden at Ocunaluftee in North Carolina where there are over eight hundred plants. The herb garden forms part of a re-creation of the way of life led by the Cherokee Indians two hundred years ago. The medicine man was one of the most important men in Indian tribes; he used herbs in his incantations and prayers, as well as for treating illnesses.

following on the occasion of the 150th Anniversary of the British Medical Association.

At the height of their civilization Greek medicine reached a level of insight which was not to be achieved again until Paracelsus 2000 years later. They gave the highest priority to personal and emotional factors in therapy. Paracelsus himself wrote that 'the whole world is an apothecary's shop and God the apothecary in chief.' It seems to me that the lack of psychological insight—into the unconscious being of man—is possibly one of the saddest neglects of modern medicine. Has it perhaps been forgotten, too, that the oath which binds a physician pledges him both scientifically and religiously?

. . . the insights of other men in other times into the eternal problem of sickness are of value precisely because they approached them in a different faith from ours and therefore ought to be re-examined and made contemporary . . .

Nothing is black and white. There are, of course, many compassionate, caring and able physicians, and, some disciples of herbalism seem to weaken their effectiveness by being too stridently self-righteous. If an unprejudiced and balanced system of healing evolves anywhere, it is likely to be in China. Chinese cooking is not famous for its wide use of culinary herbs. In fact, chefs seem to prefer only two, coriander leaves and spring onion tops. Coriander leaves, so universal, that they are called 'Chinese parsley', are the green specks sprinkled through the nation's myriad of dumplings. Spring onion tops also are used widely as both flavour and decoration. This does not mean that the Chinese ignore the rest of the green plants which thrive everywhere in their vast country.

China boasts two 'Tongrengtans', one in Beijing and the other in the Sichuan city, Chengdu. Both are large pharmacies, but with a difference. Their walls are lined with hundreds of large wooden drawers, each containing a different dried herb.

These are mixed to the individual needs of patrons, who do not leave with tiny bottles in their pockets, but with newspaper-wrapped bundles under their arms. As part of the Chengdu pharmacy there is a restaurant, again with a difference. When the diners sit at the table, they are not issued with menus; instead, they are asked how they feel. Dishes are prepared with various herb mixtures designed to set customers on the road to vitality. Some preparations are considered so beneficial they are served to everyone, like a tonic soup or the house beverage, Three Snake Wine. It is said that in ancient China people paid their doctors to keep them well and if they became ill, they stopped paying. Extending the concept to a restaurant has been more than successful. Plans

One of two Chinese Tongrengtans; this one is in Chengdu, the capital of Sichuan, and the second one is in Beijing. Both are pharmacies with a difference. In Chengdu there is a restaurant attached. A customer does not order from a menu but simply states how he feels. The food then served to him is designed to benefit his condition.

Tortellini and Cappelletti

This is from Emilia-Romagna in Italy where no salt, oil or water is added to the pasta. The milk makes the pasta easier to seal. Use Continental (Italian) parsley if possible.

SERVES FOUR TO SIX

For the parsley and Ricotta filling

2 oz/50 g (1 cup, loosely packed) parsley leaves

8 oz/225 g fresh Ricotta cheese

4 oz/100 g (1 cup) freshly grated Parmesan cheese

salt

¼ teaspoon/1.5 ml freshly grated nutmeg

1 egg yolk

For the home-made pasta

11 oz/300 g (2⅝ cups) plain (all-purpose) flour

3 eggs

1 tablespoon/15 ml milk

To cook the pasta

3½ pints/2 litres (8 cups) water

1½ tablespoons/25 ml salt

1 tablespoon/15 ml olive oil

To make the filling, chop the parsley finely. In a bowl combine the parsley, Ricotta, Parmesan cheese, salt, nutmeg and egg yolk. Mix well with a fork, or use a food processor to chop the parsley and mix the remaining ingredients. Set aside.

Now you are ready to make the pasta. Have a work surface of wood or plastic (marble is not very satisfactory), measuring 24 by 36 inches/60 by 90 cm, and a rolling pin about 1½ inches/4 cm in diameter and 32 inches/81 cm long.

Make a mound of the flour on the work surface. Make a well in the centre. Break the eggs into the well. Add the milk. Using your fingers, or a fork, beat the eggs and milk lightly together. Begin to mix the flour into the eggs with a circular movement using one hand to draw the flour from the inside of the well, the other to support the outside wall so that the egg mixture does not run out. As soon as the eggs are no longer runny, cover them with the rest of the flour and working with fingertips and palms, push and rub in the eggs to make a crumbly paste. If the dough is very moist and sticky, add a little more flour but only as much as the eggs will absorb without the dough becoming stiff and dry. Form the dough into a ball. Lightly flour the work surface and roll the dough out, giving it a quarter turn after each roll so that it opens out into an even circle. Continue to roll out the dough, turning it a little after each roll until it is ⅛ inch/0.3 cm thick.

To give the dough its final thinning, curl the far end of the dough round the centre of the rolling pin, and roll it towards you with both hands cupped over the centre of the pin. Roll up a quarter of the sheet, then slide the hands to the ends of the pin and roll quickly and lightly back and forth letting the palms of the hands push against the dough. Roll the dough up again, rolling a little more than the quarter and repeat the process. Continue until all the dough has been rolled up and stretched. It should have been rolled about 12 to 14 times. Unroll the dough, flatten out any bumps and repeat until the dough is almost paper thin and transparent. Work quickly so that the dough does not dry out. The entire rolling process should take only about 8 minutes.

Cut the dough into 2-inch/5-cm circles for *tortellini* or 1½-inch/4-cm squares for *cappelletti*. Put ¼ teaspoon/0.6 ml of the Ricotta filling in the centre of the circle or square. Fold the pasta over to within ⅛ inch/0.3 cm of the opposite edge and seal it firmly. It may be necessary to moisten the edge lightly with the milk. For the *tortellini* fold the little turnover into a crescent shape and press one end of the dough over the other, sealing well. It will look like a small bonnet. Do the same with the *cappelletti* but in this case the point of the triangle will stand up at the top like a little peaked hat. Lay the finished pasta on a kitchen towel in rows not touching each other.

To cook the pasta, pour the water into a large saucepan and bring it to the boil over a high heat. Add the salt and the olive oil. Slide the *tortellini* and the *cappelletti* into the water and cook until they are tender but still firm to the bite – *al dente*. They will rise to the top of the water as soon as they are done. If the pasta is very fresh they will take only about a minute and at the most 4–5 minutes. Lift them out of the water with a slotted spoon so that they drain, and put them into a warmed serving dish with a lump of butter. Sprinkle generously with grated Parmesan cheese.

already are being completed for a new 'Tongreng-tan' which will be nineteen storeys high, the tallest building in Chengdu.

Even with all their beneficial qualities, herbs would not be half so popular if it were not for their aromas. As with spices, usually these result from light, volatile substances called 'essential oils'. The most obvious reason they exist in plants is sexual, to attract the bees and other insects and animals which help reproductive processes. Often 'essential oils' are highly antiseptic and may prevent harmful bacteria entering cuts or wounds inflicted on the plants.

In this respect, the oil of thyme is particularly powerful, exceeding that of most spices and almost matching the strong eugenol extracted from clove, allspice and cinnamon leaf oils.

Extracted 'essential oils' play a major role in the perfumery, cosmetics, toiletry and processed food industries. The most common methods for their removal are water or steam distillation.

We sense essential oils through tiny but sensitive glands high up in our noses. Once these amazing organs register a scent and send its message to the brain, they instantly clear the way for the next sensation. This is why you have the ability to distinguish between several scents at once, yet smell nothing when breathing out. For most of human existence this capacity was essential for survival. It led hunters to their prey while protecting them from dangerous animals.

Flavour is defined as a complex appreciation of the total sensations perceived whenever food or drink is consumed. 'Taste' is only a part of flavour

Herb Butters

Herb butters make a pleasing garnish for grilled (broiled) meats and fish and as an addition to sauces and soups. The best known are Beurre Maître d'hôtel (Parsley Butter) and Beurre de Fines Herbes (Mixed Herb Butter). Parsley is one of the most popular of herbs. The Romans served it at their feasts as a palate cleanser and the Greeks made wreaths of it for weddings. Greengrocers all over the world sell it as a matter of course, and it has decorated as many canapés as there are grains of sand on a beach. Without it the widely adopted bouquet garni of French cookery could not

exist and even where the family cook does not bother with a bouquet garni, he or she will almost always add a sprig or two of parsley to the dish that is being cooked to sustain family or friends that night. Curly parsley and flat parsley, sometimes called Italian or Continental parsley, are equally popular and there is hardly an egg, fish, shellfish, meat, poultry, game, vegetable or salad dish that is not enhanced by its use. It could be called the universal herb, and since it is rich in vitamins and minerals in addition to adding delicious flavour, it more than deserves its universal popularity.

Beurre Maître d'hôtel *(Parsley Butter)*

4 oz/100 g (½ cup) butter

1 tablespoon/15 ml lemon juice

3 tablespoons/45 ml finely chopped parsley

or mixed herbs such as parsley, tarragon and chives

salt and freshly ground pepper

Cream the butter and mix it little by little with the lemon juice. Beat the parsley or herbs into the

butter and season with salt and pepper. Chill before using.

Beurre au Poivre Vert *(Herb Butter)*

1 lb/450 g (2 cups) salted butter

1 teaspoon/5 ml green peppercorns, chopped

1 tablespoon/15 ml mixed chervil and tarragon

2 tablespoons/30 ml lemon juice

1 tablespoon/15 ml finely chopped chives

2 cloves garlic, peeled and minced

1 oz/25 g finely chopped parsley

Cream the butter. Add all the remaining ingredients, mixing well. Spread slices of French bread with the mixture and arrange in rows on a baking

sheet. Bake in a preheated very hot oven, 475°F, 240°C, Gas Mark 9, for 3–4 minutes until golden brown. Serve hot.

Pesto

Basil has a longer history than almost any other culinary herb. It probably reached Europe via the Middle East from India and even to this day in France, Italy and Greece, a pot of basil is believed to keep the flies away. Its name from the Greek word basileus *means 'king' and the herb is recorded in the earliest herbals. Its culinary use is very wide as it is a favourite herb in the Far East, for example in Thai and Vietnamese cooking. In India, the plant is sacred to Vishnu and Krishna, and not much used in cooking although a tea is made from basil leaves, honey and ginger and served in winter.*

SERVES FOUR AS A FIRST COURSE, TWO AS A MAIN COURSE
2 oz/50 g (1 cup, firmly packed) fresh basil leaves
1 oz/25 g (⅓ cup) freshly grated Parmesan cheese
1 oz/25 g (2 tablespoons) pine kernels

Combine all the ingredients except the pasta in a food processor or a blender and reduce to a purée.

Basil and Pine Kernel Sauce

Basil is best used fresh and can easily be grown from seed so that it is available from spring until October. With a little care and a sunny indoor spot it can be persuaded to survive the winter.

Basil is the vital ingredient in the sauce pesto *which comes from Genoa in Italy. The famous basil and pine kernel sauce is so perfect with fresh tomatoes it seems almost to be in love with them, and is wonderful with sweet red and yellow peppers as a sauce for pasta. A tablespoon/15 ml stirred into minestrone gives the soup a wonderful lift.*

½ teaspoon/2.5 ml salt
1–2 cloves garlic, to taste
3 fl oz/75 ml (⅓ cup) olive oil
6–8 oz/225 g spaghetti, or other pasta, freshly cooked

The sauce can also be made using a mortar and pestle. Toss with the hot pasta and serve.

and is limited to sensations in the mouth of sweet, sour, salt or bitter. On the other hand, aroma, odour and fragrance are perceived only by those little glands high in the nose and it is through them that we gain full appreciation and enjoyment of flavour in food. It is interesting, and perhaps slightly ironic, that two ancient aids to survival, the 'essential oils' of aromatic herbs and spices and the human olfactory glands, now combine principally to give us pleasure. If herbs offered no further service, their contribution to living would still be substantial. Bless them.

A continuing difficulty in assimilating the knowledge of plants in general and herbs in particular is simply their extent. The world of living things is so varied that until recently botanical chroniclers were never certain that they were describing or writing about the same things. In the eighteenth century, light was cast into the confusion by the work of the Swedish botanist, Carl Linnaeus. He invented a scientific language in which every plant can be described by two Latin names. The first is the generic name, representing a class of plants similar in structure to the one described. The second distinguishes the plant from all others in the same class. Linnaeus's work is at the very foundation of the botanical sciences, but it does not solve all problems. Linnaeus lived a century or so before Darwin and therefore could not incorporate into his system the findings of evolutionary theory. We now know, for example, that common ancestry is every bit as important as structure in understanding the nature of plants. The work started by Linnaeus, however, may in our time begin to reach its full fruition. Now, for the first time, human beings can approach the plant world with tools not only capable of listing and storing vast quantities of information but of analysing, exploring and manipulating that information to produce insights, conclusions and discoveries which in earlier times would have been impossible. If we can somehow do away with ignorance, superstition and the desire to dominate our fellow beings, the combination of the intuitions of the past and the computers and tools of the future may lead us into a golden age and a new relationship with the green life around us. Perhaps we have yet to see the real benefit of the herb.

THE BLENDING OF HERBS & SPICES
by Henry Heath

The blending of herbs and spices into seasonings tends to be traditional and has always been more of a culinary art than a science. It is frequently assumed that if a little of a particular herb or spice is good then more will be better; this is not necessarily so. A good seasoning should be subtle in its impact and designed to bring out the pleasurable flavour characteristics of the main food items in any dish. The achievement of this demands skill and a knowledge of both the flavouring qualities and strengths of the individual culinary herbs and spices, both fresh and ground.

In order to remove much of the subjective guesswork out of seasoning compositions it is first necessary to assess the flavour contribution of the main food components, starting from the weakest to the strongest (Table A). In general, the weaker the flavour of the food items the lower the level of added seasoning required. This applies equally to curry blends which cater well for the differences in start materials. For example, with fish it is usual to add only lightly aromatic herbal seasonings, with lots of fresh character but little fullness of flavour, enhanced perhaps with the sharpness of vinegar and perhaps a picquancy provided by, say,

horseradish sauce. On the other hand, game and ham have high intrinsic flavours, so strong that almost no seasoning is required beyond perhaps some added bit or pungency to give the full-bodied flavour a little more interest. In the medium range of meats, such as pork and beef, one may use a wide spectrum of spices to give a flavour to suit almost any palate.

All herbs and spices have their own individual flavouring strengths and characters. The freshly cut herbs are generally lightly aromatic with a pleasant sweetness; many of the spices are sweetly fruity with a hint of citrus, others have a full-bodied, well-rounded flavour; finally there are those which are strongly pungent and frequently associated with a very spicy aroma.

It is possible to rate or classify herbs and spices, allocating to each one a rough 'flavouring index' and to list them in increasing order of flavouring strength (Table B). This cannot be precise but by using such a classification one can convert any seasoning formulation into its 'flavouring profile' or create a seasoning formulation from its desired profile.

Take for example garam masala (Table C below).

Spice	Grams	% by weight (a)	Flavour index (b)	Flavour contribution (a × b)	% flavour contribution
Black cumin seeds	15	4.69	200	938	2.54
White cumin seeds	15	4.69	290	1360	3.68
Coriander	75	23.44	230	5391	14.56
Cardamom seeds	40	12.50	350	4375	11.83
Bay leaves	5	1.56	100	156	0.42
Cloves	50	15.62	560	8747	23.65
Black pepper	50	15.62	450	7029	19.00
Nutmeg	15	4.69	350	1641	4.43
Mace	15	4.69	340	1594	4.31
Cinnamon	40	12.50	460	5750	15.55
	320	100		36,981	100

Table A: Food sources listed in order of intrinsic flavour

Herb or spice		Food basic
Parsley herb		Fish
Dill		
Fennel		
Sweet bay laurel		
Sweet marjoram		
Rosemary		Veal
Spanish sage		
Tarragon		Lamb
English sage		
Cinnamon/Cassia		
Oregano	Proportion	Chicken
Dalmatian sage	increasing	
Origanum	up the	
Savory	list	Pork
Thyme		
Caraway		
Coriander		
Fenugreek	Proportion	
Basil	increasing	
Cardamom	down the	
Celery	list	Beef
Cumin		
Pimento (Allspice)		
Clove		
Nutmeg		
Mace		Mutton
Ginger		
Pepper		
Capsicum (Cayenne)		Game
Mustard		Ham

Table B: Flavour impact of herbs and spices

	Flavour index
Freshly cut herbs	
Chervil	45
Chives	50
Coriander leaves	80
Fennel leaves	80
Garden sage	96
Thyme	125
Rosemary	130
Sweet bay	140
Dry, rubbed herbs	
Garden Mint	50
Onion (flake)	60
Tarragon	60
Savory	75
Dalmatian sage	80
Marjoram	80
Thyme	85
Rosemary	90
Sweet bay	100
Spices	
Paprika	50
Cardamom seeds	125
Dill	160
Fenugreek	200
Coriander	230
Pimento (Allspice)	260
Cumin	290
Celery seed	300
Aniseed	320
Caraway	320
Fennel	330
Mace	340
Nutmeg	350
Turmeric	400
Black pepper	450
White pepper	460
Cinnamon/Cassia	460
Ginger (dried)	475
Clove	560
Mustard	800
Cayenne (Red Pepper)	900
Chillies	1000

From the percentage formulation one might think that this garam masala was heavily that of coriander with the clove and black pepper of about equal flavouring value. In fact, one can see, from the percentage flavour contribution column, that the blended spices will have a strongly clove character backed by pepper with a reasonable backing of cinnamon and coriander. The remaining spices provide only a rounding and background flavouring effect.

If one examines the profiles in terms of the four main categories described in the text then:

Light, sweet herby notes	Medium aromatic notes	Heavy, full-bodied spicy notes	Spicy, pungent notes
Bay Coriander	Black cumin Cardamom	White cumin Clove Nutmeg and Mace Cinnamon	Black pepper
19.01%	14.37%	51.62%	19.00%

Now different meats, etc, require different proportions of these four flavour components. For a well-balanced seasoning, for a meat like beef, this should be within the following ranges:

Light sweet top notes	Medium aromatic notes	Full-bodied spicy notes	Pungency
5–10%	10–20%	20–25%	45–65%

From this can be seen that this garam masala formulation leaves room for the addition of some 25 per cent by weight of additional spices when used as part of a total curry base. This will of course be taken up by turmeric to give the desired colour and further spiciness and by chillies or red peppers to give the desired pungency or heat.

In order to use this system in reverse, in the building up of balanced seasoning formulations, it is necessary to classify the herbs and spices into the four flavouring categories and to select those members of each group which best provide a well-rounded, smooth flavour most appropriate for the dish being prepared: Table D.

Table D: Flavour characteristics of herbs and spices

Flavour contribution	Herbs	Spices
Light, sweetly herbaceous, fresh	Marjoram, Rosemary, Spanish Sage, Sweet Bay, Tarragon	Coriander
Medium, aromatic	Dalmation Sage, Fennel, Mint, Oregano	Aniseed, Caraway, Cardamom seeds, Cinnamon/Cassia, Celery seeds, Lovage
Sweetly piquant	Basil, Savory	
Heavy, full-bodied, spicy	Origanum (Wild Marjoram), Thyme	Clove, Cumin, Fenugreek, Mace, Nutmeg, Pimento/Allspice, Turmeric
Spicy, pungent		Black and White Pepper, Capsicum, Cayenne (Red Pepper), Chillies, Ginger, Horseradish, Mustard

Let us take for example the creation of a seasoning suitable for use as a yogurt-based paste on grilled cod (Table E). Here we are looking for a seasoning having the following components:

Table E:

Light, sweet herby notes	Medium aromatic notes	Heavy, full-bodied spicy notes	Spicy, pungent notes
10–20%	15–35%	0–10%	40–60%
Say 20%	30%	nil	50%
Selected from:			
Bay (5%)	Aniseed (5%)		Black pepper (50%)
Rosemary (5%)	Paprika (10%)		
Coriander (10%)	Cardamom (15%)		
Fresh coriander leaves (5%) as a garnish after cooking			

Spice	% flavour contribution (a)	Flavour index (b)	Flavour contribution (a÷b)	% by weight	Grams
Bay leaves	5	140	0.0357	6.33	6
Rosemary	5	130	0.0385	6.82	7
Coriander	10	230	0.0435	7.71	8
Aniseed	5	320	0.0156	2.76	3
Paprika	10	50	0.2000	35.44	35
Cardamom seeds	15	125	0.1200	21.27	21
Black pepper	50	450	0.1111	19.67	20

This principle can be applied to the creation of any seasoning and gives a complete latitude in the selection of specific spices within each flavouring category.

RECOMMENDED READING

Binding, G.J. *About Garlic*. Thorsons Publishers Ltd, Wellingborough 1970. History, health and recipes.

Boxer, C.R. *The Dutch Seaborne Empire 1600–1800*. Hutchinson Ltd, London 1965.

Claiborne, Craig. *A Herb and Spice Book*. Harper and Row, New York 1963. Faber and Faber Ltd, London 1965. A few notes and lots of recipes.

Culpeper's Complete Herbal. W. Foulsham Ltd, Slough 1952. Sterling Publishing Co. Inc, New York 1959.

David, Elizabeth. *Spices, Salt and Aromatics in the English Kitchen*. Penguin Books Ltd, London 1970.

Garland, Sarah. *The Herb and Spice Book*. Frances Lincoln Publishers Ltd, London 1979. Gardening, cooking, cosmetics, health and good indexes.

Genders, Roy. *The Complete Book of Herbs and Herb Growing*. Ward Lock Ltd, London 1980. Sterling Publishing Co. Inc, New York 1980. Historical introduction to herb gardens. A–Z list of herbs, culture and uses.

A History of Scent. Hamish Hamilton, London 1972. Published as *Perfume through the Ages*. Putnam, New York 1972. Just what it says.

Gordon, Lesley. *Green Magic*. Ebury Press, London 1977. Viking Press, New York 1977. Good on history and lore of plants and their influence on the human imagination.

Greene, Bert. *Kitchen Bouquets*. Contemporary Books Inc, Chicago 1979. Stories about spices and other flavourings and recipes. Fun.

Grieve, M.A. ed. Leyel, C.F. *A Modern Herbal*.

Penguin Books Ltd, London 1976. Simply a classic. Essential.

Hall, Dorothy. *The Book of Herbs*. Angus & Robertson (UK) Ltd, Brighton 1972. Gardening, lore, history, health and horticulture. Alphabetical index.

Harris, Lloyd J. *The Book of Garlic*. Aris Books, Berkeley, California 1980. See the Garlic Chapter.

Heal, Carolyn and Allsop, Michael. *Cooking with Spices*. David and Charles Ltd, Newton Abbot 1983. Very complete alphabetical listing of herbs and spices. History, botany, cultivation and recipes. Excellent set of tables at the end.

Heath, Henry, *Flavour Technology*. The AVI Publishing Co Inc, Westport, Connecticut 1978. Excellent reference for the food professional.

Hemphill, Rosemary. *Cooking with Herbs and Spices*. Angus & Robertson (UK) Ltd, Brighton 1977. History and recipes.

   The Penguin Book of Herbs and Spices. Angus & Robertson (UK) Ltd, Brighton 1959. Penguin Books Ltd, London 1966. History and alphabetical index of herbs and spices. Recipes.

The Herb Society. *The Herbal Review* (Quarterly) London. All aspects of herbs and spices.

Holton, Josie A. and Hylton, William H. *The Complete Guide to Herbs*. Rodale Press, Emmaus, Pennsylvania 1979. Comprehensive – healing, culinary, aromatic, colourful, cultivation, insect repellent, landscaping and glossary.

Lehner, Ernst and Johanna. *Folklore and Odysseys of Food and Medicinal Plants*. George Harrap and Co Ltd, London 1974. Short essays on many foods including a number of spices and herbs.

Le Strange, Richard. *A History of Herbal Plants*. Angus & Robertson (UK) Ltd, Brighton 1977. Alphabetical index of many herbs with short essays on each one.

Lowenfeld, Claire and Back, Phillipa. *The Complete Book of Herbs and Spices*. David and Charles, Newton Abbot 1974. History, alphabetical classification, recipes, drawings, cosmetic chart, glossary and herb and spice culinary charts.

Masselman, George. *The Cradle of Colonialism*. Yale University Press, New Haven, Connecticut and London 1963. The story of the Dutch quest for spices in South-East Asia. History brought vividly to life.

Parry, J. H., *The Spanish Seaborne Empire*. Hutchinson and Co Ltd, London 1965. New edition 1977. Penguin Books Ltd, London 1974.

Parry, J. W., *The Story of Spices*. Chemical Publishing Co Inc, New York 1953. Part One is an easy historical read. Part Two is an alphabetical index of spices.

Petits Propos Culinaires. Prospect Books, London. Essays and notes to do with cookery and cook books. A series of short articles and correspondences from cookbook and food writers around the world.

Pruthi, J.S., *Spices and Condiments*. National Book Trust, India. Invaluable Indian point of view on spices.

Purseglove, J.W., Brown, E.G., Green, C.L., and Robbins, S.R.J. *Spices*. Part of the Tropical Agricultural Series. Longman Group Ltd, Harlow, 1981. Two volumes. The most comprehensive and best reference for all aspects of spices. No recipes.

Redgrove, H.S. *Spices and Condiments*. Pitman, New York and London 1933. One of the subject's classics.

Ridley, H.N. *Spices*. Macmillan, London 1912. Essential for all serious students of the subject.

Rohde, Eleanor Sinclair. *A Garden of Herbs*. Hale, Cushman & Flint, 1936. Revised, Dover Publications Inc, New York 1969. Poetry and lore of various herbs. Poetic, informative and interesting.

Root, Waverly. *Food*. Simon & Schuster, New York 1980. Massive work containing essays on all the spices and many herbs.

Rosengarten, F. *The Book of Spices*. Wynnewood: Livingston Publishing Co, London 1969. One of the best and most comprehensive books ever written about spices. It's all here.

Stobart, Tom. *The International Wine & Food Society's Guide to Herbs, Spices and Flavourings*. David and Charles, Newton Abbot, 1970. Published as *Herbs, Spices and Flavourings*. Penguin Books Ltd, London 1977. Simply a classic.

Ed. Stuart, Malcolm. *The Encyclopedia of Herbs and Herbalism*. Orbis Publishing Ltd, London 1979. Extremely comprehensive survey of herbs and spices. Well written and essential. An endless source of information and inspiration.

Westland, Pamela. *The Encyclopedia of Spices*. Marshall Cavendish Ltd, London 1979. History, medicine, food, gardening, indexes, charts, recipes, botany and cultivation.

Wilson, Constance Anne. *Food and Drink in Britain*. Constable, London 1973. Harper & Row, New York 1974. Peregrine Books, New York 1976. Meticulous research. Interesting writing which goes far beyond Britain alone. Excellent references.

LIST OF RECIPES

GENERAL INDEX

Compiled by Valerie Lewis Chandler, B.A.,
A.L.A.A.

Illustration Acknowledgments

Front Jacket: Christine Hanscomb and
    Lodge Cheeseman
Back jacket: House Food Industrial
    Company Limited (Japan)
Blackrod Limited: 25, 38, 71, 81, 97, 128,
    130, 131, 132, 137, 157, 158, 161, 170–1,
    172, 174
Bodleian Library, Oxford: 41
British Library: 153
British Museum: 43, 155
Colmans of Norwich: 129
Mary Evans Picture Library: 62
Lyn Gambles: 27, 98, 99, 139, 146, 178–9,
    180
House Food Industrial Company Limited
    (Japan): 9, 10–11, 12, 21, 29, 32–3, 34–5,
    36, 39 (top and right), 40, 49, 50, 51, 52,
    53, 55, 60, 63, 65, 67, 68, 73, 74, 75,
    76–7, 78–9, 85, 88–9, 90, 92, 94, 100,
    103, 105, 107, 108–9, 110–1, 112, 113,
    114, 115, 118, 119, 121, 122, 124, 126,
    134, 135, 141, 148–9, 150, 151, 162, 163,
    164, 165, 167, 168–9, 177
IGDA, Milan: 18–19, 44 (Bibliothèque
    Nationale), 58–59 (Rijksmuseum)
Lodge Cheeseman: Half title page and
    title page
Nigel Maslin: 31, 39 (above), 145